THE NEW SECRET LANGUAGE OF
SYMB◆LS

THE NEW
SECRET LANGUAGE OF
SYMBOLS

AN ILLUSTRATED KEY TO UNLOCKING
THEIR DEEP & HIDDEN MEANINGS

DAVID FONTANA

WATKINS
Sharing Wisdom Since 1893

The New Secret Language of Symbols
David Fontana

This paperback edition first published in the United Kingdom
and Ireland in 2010 by Watkins, an imprint of
Watkins Media Limited
Unit 11, Shepperton House
89–93 Shepperton Road
London N1 3DF

enquiries@watkinspublishing.com

Conceived, created and designed by Watkins Media Limited

Editor: Peter Bently
Designer: Gail Jones
Managing Editor: Christopher Westhorp
Managing Designer: Manisha Patel
Picture Research: Julia Ruxton
Commissioned artwork: Neil Gower, Olaf Hajek, Katarzyna Klein, Clare Melinsky,
    Gary Walton, Mark Watkinson

British Library Cataloguing-in-Publication Data:
A CIP record for this book is available from the British Library

ISBN: 978-1-78678-227-4

10 9 8 7 6 5 4 3 2 1

Typeset in Scala and Democratica
Colour reproduction by Colourscan
Printed in Malaysia

Notes:
Abbreviations used throughout this book:
CE Common Era (the equivalent of AD)
BCE Before the Common Era (the equivalent of BC)

Pressure on space has meant that the date, artist and other background information have not always been given
in picture captions: the author has chosen instead to say more about symbolism. For further information about
the paintings and objects reproduced in this book please refer to the Acknowledgments & Picture Credits,
which begin on page 188.

contents

PART I
INTRODUCING SYMBOLS

THE SYMBOLIZING MIND

WORLDS IMAGINED
In the Middle Ages and the Renaissance, intellectuals striving to understand the cosmos wove elaborate symbolic systems. This Ottoman miniature, from the *Zubdat al-Tawarikh* (*The Fine Flower of Histories*), dated 1583, shows an Earth-centered cosmos with the signs of the Zodiac and the lunar mansions.

We humans have an inborn ability to think in terms of symbols. This derives, at the most fundamental level, from a willingness to allow one thing to stand in for another. We see a picture and it stands in for a landscape or a face; we read words and they stand in for concepts. Without this facility we would never have invented either mathematics or language. Numbers express quantity, which is philosophically a sophisticated concept (it's an abstraction, like redness or cowardice) but one that in practice we find ourselves using with ease and without ambiguity. Words are more complex, however. They are sounds or marks on a page or screen that stand for objects, events, emotions and so on that are not necessarily present at the time of speaking or writing. For example, a simple word such as "house" can immediately conjure up in someone's mind an extensive set of concepts to do with physical buildings, interiors, homes, security, and perhaps even a mortgage and other liabilities. To put it another way, a word can be rich and complex in its associations, even though its basic meaning may be straightforward. This is the essence of symbolism.

Humans may be unique in their symbol-making ability, and its absence in other primates may be one of the reasons why they have failed to develop comparable linguistic skills. We take language for granted, yet if we think about it for even a moment we recognize what an extraordinary achievement language actually is. The mind allows particular words to conjure up a whole wealth of meaning, involving abstract concepts, visual images, imaginative ideas, memories, hopes and fears, longings and regrets, and much more besides.

KEYS TO UNDERSTANDING

Symbol-making has something mysterious, even magical, about it. For without it we would lose much of the rich inner landscape of the human mind. The associations that surround commonplace symbols such as house, dog, hair, sea and moon give us a source of value in our lives—a semantic and emotional density. If we take the moon, for example, we know, without any great depth of reading or other cultural experience, that it is more than just a changing yellow disk in the nighttime, morning or afternoon sky. We may think of its long-established association with romance (the movies have done much to reinforce this link, though the notion predates movie-making by many centuries); and we may think too of a different kind of romance—namely, the adventure and wonder

SPEAKING STONES
A stone tablet that forms part of a Mayan calendar. These intricate designs are actually words in the written Mayan language. The development of writing is one of the most complex and intricate forms of symbol-making.

of the American moon landing in 1969. When we look at the moon, or read about it or even merely think about it or mention it casually to someone, such different associations can be simultaneously present in our minds, though not at the conscious level.

As we shall see, there is an important difference between, on the one hand, symbols that have accumulated their meanings organically, over time, in a complex interplay of conscious and unconscious responses; and, on the other hand, symbols that have been deliberately chosen or devised. This latter category of symbols should more properly be referred to as *signs*. They serve a symbolic purpose, but only because we have decided to use them in that way. By contrast, a circle, for example, carries intrinsic meaning for us by virtue of what it actually *is*—that is, a line that has no beginning and no end. This line immediately suggests to us the idea of completion, of wholeness, of totality, perhaps even of eternity. We have not learned this idea from other people: it seems intrinsic to the circle itself. Our minds intuitively respond to the circle

in this way. Between our mind and the circle there is a natural, immediate communication of meaning —an intellectual intimacy. There is more to be said about circles, but this example helps us to see that the mind regards true symbols as having an intrinsic and universal power to communicate something far beyond themselves.

ACROSS TIME & SPACE

So far we have spoken of symbol-making from a modern, Western perspective, while implying that the ideas expressed are universally valid. That is true. Yet our intellectual horizons are culturally determined. Differences of belief and social practice, as well as environmental differences (including climate, landscape, flora and fauna) take our conscious and unconscious minds in different evolutionary directions. Belief systems and cultural influences intersect, complicating the picture. It is when we extend our focus to cover other centuries and other cultures that symbolism becomes truly fascinating.

SIGNS, EMBLEMS & SYMBOLS

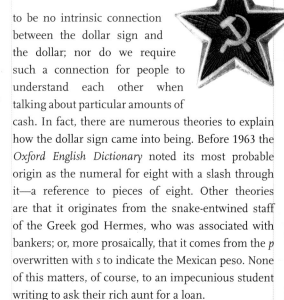

RED STAR
(opposite) The Morning Star, herald of a new dawn of Marxism, and the hammer and sickle, denoting industrial and agricultural workers, were widely used communist emblems.

GREAT WESTERN
As its company emblem Britain's Great Western Railway adapted the ancient arms of London (below left) and Bristol (below right) to suggest historical continuity, vigor and prosperity.

True symbols resonate with meanings that have evolved organically over time, whereas signs are graphic notations consciously chosen with the express purpose of *conveying* meaning: the difference is one of efflorescence versus intention. There is also a third category, namely emblems, which in their mode of operation have more in common with signs than with symbols—although in their visual appearance they may resemble symbols.

A common sign almost universally understood is $, meaning dollar. To our modern minds there is something arbitrary about this shape: there seems to be no intrinsic connection between the dollar sign and the dollar; nor do we require such a connection for people to understand each other when talking about particular amounts of cash. In fact, there are numerous theories to explain how the dollar sign came into being. Before 1963 the *Oxford English Dictionary* noted its most probable origin as the numeral for eight with a slash through it—a reference to pieces of eight. Other theories are that it originates from the snake-entwined staff of the Greek god Hermes, who was associated with bankers; or, more prosaically, that it comes from the *p* overwritten with *s* to indicate the Mexican peso. None of this matters, of course, to an impecunious student writing to ask their rich aunt for a loan.

Other signs are more sharply representational—for example, a roadside silhouette of a leaping deer should make a driver automatically more observant. Three-dimensional signs also vary in their obviousness—their "etymology", as it were. When you close your fist and lift your thumb to indicate approval, the reason for doing so, historically, is less clear than the reason you point with one finger to show someone a rainbow.

Emblems, like signs, are devices invented by the conscious mind to serve particular purposes, but they differ from most signs in being strongly pictorial. The leaping deer might be used, in color with green eyes and dappled brown skin, as the emblem for a courier company. Of course, the deer is also a symbol, with associations of shyness and speed. Trademarks and logos, which work as a visual shorthand for commercial organizations or their products, are usually signs (when they serve as triggers for identification), but they can also be emblematic (when they visualize certain values, such as fleetfootedness). It is usual to think

DOMINE · DIRIGE · NOS   VIRTUTE · ET · INDUSTRIA

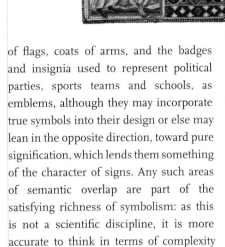

of flags, coats of arms, and the badges and insignia used to represent political parties, sports teams and schools, as emblems, although they may incorporate true symbols into their design or else may lean in the opposite direction, toward pure signification, which lends them something of the character of signs. Any such areas of semantic overlap are part of the satisfying richness of symbolism: as this is not a scientific discipline, it is more accurate to think in terms of complexity than of muddlle.

TRUE SYMBOLS

Compared with emblems and signs, which typically represent concrete entities, true symbols often stand for more elusive and profound concepts that cannot readily be put into words. Their value is evidenced by the fact that many of them have retained their meanings across centuries and cultures. Like an alternative language, they hint at things unseen—for example, aspirations, longings and fears, together with dimly grasped concepts such as divinity, the soul, faith, immortality, innocence, majesty, purity, transcendence. One of their features is that their meaning is often grasped intuitively, without the need for much explanation. Religious symbols such as the cross in Christianity, the crescent in Islam, the *menorah* in Judaism, the Dharma wheel in Buddhism, the *taiji* in Daoism (see page 13), the *aumkar* in Hinduism, and many other true symbolic devices become hallowed not only through usage but also through their intrinsic power to communicate important truths. They are the concentrated repositories of supreme meanings—distillations of life-changing knowledge and insight.

INNATE PROFUNDITY

Many true symbols are said to have arisen spontaneously from the unconscious by virtue of some profound intuition deep in the inner recesses of our minds. Often such symbols prompt an immediate emotional response, even in those to whom they are unfamiliar— as if tugging at memories just tantalizingly beyond recall. Consequently they are sometimes described as the meeting-point between different realities— an outer, finite reality that can be seen and touched, and an inner, infinite reality accessible only through meditation and dreams. True symbols, in one sense, create themselves. Signs and emblems are quickly forgotten once they have outlived their usefulness, whereas true symbols live on because they relate to the lasting qualities of spirit. Delving beneath layers of specific cultural significance we make important discoveries about what it means to be human.

CROSS OF CHRIST
An enameled and jeweled altar cross depicting scenes from the Old Testament. The image of Christ suffering for our sins is arguably the most explicitly emotional of all religious symbols. This cross is French or Flemish, ca. 1165.

PORTALS TO DIVINE POWER

The mind is one of the greatest of all mysteries—a boundless, ever-expanding universe inside us. Our memories and our conscious thoughts may give us some idea of where the mind begins, but the question of where it ends remains unanswerable. Beyond all that we summon into our thought lies that great store of all the experiences that have gone to make up our lives, extending far beyond the reach of consciousness. And at even deeper levels the mind embraces what the Swiss psychologist Carl Gustav Jung (1875–1961) called "the collective unconscious", the area of our psychological lives that he considered we inherit in much the way that our physical bodies inherit their physical characteristics. Associated with these deeper levels of our being is the soul or spirit, that part of ourselves that the world's great spiritual traditions insist is our eternal essence, the ineffable self that transcends the transient world of the senses.

PATHS TO AWARENESS

Those symbols that have lasting, universal appeal may in fact originate in the collective unconscious of humankind: hence their ability to serve as portals back into these deeper levels. Frequently such symbols make their appearance in dreams, those nightly adventures created for us by the unconscious and acted out

HIGHER POWER
The painted ceiling of the Meenakshi Sundareswarar Temple in Madurai, South India. The design is that of a stylized 1,000-petaled lotus flower, symbol of higher consciousness as embodied in the temple's deities, Sundareswarar ("Fair Lord") and Meenakshi, forms of the god Shiva and his consort Parvati.

THE GREAT ULTIMATE

within the magical theater of the sleeping mind. They can also be used as objects on which to concentrate during meditation. Helping to still the conscious mind and quieten its habitual chatter, meditation allows the subtle language of the unconscious to emerge into awareness, bringing us insights into hitherto undiscovered aspects of ourselves. If we meditate upon a symbol that has a particular attraction for us, it has the potential to reveal ever deeper levels of meaning, and to lead us ever closer to the spiritual source at the center of our being. We can choose either to sit in meditation with eyes closed, visualizing the symbol; or we can sit with eyes open, focusing gently on an image of the symbol placed in front of us. There is no better way to connect with the profound truths expressed in symbols than using them, in meditation, as mirrors to enhance our self-understanding.

One of the world's most recognizable symbols is the one known in the west as the YIN-YANG symbol (below). The TAIJI (or *t'ai chi*, "Great ultimate"), to give it its proper name, encapsulates in a graphic form the core principles of chinese Daoist thought. The circle represents the limitless, infinite nature of the universe, while the two areas within it represent opposite but complementary forces that constantly interact with one another to shape the cycle of life. The dark area is *yin*—passive, female and nocturnal. The white area is *yang*—active, male and associated with the day. *yin* represents the primordial, the instinctive, intuitional and pliable. *yang* represents the creative, the rational and the unyielding. The *taiji* image speaks of constant movement and a world in dynamic balance; a realm of existence containing two fluctuating impulses that are intimately connected and mutually interdependent—as one advances, the other retreats.

MYTH & SYMBOL

When we think of the world's great treasure-house of mythology, we might imagine at first that its interest to us is primarily dramatic or historical. Perhaps the quest of Jason and the Argonauts for the Golden Fleece, or the great battles in the Norse sagas, offers a harmless and pleasant way to enthrall a child or to evoke a lost world of the imagination. In fact, many of the great myths and legends of the world—in particular, those of ancient Egypt and Greece— contain extraordinary symbolic insights into profound areas of the human mind, and also have the power to unlock for us the path to our personal unconscious and to the collective unconscious. The great pioneer of this line of thought was Carl Jung, who described the collective unconscious as containing what are known as the archetypes—that is to say, innate psychological and spiritual energies that motivate us instinctively toward enduring values such as love, truth and heroism, and toward fundamental themes such as God, creation, nature, wisdom, birth and death (see pages 15–17). Each of the archetypes carries layers of complex meaning, which are often most readily approached and understood through the symbolism of ancient myths. Sometimes this symbolism takes the form of symbolic objects such as rings and hidden treasure, creatures such as dragons and many-headed dogs, and landscape features such as caves, rivers, the sea and mountains; and sometimes it takes the form of symbolic motifs such as journeys, romance, battle, heroism and loyalty. Mythic archetypes can also represent the negative forces against which

TAIJI

The *taiji* represents the perfect interplay and balance of *yin* (represented by the dark area) and *yang* (represented by the light area), the two forces that make up the universe in Chinese thought (see box, above). Each *yin* and *yang* section contains a spot of the complementary element to indicate that it is turning into the other. A version of the symbol forms part of the flag of South Korea.

humankind has to contend, both within the self and embodied in other people, such as betrayal, greed, cruelty, pride and selfishness.

What marks out certain myths and legends as archetypal is their enduring ability to engage the mind. We immediately recognize that they symbolize the most vital concerns and experiences of our lives. A struggle between a hero and a monster may haunt us precisely because we too, inwardly, are engaged in a struggle—for example, between faith and doubt. We should not assume that a legend of ancient Greece or Mesopotamia is of merely historical interest: it may express a vital aspect of our inner being. This explains the survival of ancient myths and legends into our own time, long after the beliefs they incorporate have faded into the dimly perceived legacy of history.

Archetypes are also encountered during the explorations of deeper levels of the mind that take place during psychotherapy. Analysts working with dream material, childhood memories and neuroses, and adult depressions, fears and aspirations, have found it illuminating to draw comparisons with the typical themes of myth and folktale. Modern psychoanalytical psychology, which originated with Sigmund Freud, Carl Jung and their followers, has in effect simply rediscovered what was known in detail by the ancients. In particular, the subjects surrounded by taboos in modern times, such as incest and unorthodox feelings about the father or mother, become clarified in myth (think of Cronos castrating his father Uranos as narrated by the poet Hesiod). The archetypes of myth are important tools in our quest for self-knowledge.

WISDOM INCARNATE

Many myths arose around the Buddha that served to convey his special enlightened nature and supreme wisdom. This wisdom is both utterly profound and remarkably simple: awareness of things as they really are. To his right is a wheel representing the Dharma, his teachings; and his hands are in the symbolic gesture of instruction. Another common symbol is the *ushnisha* or "wisdom bump" on the top of his head, while the *tilaka* on the brow denotes the "third eye" of insight.

CARL JUNG & THE ARCHETYPES

BA BIRD
(left) For Egyptians the *ba* bird was the soul as pure archetype, cleansed and blessed in the afterlife. Reign of Osorkon II (872–837BCE).

Although, as we have seen, the concept of archetypes is particularly associated with the work of Carl Jung, it originated with the Hellenistic–Judaic philosopher Philo Judeus, or Philo of Alexandria (lived ca. 20BCE–ca. 50CE), who used the term to represent the *Imago Dei*: the aspects of the Divine accessible to man. Jung employed the term archetype more widely to stand for the "universal images that ... make up the contents of the collective unconscious"; although they are in themselves formless energies, he believed, they emerge into the conscious mind as symbols. Philo, on the other hand, maintained that the archetypes are what endures when the soul has been progressively purified of its selfish and egotistical desires and recognizes its unity with the Divine.

ANIMA & ANIMUS

Jung considered that the archetypes are symbolized most frequently in human form. Two examples are the Anima and the Animus, which represent respectively the feminine side of the male and the masculine side of the female. We each carry the qualities of both sexes within us, and the male will ideally be in touch with his Anima, and the female with her Animus. However, if the Anima or Animus becomes dominant, the balance of the self is undermined. Jung argued that a man dominated by the Anima is exaggeratedly moody and emotional, and a woman dominated by the Animus exaggeratedly over-assertive and ruthless. Anima and Animus simply provide balance and prevent overly masculine

THE DEVIL
This medieval door decoration depicts the Devil, the classic Shadow figure of Christian tradition, as a warning against sin. He has goat's horns, a feature derived from the Greco-Roman god Pan, the lord of nature and a symbol of base desires and unbridled appetites—but also of the joys of nature.

TILL EULENSPIEGEL
(right) A banknote of 1921 shows Till Eulenspiegel, a trickster of German legend. The image alludes to his name, which means "Owl Glass": Till is the archetypal Fool who holds a mirror up to so-called "wise" folk.

at times of stress, making us act out of character in ways we subsequently regret. It may also be projected outward, resulting in the victimization of others or of minority groups or nations. The potential dangers of this are obvious; nevertheless, the Shadow is not entirely negative. Once its energies are recognized and socialized, they may help us to discover necessary powers of self-assertion or self-determination.

Another potentially troublesome archetype is the Trickster. The Trickster represents those things that go unaccountably wrong, that snatch away the fruits of success, play cruel games, and challenge or upset the accepted order of things. At an inner level the Trickster prompts self-doubt, reminding us of our anxieties; we appear foolish just when we most want to impress. Like the Shadow, however, the Trickster is not entirely negative, for it can sometimes prompt desirable changes. It can also help us find the unconventional side of ourselves, or remind us that we are indulging in self-deception. Furthermore, it can remind us that life is unpredictable, that we should not take ourselves too seriously, or become complacent, or imagine that anything in this life is permanent or success always assured. In history the Trickster was personified by the court jester or the fool, the only individual allowed to poke fun at the established order. In Norse mythology the role was filled by Loki, who continually upset the plans of the other gods. In African folklore the Trickster is often a hare. Brought by African slaves to America, this tradition combined with Native American rabbit

or overly feminine behavior. Like all archetypes, the Anima and the Animus can be projected outward in the form of idealized images of the opposite sex, leading the male to be forever seeking an impossibly beautiful and adoring woman to love, and the female to search in vain for a paragon of the male virtues to protect and cherish her.

In myths and fairytales the Anima often appears as the imprisoned princess or the mysterious young woman who guides the hero when lost or helps him return after his dangerous mission. The Animus typically appears as a courageous and resourceful young man who may nevertheless imperil himself through a willful and headstrong nature.

THE SHADOW & THE TRICKSTER
Another important archetype is the Shadow, the negative side of the personality, the sum total of all the instinctive primal qualities that we hide even from ourselves. If the Shadow is not acknowledged, Jung believed, it remains liable to burst out uncontrollably

trickster tales to produce Brer Rabbit. In the natural world the wind, capricious and essentially beyond our control, provides one of the most enduring Trickster symbols of all.

THE HERO & THE WISE PERSON

The Hero represents all that is best in us: noble ideals, self-sacrifice, honorable aspirations. He is an aspect of us all, male and female, the symbol of the best we can aspire to. Again, he can also be projected onto the outside world—for example, as the perfect leader for whom we search without success, the superman who will solve all our problems. The Hero is a favorite archetype in Wild West and war movies. We find him also in fairytales, often on a quest for a magical object (a treasure, a sword, a ring, the Grail) that will right all wrongs. Internalized, he becomes a symbol of our own search for our true self, the profound secret of our own being. He also appears in tragic myths and archetypal stories where he may be undone by a single flaw in his character—Achilles killed by a wound to the heel, his only vulnerable spot; Hamlet undone by his indecision; Caesar by his refusal to heed the soothsayer; Lear by his failure to distinguish love from flattery. In his flaws the Hero symbolizes human vulnerability and reminds us that even heroes are inevitably defeated by their own mortality. As Shakespeare wrote in *Cymbeline*: "Golden lads and girls all must, / As chimney-sweepers, come to dust."

Along with the Hero, we also carry within us the archetype of the Wise Person, typically symbolized by the wise old man or woman, the sage or wizard, or a parent, who has the ability to guide, heal and inspire and may also possess supernatural powers. Just as we can project the Hero outward, so we can also project the Wise Old Man or Woman, instead of learning to find him or her within ourselves. In consequence we may assume that others always know better than we do—for example, the TV scientist, the persuasive politician, the self-proclaimed healer. This helps to explain why we are often so easily deceived by false gurus and prophets.

HERO VERSUS SHADOW
The battle—known as the Centaurmachy —in Thessaly between the Lapiths, a warrior race, and the violent, lustful Centaurs has been interpreted as the inner conflict between the Hero and Shadow archetypes. This detail comes from a Greek vase, sixth century BCE.

NARRATIVES OF FAITH

THE SOARING SOUL
As seen here in Wells Cathedral, England, the pointed arches, vaulting and pinnacles of Gothic architecture draw the eye —and spirit—upward, in the direction of heaven.

DIVINE MOUNTAIN
Begun in the 1100s, this temple at Angkor Wat, Cambodia, was dedicated to the god Vishnu. As with many other Hindu temples, its towers represent Mount Meru, where the gods reside. The central tower rises above the temple's main sanctuary, the focus of worship.

The great spiritual traditions of the world have frequently relied on symbols, in the form of both narratives and images, to represent realities that are difficult or impossible to express in words. These narratives and images are intended to be taken not as literal truth but as pointers in the right direction. For example, each of the great traditions has creation narratives that convey profound lessons about the nature of man, his relationship with the physical world, and his spiritual destiny. The biblical narrative of the creation of the first humans and their expulsion from Eden illustrates the perils of disobedience to God (or of rebelling against the laws of nature), of seeking the knowledge of the intellect instead of the wisdom of the spirit, and of desiring to take from the Earth that which is not freely given. Each of these perils is as real today as it was when the narrative was composed (probably in the sixth century BCE).

ART, ARCHITECTURE & RITUAL

Spiritual truths are expressed not only in stories (presented in scriptures and other sacred texts) but also in ceremonial objects, in art and in sacred architecture. Episodes from a story, of course, may be depicted in painting or sculpture, as well as, sometimes more obliquely, in sacred objects such as screens, chalices, bowls, caskets and candlesticks. The value of a sacred building, whether a temple or a church, is that it offers a multi-faceted embodiment of sacred themes and events. The walls, floors and windows offer two-dimensional surfaces on which depictions may be displayed, while the horizontal surfaces offer a way to exhibit sacred objects. The overall structure of a sacred building will also usually be significant. Its symbolism may combine sacred narrative and sacred geometry: for example, in a Christian church the cross plan and the dome, often found together (as in St. Peter's

Basilica, Rome), suggest the crucifixion of Jesus and the vault of heaven.

Churches are implied narratives in architecture, combined with more explicit narratives in sculpture, painting and glass. At a time when many were illiterate, these were ways of teaching the faithful about their religion. In Europe, Gothic churches were built in the form of a cross and aligned to the East and the birthplace of Christ. Their altars spoke of Christ's sacrifice and the tomb in which his body was laid. The pointed Gothic arches symbolized praying hands and served as ever-present reminders of the importance of prayer in spiritual life. The sculptures and carvings of saints symbolized the saintly virtues. The painted walls bore symbolic narratives of Christ's birth, of his miracles and his teaching, and of his journey to death on the cross. Ceiling paintings symbolized the need to raise the eyes and the spirit from the temporal to the eternal world.

An object provides a focus for our thoughts, whether prayerful or meditative. For example, the crucifix was a symbolic reminder that earthly life and physical suffering are inseparable, while ever-present images of grapes, of corn, of fishes, of the eagle and the dove each carried its own specific symbolic meaning which the congregation would know and understand. The emphasis was upon turning the mind toward Christ and God, remembering the brevity of human life, refusing to be ensnared by the world, the flesh and the devil. Physical life had a purpose beyond itself, and a church was a living monument to that fact.

Comparable meanings exist in the sacred buildings of other sacred traditions, different in detail but carrying the same message that the physical world is not the ultimate reality, and that men and women must focus upon the imperishable truths of the spirit, as distinct from the impermanence of earthly life. Islam utilizes geometrical shapes rather than living forms to convey symbolic messages, but the concern is again to turn the mind of the believer to God. Hinduism, which has no qualms about the body, uses expressive sculptural forms to convey the bountiful nature of the divine.

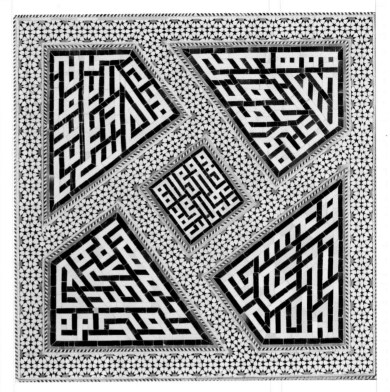

MYSTIC EXPERIENCE

Religious experience, a product of faith rather than reason, has always sought to express itself by non-rational means. Hence the significance, in different religions, of light, fire, water and, for mystics, ecstasy—the body offered a useful analogy of the ultimate transfiguring experience. Angels, in the three great monotheistic religions (Judaism, Christianity, Islam), are deeply evocative of life beyond temporal constraints, their flight and their heavenly music reinforcing the symbolism of transformation. Yet in both Judaism (Kabbalah) and Christianity (John 1:1) the word too had an important part to play—not as language but as ineffable mystic energy. Comparable to this is the sacred syllable *Om*, or *Aum*, recited at the beginning and end of all Hindu and Jain prayers. Said to represent the supreme reality, or *brahman*, according to many Hindu philosophers *Om* was the first sound or vibration and contains the essence of true knowledge.

SACRED PATTERNS
Islam forbids pictorial representations of the Divine in mosques, so mosque decoration glorifies God through the astonishingly varied use of calligraphic, floral and geometrical patterns. This ceramic panel from the Friday Mosque of Isfahan, Iran, contains five extracts from the Quran in a highly stylized script.

SECRET SYMBOLS

MYSTIC SECRETS
Mystic societies such as the Rosicrucians used a host of symbols, many drawn from biblical and alchemical traditions. However, what such symbols meant in a particular context was often known only to the initiates who used them. *The Tree of Knowledge of Good and Evil*, from a German work entitled *Secret Symbols of the Rosicrucians* (1785–1788).

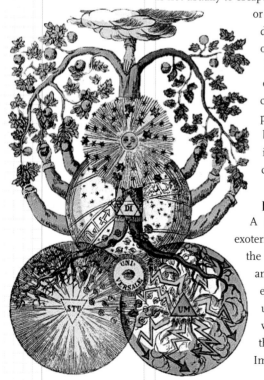

It is no coincidence that the bestselling novel by Dan Brown about occult symbolism and the secret lineage of Christ is entitled *The Da Vinci Code*. We speak of *decoding* symbolism, and this reflects the character of the enterprise when we attempt to explicate the meaning of an enigmatic symbol. The more complex the symbol, or the more remote it is from us in its cultural milieu, the more appropriate this verb feels.

Symbolism is a language ideally suited for communication between initiates who subscribe to a particular set of beliefs, especially when those beliefs are seen to be powerful, unorthodox, subversive or dangerous in some way. It offers a visual codebook to which outsiders are denied ready access.

The purpose of concealment through symbolism is not usually to escape some anticipated punishment or persecution. Those who have dealt in esoteric symbols have often laid claim to special knowledge—usually the kind of insight that is thought to confer power. Reserving this power for initiates has always been a compelling motivation in the way closed groups have communicated with each other.

PATHS TO GOD

A symbol can be described as exoteric or esoteric in form—from the Greek words meaning "outer" and "within" respectively. The exoteric meaning is one that is understood by the layperson, whereas the esoteric meaning is the preserve of a narrower circle. Implicit in esoteric thinking is the idea that some knowledge is secret, that for some reason it must be hidden from a mass audience. If such knowledge were to fall into the wrong hands, it might be misused. In any case, spreading this knowledge too thinly might weaken its efficacy.

A particular symbol may well have one meaning, rooted in traditions established over many centuries, to the educated general public; and quite another meaning to someone who has attained privileged access to more profound insights. For centuries Western civilization had as part of its literary canon the medieval European legends of the many quests for the Holy Grail. This fabled chalice was supposedly the vessel used at the Last Supper, and subsequently held out by Joseph of Arimathea to catch drops of Jesus' blood as his life ebbed away on the cross. Believed to possess miraculous powers, the Holy Grail has long been a symbol of something much sought after that has remained elusive or unattainable. A more recent interpretation is that the Grail is not an artifact after all but a secret—a revelation that will challenge the foundations of the modern world. One version of this theory (expressed in the book *Holy Blood, Holy Grail* by Baigent, Leigh and Lincoln) is the notion that, instead of dying on the cross, Jesus lived to marry Mary Magdalene and father children whose Merovingian lineage continues today: the Grail, according to this view, symbolizes Mary as the receptacle of Jesus' bloodline. These ideas are linked with the supposed existence of a secret society, the Priory of Sion, whose grandmasters are said to have included Leonardo da Vinci and Jean Cocteau, and with the role of the Knights Templar as the society's secret military arm.

All this illustrates not necessarily the functioning of symbols within secret societies (this is *speculative* history, after all), but certainly the way in which esoteric symbolism strikes a chord with many people in the

Rosicrucianism (see pages 48–49), the Kabbalah (38–39) and quasi-scientific systems such as alchemy (60–61) all employed symbols in a similar way, primarily because it was felt that these systems represented profound truths which might be dangerous in the hands of those who had not undergone the preparation necessary to practice them correctly.

To the uninitiated, alchemical teachings sometimes appear to be examples of obscurity for obscurity's sake. Many alchemical texts are virtually unreadable, and defy the attempts of even the most dedicated practitioner to make use of them in any effective way. Some alchemical texts openly admit to the use of secrecy. The *Rosarium Philosophorum* states: "Wherever we have spoken openly, we have said nothing. But where we have written something in code and in pictures, we have concealed the truth." However, alchemy should not be too readily dismissed. There may be no evidence that it is of value in turning base metals into gold (its perceived purpose in the popular mind), but viewed as a spiritual practice intended to turn the base metal of the self into the gold of the spirit, it begins to make sense. Carl Jung studied the system with this aspect in mind, and concluded that alchemy was an inner discipline that can throw much light upon the process of transformation that takes place in patients as they progress in psychotherapy and their personalities become more fully integrated.

Alchemy and Rosicrucianism both belong to the esoteric wisdom tradition of the West, sometimes referred to as Hermeticism. Theosophy, Gnosticism and various Western manifestations of the Kabbalah are elements in the same shifting kaleidoscope of ideas. The term Hermeticism derives from Hermes Trismegistus, who combines characteristics of the Greek god Hermes and the Egyptian god Thoth. Within this long, broad tradition of occult belief, symbols function almost like sacred texts, being richly ambiguous in ways that keep their interpreters tirelessly engaged in crosscurrents of exegesis.

LIBERATING THE SPIRIT

This picture comes from one of the most richly illustrated alchemical works, the sixteenth-century treatise *Splendor Solis* (*Splendor of the Sun*). It shows the symbolic process of "boiling the body" to release the spirit, represented by the white bird. The image was probably produced in Augsburg, Germany, late 1500s. (See also pages 60–61.)

Wesern world today. Yet throughout history there have indeed been countless sects, fraternal societies and special interest groups claiming to have preserved and guarded the wisdom of the ancients, protecting it from being adulterated by wider exposure.

CULTISH MYSTERIES

In the popular imagination, a secretive veil of symbolism is probably the best-known aspect of perhaps the largest of all esoteric societies, the fraternal organization known as the Freemasons (see pages 158–159). Masons advance by acquiring deeper knowledge of the "sacred law" and over time they become familiar with forms of communication known only to other freemasons, by means of gestures, signs and passwords.

PART 2

THE WORLD OF SYMBOLS

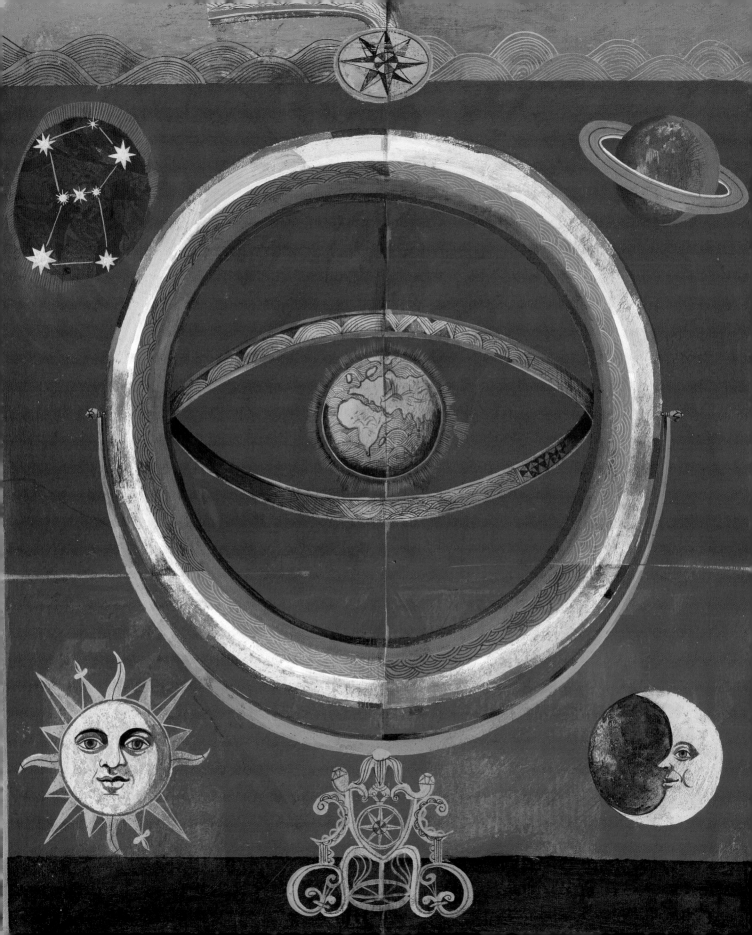

COSMOS

HUMAN BEINGS ONCE SAW THE EARTH AS LYING AT THE HEART OF A UNIVERSE OFTEN CONCEIVED AS SPHERICAL AND CONSISTING OF MULTIPLE LAYERS—THE DOMAIN OF DEITIES AND POWERFUL COSMIC FORCES. EVEN TODAY THE HEAVENS REMAIN, FOR MANY, REPLETE WITH PROFOUND SIGNIFICANCE.

heavenly bodies

Apparently moving around the world in eternal and regular cycles, the heavens have intrigued humankind from the earliest times. The heavenly bodies were seen as reflecting and in turn influencing the nature and course of life on Earth.

STARS
In many cultures the stars have been held to influence the lives of humans (see pages 30–31). Individual stars might represent angels, seeds of life, or pinpricks of the divine light beyond the celestial sphere. The Milky Way is a celestial road, bridge or river, symbolizing the link between the human and divine realms.

COMETS
Comets and meteors are universally seen as omens, heralding momentous events on Earth or in the cosmos. Some claim that the Star of Bethlehem may have been Halley's Comet, which appeared in 12BCE and also in 1066, boding ill for Harold II of England but not for William of Normandy, who conquered Harold's kingdom.

PLANETS
The planets took on the symbolism of the ancient deities whose names they bear. Blood-red Mars is warlike and violent, while the slow-moving giants Jupiter and Saturn denote cosmic majesty and mystery respectively. Mercury was two gods to the Greeks: Apollo at dawn and Hermes at dusk. Venus has a similar dual identity as the Morning or Evening Star, the sun's bright herald or postilion. It was the bringer of light and linked with goddesses of fertility and love, and later with the Virgin Mary. In Mesoamerica, Venus was a potent masculine force, and its rising was a propitious time for war.

STAR FACTORY
Stars are often stylized as a pentagram, a five-pointed symbol of renewal. Some "stars" are in fact galaxies, like the Whirlpool Galaxy (left), a "star factory" where new stars come into being.

sun

The most brilliant heavenly body, the sun is an almost universal symbol of life, light and creative renewal, of supreme sovereignty and royal power. As the giver of light it is the symbol of divine wisdom, enlightenment and profound and esoteric knowledge. It also represents the light of inspiration, creativity and the arts, represented by the Classical solar god Apollo, leader of the Muses. Thousands of sacred monuments around the world are aligned with the points on the horizon where the sun rises on the longest and shortest days of the year, crucial calendar markers in ancient times. The date of Christmas probably reflects the Church's attempt to Christianize the popular Roman festival of Sol Invictus (see opposite), which was celebrated in the days after the winter solstice, the darkest period of the year.

In most pantheons the sun is either the greatest deity or a supreme manifestation of that deity's power. In Egypt the sun god Ra was the great protector, his powers and blessings mediated by the pharaoh, who was both "Son of Ra" and also the sun itself, the solar god Horus personified. The Egyptians had several forms of the sun god to represent the sun throughout the day—and also the night, when he passed through the underworld (see below). The Inca called themselves "Children of the Sun" and swathed the Cusco temple of the sun god Inti in gold, which was said to be his sweat. For the Aztecs, only mass human sacrifice could slake the sun's thirst for blood and guarantee his daily rising.

As the giver of warmth, the sun represents energy, passion and youthful ardor. It is most often conceived as male, but as the source of life it may be female, as in Japan and in Native American and Oceanian traditions.

SUN KING
Radiating brilliance over all, the sun embodies the power and mystique of sovereigns. Louis XIV of France (ruled 1643–1715) cultivated the image of himself as Sun King (*Roi Soleil*), around whom court and nation revolved. The sun motif was used liberally at the Palace of Versailles (above, a fence detail).

THE LORD OF ALL

No people evolved a more complex and subtle solar symbolism than the Egyptians, who represented RA (or RE), the sun and supreme creator, in manifold forms. The SCARAB god KHEPRI (right) was the sun at dawn, its daily reemergence from the UNDERWORLD resembling the dungball pushed up by a scarab from its nest. Just as the dungball contains and nourishes the beetle's egg, the sun nourishes creation anew as it begins its daily journey. The FALCON-god HARAKHTY, whose name means "HORUS-of-the-Horizon", was the sun rising to its zenith, where it hovered overhead like a soaring bird of prey; the falcon wearing a sun-disk was the most common Egyptian solar symbol and also a potent emblem of royal power. RAM-headed ATUM, or RA-ATUM, was the evening sun god, who descended into the underworld to defend the world from chaos and destruction before rising anew as KHEPRI. The ATEN was the visible disk of the sun. It was venerated in the reign of AKHENATEN (ca. 1353—1332BCE) as the supreme deity and lord of life.

1

2

3

4

5

6

THE SUN OF NATIONS

As a symbol of sovereignty, freedom and renewal the sun is found on several national flags, such as those shown here (from top to bottom): The ancient flag of JAPAN (1) shows the rising sun, reflecting the Japanese name of the country, *nihon* or *nippon*, literally the "source of the sun" or "land of the rising sun". The shinto sun goddess, AMATERASU, is the traditional ancestor of the emperors of Japan. The emblem on the flags of URUGUAY (2) and, below that, ARGENTINA (3), is the SUN OF MAY, commemorating a rebellion against the Spanish in May 1810, which both countries regard as a key step on the road to nationhood. The flag of TAIWAN (4) is that of the pre-1949 REPUBLIC OF CHINA, and symbolizes the dawn of a new era following the downfall of the Qing dynasty in 1911. The forms of the Uruguayan and Taiwanese flags are both influenced by that of the United States. On the flag of ANTIGUA AND BARBUDA (5), the sun dawns from a blue sea amid a "v" for victory to celebrate independence from Britain. The sun's black background honors African heritage, as it does on the flag of MALAWI (6), another former colony.

SOL INVICTUS

(*above*) The Greek sun god Helios was revered in Rome as Sol Invictus, the Unvanquished Sun, whose midwinter rebirth was celebrated on December 25. The Church chose this date to mark the birth of Christ, the "Sun of Righteousness", who at times was depicted like Sol in his solar chariot. (See also Phaëton, right.)

SWASTIKA

(*left*) Corrupted by the Nazis in Germany, the swastika is an ancient solar symbol found in similar forms from Mesoamerica to East Asia and the Celtic world. It represents dynamic creative forces swirling eternally around a cosmic center.

JAGUAR SUN

The Mayan sun god Ahau Kin, "Lord of the Face of the Sun", was sometimes shown with features like a jaguar, the Mesoamerican king of beasts. At night Ahau Kin traveled through the underworld as the Jaguar God.

HUITZILOPOCHTLI

The "Hummingbird of the South" was the sun god, war god and supreme national deity of the Aztecs. Identified with the sun, Tonatiuh, Huitzilopochtli was central to the Aztec cult of human sacrifice, which took place on a huge scale to satisfy his thirst for blood.

PHAËTON

The son of Helios symbolizes foolhardiness. He pleaded to be allowed to drive his father's solar chariot and Helios reluctantly agreed. But Phaëton could not control the sun god's horses and ran amok. To end the chaos, Zeus killed Phaëton with a thunderbolt.

DAZHBOG

The name of Dazhbog, the sun god of the pagan Slavs, means "god who gives". The brother of the Fire God, Dazhbog lived in an eastern paradise from where, like the Greek Helios, he rode forth daily in a sun chariot. The Russians, the most easterly Slavs, were said to be his offspring.

ECLIPSE

Solar eclipses were widely seen as evil omens. For the Inca, they signaled that the sun god Inti (above) was angry: an eclipse preceded the Spanish conquest of Peru. An eclipse probably explains the Japanese myth that tells how the sun goddess once hid in a cave, plunging the world into darkness.

SUN CROW

In Chinese tradition the sun represents *yang*, the male principle. It is inhabited by a three-legged crow, whose legs symbolize the dawn, noon and setting sun. Chinese myth recounts how there were once ten suns, but nine were slain by the divine hero Yi the Archer.

CELTIC CROSS

Representing the sun radiating to the four directions from the center of cosmic creation, the Celtic cross was a prehistoric pagan symbol that was adapted as the characteristic cross of Celtic Christianity. Celtic deities of light, such as Lugh or Lugus, may have once been sun gods.

moon

The moon and the sun appear to be about the same size when viewed from Earth, and from this coincidence no doubt sprang the universal idea that they are a cosmic pair, the presiding bodies and chief symbols of day and night, light and dark. In cosmologies they may be husband and wife or incestuous brother and sister. Alternatively, the sun and moon may be the eyes of a god, as in Egypt (Horus), China (the cosmic giant Pan Gu) and Japan (Izanagi).

In most cultures the moon is female, no doubt owing to the relationship between the lunar and female fertility cycles—the words "moon", "month" and "menstrual" are all related. For the Akan people of Ghana, the moon is the supreme symbol of creation, represented by the goddess Nyame. More often, the moon cedes second place to the sun as creator; however, the moon is consistently a symbol of female fertility and power, and in ancient times it was associated with the great goddesses such as the Egyptian Isis and the Greek Artemis (Diana), the virgin hunter. Artemis was merciless in defence of chastity, reflecting the ambiguities of a heavenly body that presided benignly over fertility, tides and time, yet also over the hidden menaces of the dark night.

However, the moon is sometimes male, as in Japan, where the counterpart of the sun goddess Amaterasu is the moon god Tsukiyomi. In Oceania, the sun was female and the moon male because women worked by day and men fished by night. In Egypt the ever-changing moon represented magical transformation and hence occult wisdom, embodied in the ibis-headed god Thoth, his bill curved like the crescent moon. Hermes, his Greek equivalent, was the psychopomp, or guide of the dead, symbolized by the moon as light in the darkness.

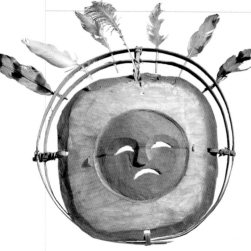

TARQEQ

(*left*) The Moon Spirit of the Inuit represents fertility, morality and the spirit of animals. Tarqeq punishes human transgressions with disease, storms and failure in hunting. On this Tarqeq mask from western Alaska the white border round the face denotes air, the hoops are the levels of the cosmos and the feathers symbolize stars.

ISLAMIC MOON

The crescent moon widely used as a symbol of Islam derives from the Ottoman empire, which in turn probably adopted it from the banner of Constantinople, the capital of the Byzantine empire conquered by the Ottomans in 1453. It originally symbolized Artemis, the patron goddess of Byzantium, Constantinople's ancient forerunner.

PHASES OF THE MOON

The phases of the moon—new, waxing, full, waning, new (below)—widely symbolize the eternal cycle of becoming, dissolution and recreation. In China, the New Year begins at the first NEW MOON after midwinter, which represents the potentiality of all growth. The FULL MOON represents the fullness of YIN: receptivity, passivity, darkness, femininity and moisture. In Chinese tradition the brightest full moon occurs in the eighth lunar month, and on this day falls the Moon Festival (the Mid-Autumn Festival), when the family comes together to share meals and eat circular cakes that symbolize the full moon. In Buddhist tradition the bright full moon symbolizes purity and serenity.

In India, the CRESCENT moon is the emblem of SHIVA as cosmic transformer. It is also linked with the Egyptian THOTH and the classical HERMES or MERCURY, gods of transition and transformation. The Maori explained the lunar waxing and waning as a constant battle between the moon and another god. Incidentally, the word crescent means "waxing" (Latin *crescere*, to grow), whereas the "crescent" with horns pointing to the right (east)—often found in lunar symbolism (right)—is in fact a waning moon.

LUNAR BABOON

Baboons were lunar animal for the Egyptians, since they were awake before dawn and heralded the sun. The lunar god Thoth often took the form of a baboon, wearing a headdress representing the full moon within a crescent moon. This device in turn symbolized the various phases of the moon and the transformation of the soul.

MAN IN THE MOON

Western folk tradition discerns on the moon's surface the figure or face of a man. He was often said to have been sent there for gathering sticks on the sabbath.

MOON MADNESS

The light of the moon was widely associated with baleful influences and mental instability, which was why the mentally ill were once said to be "lunatic" or "moon-mad". Its effects were strongest at the full moon: in eastern European folklore, this was the time when werewolves metamorphosed into their lupine forms.

IMMACULATE CONCEPTION

Depictions of the Virgin of the Immaculate Conception may show the moon at the feet of the Virgin Mary as a symbol of her purity —the Immaculate Conception refers to the belief that she was conceived without inheriting humankind's sinful nature. This tradition was popular in Spanish sacred art in the seventeenth century.

HARE IN THE MOON

The equivalent of the man in the moon in many East Asian and American traditions is a hare or rabbit. In Chinese myth the lunar hare holds a pestle and mortar with which it mixes the elixir of immortality. In traditional Chinese belief the moon is a source of life, which begins in the womb with the creation of the "moon-soul" (*po*).

ASTROLOGY

One of the most ancient and complex of symbol systems, astrology is the study of the movements of the stars and planets and their supposed influences on the world. Originating in ancient Babylonia, it was developed by the Greeks and Romans, elaborated by the medieval Arabs and in recent times has embraced Uranus and Pluto. Astrology's principles have changed little in two millennia, and only since the seventeenth century has it been distinct from "scientific" astronomy. For many it continues to symbolize humankind's intimate connection with the cosmos.

Astrology works on the Hermetic principle ("As above, so below"): what occurs in the greater cosmos (macrocosm) is reflected in the smaller cosmos (microcosm) of our own world. The ancients were fascinated by how the seven moving (or apparently moving) planets (sun, moon, Venus, Mercury, Mars, Saturn, Jupiter) shifted in a regular pattern in relation to each other and to the Earth, against the backdrop of "fixed" stars. This backdrop was divided into twelve "houses", each named for its "ruling" constellation. Together, these are known as the Zodiac, from the Greek for "animal", since all but one are symbolized by living creatures (left). On this eighteenth-century chart (right) of the northern celestial hemisphere, the Zodiac lies around the "celestial equator" (the Earth's equator projected into space).

The particular qualities of the stars and planets, and their relative positions, are said to influence the lives of individuals and even of nations. The astrologer works out these influences at any one time by "casting" a horoscope, or map of the heavens. The horoscope for the time of a person's birth is believed to offer an insight into his or her character and destiny.

LIBRA, THE SCALES (September 23–October 22) The Earth at the equinox; linked with intellect and intuition in balance; and the element of air.

VIRGO, THE VIRGIN (August 22–September 22) A transitional time of harvest; linked with dependability, honesty, critical analysis; and the element of earth.

LEO, THE LION (July 23–August 21). The solar sign par excellence, ruling high summer, Leo is linked with power, pride, courage, ambition; and the element of fire.

SCORPIO, THE SCORPION (October 23–November 21) Nature in retreat, the onset of dark days; linked with intensity, emotional depth, tenacity, perception; and the element of water.

CANCER, THE CRAB (June 21–July 22) Linked with calmness and sensitivity, creativity and independence; and the element of water.

CHINESE ASTROLOGY

chinese astrology is used throughout the far east and its basic principles, like those of western astrology, rest on the idea that changes in the heavens (TIAN) influence events on earth. however, unlike western astrology, it encompasses meteorological phenomena such as THUNDER and RAINBOWS. it also ties in with the cosmology of the FIVE ELEMENTS and YIN and YANG (see page 88).

chinese astrologers divide the heavens into twenty-eight "lodges" (XIU), reflecting the lunar month: the

MOON dwells in a different lodge every night. however, there is also a zodiacal system of twelve constellations: RAT, OX, TIGER, RABBIT, DRAGON, SNAKE, HORSE, RAM (or SHEEP/GOAT), MONKEY, ROOSTER, DOG and BOAR (below). each has its own character and influences, and each presides over one year of a twelve-year cycle. this cycle operates in conjunction with yin, yang and the five elements to produce a sixty-year cycle beginning with the year "yang wood rat" and ending with "yin water boar".

SAGITTARIUS, THE CENTAUR OR ARCHER (November 22–December 22) Linked with strength and intellect in balance, purposefulness, inspiration, moral force; and the element of fire.

CAPRICORN, THE GOAT OR GOAT-FISH (December 23–January 19) The sign in winter's depths; linked with reflection, caution, inner creativity; and the element of earth.

AQUARIUS, THE WATER-CARRIER January 21–February 19) The time of returning light; linked with hope, vision, compassion, sharing of wisdom; and the element of air.

PISCES, THE FISHES (February 20–March 20) A fluid time as spring nears; linked with adaptability, sensitivity, emotion, dreaminess; and the element of water.

GEMINI, THE TWINS (May 20–June 21) Linked with intellect, adaptability, duality and contrasts of character; and the element of air.

TAURUS, THE BULL (April 20–May 19) The time when Earth's creativity is most rampant; linked with determination, strength, courage; and the element of earth.

ARIES, THE RAM (March 21–April 19) Astrologically the first sign of the Zodiac; coinciding with the start of spring, the sign is linked with energy and impulse; and the element of fire.

NATURE

PRIMITIVE SOCIETIES WERE CLOSER TO THE NATURAL WORLD AND MORE LIKELY TO DIFFERENTIATE ITS OPPORTUNITIES AND ITS DANGERS—THE GENERALIZED IDEA OF NATURE AS A BEAUTIFUL, IF UNSETTLING, WILDERNESS DID NOT EMERGE UNTIL THE EIGHTEENTH CENTURY.

land & sea

Inevitably, humankind has projected its deepest longings onto distant views within a landscape—the clouds, the sea's horizon, the night sky. The physical world forms a topography of the unconscious—our dreams and our anxieties.

ISLANDS
An island is a symbol of the isolated self or ego, though John Donne famously affirmed human interdependence when he wrote: "No man is an island, entire of itself." An island is also a refuge, even a paradise. The "Islands of the Blessed" are home to the virtuous dead in both Greek and Celtic traditions.

HILLS & MOUNTAINS
Mountains have spiritual significance as meeting-places between Earth and heaven. Hinduism and Buddhism both envisage a cosmos constructed around the conical shape of Mount Meru. As in Dante's *Purgatorio*, the higher you climb the mountain, the closer you approach enlightenment or salvation.

SEAS, LAKES & SPRINGS
The sea brings to mind infinite freedom and brave adventure—but also unfathomable depth (the unconscious). Its immensity can be both exhilarating and terrifying. Waves stand for the force of passion, which can overwhelm us, as in the Greek myth of Hero and Leander. Fresh water implies fertility. Whereas springs and streams represent the gushing life-force, ponds have the quiet stillness of the womb. Lakes are traditionally the Earth's eyes.

RIVERS
Constantly in flux, rivers symbolize the relentless onward flow of life. Following a river to the sea is a symbol of the attainment of higher consciousness. In India the Ganges, personified as the goddess Ganga, is the cleansing river that flows from the god Shiva's tresses.

trees

The largest members of the plant kingdom, trees furnish a symbolism that is both rich and, in many aspects, universal. Deciduous trees are the supreme symbols of cyclical growth, decay and regeneration; but deciduous and evergreens alike represent strength, constancy, fortitude and longevity. With roots under the earth and branches in the sky, trees are bridges linking the three realms of underworld, earth and the heavens. In Pueblo traditions of the American Southwest, for example, it is often up a tree that humankind emerges into the world from its birthplace underground. Trees link the four elements: they feed on earth and air, exude water (sap), and burn to fuel a fire. During the old northern European winter solstice feast of Yule, the burning of a deciduous oak log and the adornment of evergreen fir trees with lamps symbolized the rebirth of nature, and the return of light and life from the dark sleep of midwinter.

Trees were commonly understood as the dwellings of spirits, and groves and clearings within the dense, dark forests were natural sacred spaces. The Celts worshiped among trees, and the word *nemeton* means both "grove" and "sanctuary". The forests were home to the Horned God, an antlered Celtic deity linked with fertility. For the Buddha, trees were symbols of the calm awareness of the meditative state, and he taught in secluded forests. The "Forest Tradition" of meditation persists today in Theravada Buddhism.

BANYAN
The banyan (*Ficus benghalensis*) is India's national tree. Growing from the crown of a host tree down to the ground, it is a likely model for the inverted world tree of the *Upanishads*.

TWO TREES, ONE ROOT
A variant of the cosmic tree has twin trunks stemming from a single root, or with interlaced boughs. This represents the dualism of opposing but complementary forces—life and death, Earth and heaven, body and spirit.

COSMIC TREE
The cosmic center and source of all being is often envisioned in the form of a great tree, the axis of the world that permits communication between the Earth and the heavens. In the *Upanishads* and the *Zohar*, the cosmic tree is inverted, having its roots in the heavens, the origin of all existence.

DATE PALM
Originally a Roman symbol of military triumph, palm fronds were thrown to hail Jesus as the Messiah. Hence in Christian symbolism the palm represents dying for the faith but also ultimate victory over death. In Arab tradition the date palm is the tree of life. In the Quran, Mary (Maryam) bore Jesus (Isa) in the desert beneath a palm tree that at once produced ripe fruit and a spring.

THE SACRED OAK

The mighty OAK is a widespread symbol of masculine vigor and strength, and has often been linked with powerful male deities such as ODIN. Perhaps from its ability to withstand LIGHTNING, the oak was especially hallowed to thunder gods such as ZEUS and JUPITER, THOR and the Celtic TARANIS. The oak was the ancient Celts' most sacred tree, and Pliny the Elder (23—79CE) derives the word "druid" from the Greek *drys* (meaning "oak"). The druids, said Pliny, collected their sacred MISTLETOE only from oaks. The Celts worshiped chiefly in oak clearings; and the Drunemeton, or "oak GROVE", was the chief sanctuary of the Galatians, the Celts of Anatolia. The oak symbolized steadfastness, bravery—the "heart of oak"—and victory. Winners at the ancient Pythian Games at Delphi in Greece wore oak-leaf CROWNS; and several armies award oak-leaf badges to soldiers for conspicuous bravery in battle.

Yet oaks also have feminine associations. As one of the mightiest living things to grow from the soil, the oak is sacred to earth goddesses and mother goddesses as widespread as the Greek HERA and the Native American MOTHER EARTH. Hera and her consort, Zeus, were ritually "wed" in an oak grove, perhaps representing the union of EARTH and SKY. The female tree-spirits of the Greeks were the DRYADS, literally "oak-nymphs".

The oak is also associated with prophecy and divination. At the Greek oracle of Dodona, originally sacred to the mother goddess DIONE and later also to Zeus, the priest or priestess interpreted the rustling of oak leaves as the voice of the gods.

LIME OR LINDEN
Long-lived and bearing sweet-scented medicinal blossom, the lime tree (also called the linden tree) was held to inspire truthfulness. Scythian diviners wrapped a leaf of the lime tree around their fingers, and in many parts of Germany village assemblies and courts once sat beneath the tree. It also symbolized friendship—the lime tree was where lovers met and villagers held communal feasts.

TREE OF DEATH
Trees may be explicitly linked with sacrifice or death, like the tree of knowledge in Genesis, the fruit of which bestowed the curse of mortality on humankind. For Christians, its counterpart is the cross, the "tree" of the Crucifixion (and eternal life in Christ). In Norse myth, Odin hanged himself for nine days on Yggdrasil, the cosmic ash tree, in an act of self-sacrifice to obtain the runes of prophecy.

ACACIA
The sacred shittah wood of the Israelite tabernacle was acacia and so, in one tradition, was Christ's crown of thorns. The red or white acacia flowers represent the duality of death and eternal life.

HAWTHORN
In European folklore the hawthorn (may) is a tree of powerful magic. In the British Isles, may blossom was hung around house doors on May 1 to avert evil, but it was unlucky to bring the blossom inside before then.

HOLLY
Bearing fruit in mid-winter, the evergreen holly symbolized new life in pagan Rome. It was later linked with the crown of thorns, its berries representing drops of Christ's blood.

LAUREL
The laurel (bay) denotes chastity and triumph. A nymph, Daphne, turned into a laurel to avoid the lust of Apollo, god of light and inspiration. He made the tree sacred, and its leaves crowned poets and victors.

THE THREE FRIENDS OF WINTER

In Chinese tradition, the **PINE** (*song*), **BAMBOO** (*zhu*) and **PLUM** (*mei*) are known as the "Three Friends of **WINTER**". The evergreen pine withstands harsh weather and symbolizes constancy and endurance in adverse times. It is a common emblem of longevity or immortality, often found alongside symbols such as **PEACHES** and **CRANES**. A gift decorated with nine pine trees conveys a wish for long life, because the Chinese for "nine" sounds like the word for "forever". Pine has stood the ultimate test of time, like a wise person who has endured much.

Bamboo (technically a grass) is also an evergreen, and shares that symbolism with the pine, as well as representing versatility, since bamboo has so many uses, from food to scaffolding. Its suppleness makes it an emblem of fortitude and flexibility. The deciduous plum (*prunus*) has a special symbolism as the first tree of the year to blossom, before even the celebrated

CHERRY. Its delicate red, white or pink blossoms foretell the **SPRING** and symbolize hope, beauty, virginity and—since it flowers only briefly— the impermanence of existence. It also denotes courage in adversity, or "braving the frost", as one poet put it. The "Three friends of winter" are like the ideal confucian scholar-official: steadfast in all (political) weathers.

ALMOND

In the Levant the almond tree blossoms first, making it an ancient symbol of new life. Its sweet nuts represent concealed treasures, especially spiritual ones. The almond stands for Christ, who is God (the nut) clothed in mortal flesh (the shell); or for the Virgin, the sacred vessel containing Christ: the image derives from the "ripe almonds" of Numbers 17.8. Christ and Mary may be depicted within a mandorla, an almond-shaped halo.

HAZEL

In European lore the hazel represents divine insight, magical knowledge and fertility. It was the traditional material of a magician's wand, and in Irish myth nuts from a magic hazel tree were eaten by a salmon, imbuing it with universal wisdom. The hero Finn acquired this wisdom when he tasted the fish. Norman peasants would touch a cow three times with a hazel stick to make it lactate, and hazelnuts were thrown at German weddings.

YEW

Bearing toxic berries, the yew tree has symbolized death since ancient times. Yet this evergreen is also linked with immortality, since it is among the longest-lived of trees. Both traditions account for the centuries-old English custom of growing yews in graveyards (above). Branches of other evergreen foliage were commonly cut to decorate the house at Christmas, but yew was never used for fear that it would bring death to the family in the coming year.

OLIVE

Providing food and oil for cooking and light, the olive was sacred to Athene. It is a tree of peace, since an olive branch announced to Noah the end of God's wrath (Genesis 8.11).

CYPRESS

Shakespeare's "sad cypress" has long been linked with death: it was once sacred to Hades, Greek god of the underworld. But in Asia it is a revered symbol of longevity; the "Cypress of Abarqu" in Iran is 4,000 years old.

RED CEDAR

(right) The giant red cedar is an emblem of solidarity among Pacific Northwest native peoples, for whom its fibrous bark and soft yet durable wood was long a staple material. Sacred heraldic clan poles ("totem poles") are still made from it.

ASH

The Norse world tree Yggdrasil was an ash with its roots in three underworld springs and its canopy spreading over the heavens. It represented the unity of all existence. For the Greeks the ash was an emblem of strength: spear shafts were made from it.

CEDAR

Growing straight and tall, living to great ages and furnishing scented wood of remarkable durability, the cedar is linked with longevity, eternity, and the celestial or spiritual realm. King Solomon's temple was partly built of cedar (1 Kings 6.1).

FIG

The fig tree (*ficus*) is a key food source in many regions and represents sustenance, plenty and reproduction. It is the tree of life in Egypt and much of Asia, and in Islam a forbidden tree of paradise. Buddhists revere the tree as a symbol of the Buddha's enlightenment beneath a pipal (*Ficus religiosa*).

MULBERRY

The sweet fruit of the mulberry starts white or green, then turns red and finally purple or black, symbolizing the stages of life: innocence, vigor and decline. In Chinese myth it is a cosmic tree: the sun's home is a giant mulberry located beyond the eastern horizon.

TAMARISK

Said to have originated in heaven, the desert tamarisk is traditionally revered in the Near East. The biblical manna may have been the sweet resin of the tamarisk, and Abraham planted one in Beersheba (Genesis 21.33). One tradition claims that the tree of knowledge in Eden was a tamarisk. In China the tree shares with the pine associations of longevity and resilience (see box, opposite).

POPLAR

During the American Revolution, fast-growing poplars and other trees were planted as symbols of "growing freedom". French revolutionaries followed suit, adorning the trees with tricolored ribbons and the "Cap of Liberty" (see page 153).

WILLOW

In China, the willow represents resilience and flexibility and has protective powers. A branch of willow wards off evil spirits, and the Buddhist goddess Guanyin uses a willow branch to sprinkle healing nectar on the poor and sick. In the Bible, the sorrowing Israelites hang their harps on willows by the waters of Babylon (Psalm 137) and hence the weeping willow in particular is associated with mourning. Thus in England it was unlucky to burn willow in the house or to use a willow withy to drive animals.

KABALLAH

Kabbalah is an esoteric wisdom tradition that evolved within medieval Judaism but has roots in ancient Jewish mysticism. The central work of Kabbalah is the *Sefer Ha-Zohar* ("Book of Splendor"), or *Zohar*, written in Aramaic in Spain ca. 1200 by Moses de León. Kabbalah itself is a Hebrew word meaning "oral tradition", and kabbalistic lore claims that the first to receive the secret wisdom was Adam. But after the Fall the wisdom was lost until Abraham, the first patriarch of Israel, was initiated by the priest–king Melchizedek (above).

Kabbalah offers a complex symbolic explanation for the origin of the cosmos, and the relationship between God, humankind and the rest of the created material world. According to Kabbalah, all phenomena have their origin in the *Ain Sof Aur*, or "Limitless Light", a mystical term for God as the First Cause or fount of all, neither matter nor spirit but the source of both. The manifested universe proceeds from the *Ain Sof Aur* in a series of ten emanations or *sefirot* ("countings"), beginning with Kether (the Crown) and ending in Malkuth (the Kingdom), the world of manifest phenomena. Each *sefirah* represents a different aspect of God, who made the universe in his image. Spiritual enlightenment can be gained by studying the esoteric symbolism of the *sefirot* and the highly complex relationships and pathways that connect them. These are represented in symbolic form by the kabbalistic "Tree of Life" (opposite).

The *sefirot* have been compared to the system of *chakras*, which like the *sefirot* are represented visually as spheres that map the ascent of spirit (see pages 100–101). Both systems offer not only a symbolic explanation of the connection between spirit and matter but also a path to human transformation. The *sefirot* have also been related to mythic archetypes and to the cards of the Major Arcana in Tarot (see pages 122–123).

THE FOUR WORLDS

Kabbalah acknowledges four "worlds", or levels, of manifestation descending from the AIN SOF AUR (see main text) to the world of matter. Each contains the ten SEFIROT to a greater or lesser degree, and each is mystically linked to a letter of the TETRAGRAMMATON (see below, left). The first world, ATZILUTH (emanation), is the purest of the four, replete with the infinite light of Ain Sof Aur. The second world is BERIAH (creation), where archangels dwell and creation comes into being but does not assume manifest form. This occurs in the third world, YETZIRAH (formation), identified with Yesod on the TREE OF LIFE. The process of manifestation is complete in the fourth and "densest" world, ASSIAH (action). Assiah has two sublevels, spiritual and physical. The latter is the material world as we know it.

THE UNIFICATION OF THE FAITHS
For kabbalists God is unchanging and eternal; hence it is only externally that Judaism, Christianity and Islam differ. This eighteenth-century symbol of the union of the three faiths (above) is by Rabbi Jakob Emden.

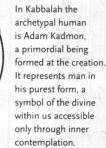

ADAM KADMON
In Kabbalah the archetypal human is Adam Kadmon, a primordial being formed at the creation. It represents man in his purest form, a symbol of the divine within us accessible only through inner contemplation.

TETRAGRAMMATON
The Tetragrammaton ("four letters") is the sacred name of God, written in Hebrew with four letters (YHWH). The four letters are imbued with a mystical power and the name is so sacred that it may never be spoken.

KETHER "Crown", first emanation; the potential of all existence, radiant with *Ain Sof Aur*.

BINAH "Understanding", third; the womb of becoming, or the mystical "mother" of creation.

GEVURAH "Strength" or "Justice", fifth; the stern judgment of God, balancing Hesed.

HOD "Splendor" or "Majesty", eighth; the glory of creation that nears fruition with the divine gift of form.

YESOD "Foundation", ninth; where spirit is transformed into material reality, coming into being.

THREE PILLARS Divine Will (center), Justice (left) and Mercy (right), or neutral (center), female (left) and male (right), the pillars are linked by thirty-two pathways.

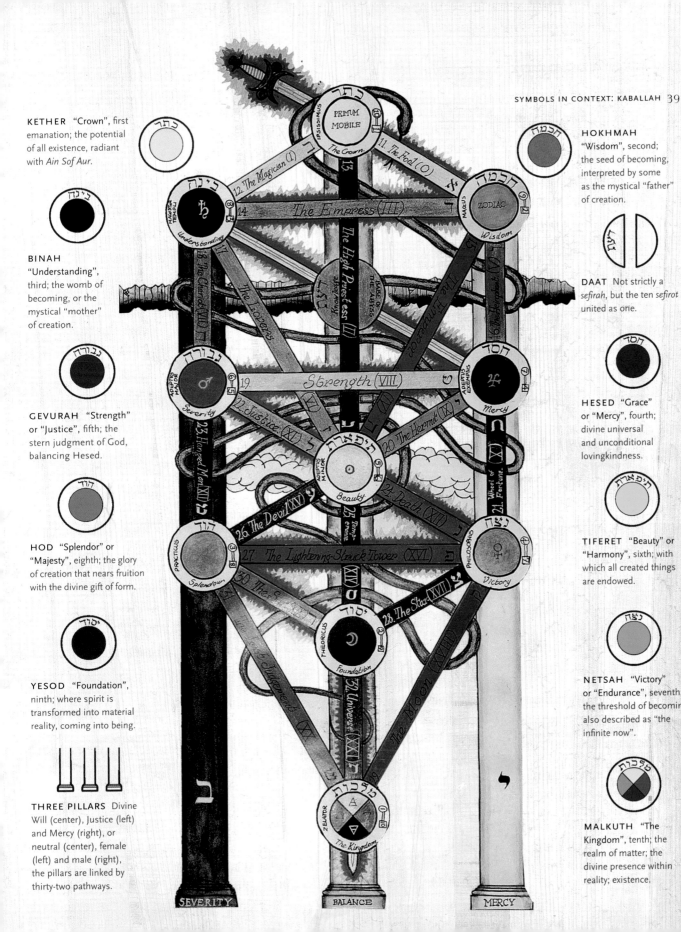

HOKHMAH "Wisdom", second; the seed of becoming, interpreted by some as the mystical "father" of creation.

DAAT Not strictly a *sefirah*, but the ten *sefirot* united as one.

HESED "Grace" or "Mercy", fourth; divine universal and unconditional lovingkindness.

TIFERET "Beauty" or "Harmony", sixth; with which all created things are endowed.

NETSAH "Victory" or "Endurance", seventh; the threshold of becoming, also described as "the infinite now".

MALKUTH "The Kingdom", tenth; the realm of matter; the divine presence within reality; existence.

fruits

Fruits (which in functional terms are simply containers for seed) stand self-evidently for "fruitfulness"—the generosity and fertility of the earth. Classical painters showed fruit in variety and profusion spilling from a cornucopia or "horn of plenty". Yet fruit has negative associations too—most notably the "forbidden fruit" of "the tree of knowledge of good and evil" that stood in the garden of Eden in the Book of Genesis. In Christian tradition, the sinfulness of humankind is attributed to Adam and Eve eating the fruit and losing their primal innocence; in Judaism this act initiates a pattern of human disobedience to God. The Bible does not state what the species of tree was, but Christian art has tended to depict the fruit as an apple, especially in the West. A man's "Adam's apple" is said to have arisen where a bit of the forbidden fruit stuck in Adam's throat. Behind this lies a Latin pun: the word *malum* means both "apple" and "evil". However, ancient writers also identified the tree as a tamarind or a fig, among others.

Fruits are linked with sexuality, from their role as the seed-laden creators of new life and also, as in the case of the barren, seedless banana, from their shape.

STILL LIFE
European artists in the seventeenth century used fruits in abundance to symbolize the cornucopian bounty of God's creation. Yet there was often an implied overtone of mortality: some artists showed fruit past its prime, in the first stages of decay.

LEMON
With its combination of sweetness and sharpness, of fragile flower, tough rind and juicy pulp, the lemon stands for fidelity through the vicissitudes of love.

BERRIES
Often deep-red in color, berries may be associated with life or blood. In Christian tradition, the elderberry has connotations of remorse: tradition has it that Judas hanged himself from the branch of an elder tree.

PEAR
The Romans used the same word (*pirus*) for the pear and the male genitalia, a link that lasted into the Renaissance. In Greek myth pears are sacred to the goddesses Hera and Aphrodite; in Roman, to Pomona.

POMEGRANATE
This many-seeded fruit denotes fertility, but also temptation. Persephone, the daughter of Demeter, Greek goddess of the harvest, ate six seeds and became the prisoner of Hades in the Underworld.

PEACH

An auspicious symbol of longevity in China and Japan, the peach had a different meaning in Christianity: a peach with a leaf attached was a symbol of truthfulness. This refers to an ancient use of this image to symbolize the tongue speaking from the heart.

APPLE

Apart from its link to original sin (see main text, opposite), the apple has a wealth of symbolism in the West. The Golden Apples of the Hesperides are the fruit of immortality. Christian scholar Origen interprets the apple mentioned in the Song of Solomon as an image of the sweet, rich Word of God.

FIG

The fig is linked with sexuality, and with Dionysus (Bacchus), the Classical god of wine. The withered fig is a church whose branches have been blighted by heresy. In Buddhism the fig is holy: the *bodhi* tree under which the Buddha awakened was a fig.

FRUITS OF THE ORIENT

In china, the LYCHEE (unknown in the west until modern times) is a symbol of good fortune, because its name sounds like the chinese word for "interest" in the financial sense, and like another word meaning the birth of a baby son. The APPLE, similarly, has connotations of harmony, as its name in chinese is phonetically indistinguishable from the word for "peace". such puns are accorded great significance in china—no two lovers would ever wish to share a PEAR, since the word for that fruit is a perfect homonym of the word for "separation" (even though, since the pear tree itself is long-lived, there is also an association with longevity, one of the prime blessings in chinese tradition). CHERRY blossom is a national symbol of japan, and an emblem for the samurai caste—its brief but breathtaking beauty represents the fleeting nature of a warrior's life, while crushing the fruit's red flesh denotes self-sacrifice through bloodshed.

GRAPE

This fruit represents the wine that Christ compared to his blood at the Last Supper, and his resurrection, but it can also suggest Bacchanalian licence. In the Hebrew Bible the vine is blessed abundance.

APRICOT

The Chinese associate apricots with education —Confucius is said to have taught his students under an apricot tree.

BANANA

The banana plant dies after bearing one crop of seedless fruit, which for Buddhists makes it a symbol of the futility of worldly goods (in fact, the plant propagates by rhizomes in the soil). In dreams, the banana's phallic shape links it with male sexuality.

DATE

The date was the sacred tree of the Babylonians. In the Hebrew Bible it denotes the just citizen, enriched by the blessings of God. In Islam it is linked with Mary (Maryam), who in the Quran bears Jesus (Isa) under a date palm.

JUJUBE

In Chinese the words for "jujube" and "soon" sound alike (*ji*), hence the fruit symbolizes a wish that a bride will swiftly have children.

ORANGE

A symbol of marriage, orange blossom is traditionally worn by the virgin bride. The shape and color also link it with the sun. (See also MANDARIN, page 43).

PERSIMMON

Starting off bitter and sweetening dramatically as it ripens, this fruit is a Buddhist symbol of spiritual transformation.

FRUITS IN PLENTY

said to be the horn of the goat-nymph **AMALTHEA** who suckled **ZEUS**, the **CORNUCOPIA** gave forth an unending bounty of fruit. It was an attribute of the fertility goddess **DEMETER** (the Roman **CERES**), and also features in art with **DIONYSUS** (**BACCHUS**), the god of wine and revelry, as well as with **FLORA**, goddess of flowers, and allegorical deities such as **FORTUNA**, **PAX** and **CONCORDIA**. As a general symbol of abundance it features in the **ARMS** of New Jersey, North Carolina and Idaho, and on several national emblems.

A **BASKET OF FRUIT** appears alongside the goddess **POMONA** (see page 53) and is also a symbol of the sense of taste. **ANGELS** may bring baskets of fruit to **CHRIST** in the wilderness. A **BOWL OF FRUIT** may represent either the virtue of **CHARITY** or the vice of **GLUTTONY**.

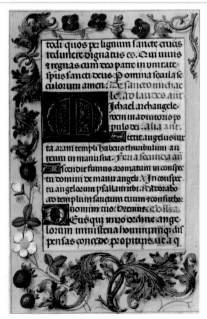

CITRON

(*right*) Resembling a large lemon, the citron (right) is the sacred etrog fruit of Judaism. A variety of citron that sprouts finger-like shoots at its base is known in China as "Buddha's Hand" (*Foshou*) from its resemblance to the Buddha's hand gesture known as *bhumisparsamudra*—touching the ground to call the earth to witness his enlightenment. By a play on words in Chinese the citron also symbolizes long life (*fu*) and happiness (*shou*). The citron, peach and pomegranate make up a trio known as the "Three Plenties" or "Three Abundances", respectively symbolizing prosperity, long life and many progeny.

STRAWBERRY

Its shape—and its red voluptuousness—made the strawberry a symbol of female sexuality and it was an ancient symbol of Venus, the Roman goddess of love. In parts of France, newlyweds shared a bowl of strawberry soup as an aphrodisiac. Another folk tradition claims that if a couple eat two halves of the same strawberry, they will fall in love. As a summer fruit the strawberry is also associated in mythology with the sun, and represents the summer in Native American traditions.

PINEAPPLE

Stone pineapples, often mistaken for pinecones, adorned the walls and gateposts of many eighteenth-century European mansions. At the time few Europeans could afford pineapples or other exotic fruits that had to be imported by sea over great distances from the tropics, or grown in heated glasshouses. Because they were prohibitively expensive for most people, pineapples often became self-conscious symbols of wealth and abundant hospitality.

CHESTNUT

In China, a play on words means that chestnuts ($lizi$) symbolize the begetting (li) of progeny (zi). In Scotland, at Halloween, lovers would often place two chestnuts together in the fire. If the nuts burned steadily together the sweethearts' courtship would fare well; but the opposite would be true if either of the nuts burst and they sprang apart.

PLUM

For the Native American Pawnee, the wild plum is a symbol of fertility. In China the plum tree is one of the "Three Friends of Winter" (see page 36), and its unripe fruit represents the pupil in contrast to the master. To Christians the plum denotes fidelity and independence.

WALNUT

Nuts are widely linked with fertility and new life (see **HAZEL** and **ALMOND**, page 36). The Romans ate stewed walnuts to enhance fertility, although the writer Pliny the Elder warned against the tree's harmful shade. The kernel within the tough shell symbolizes profound wisdom that is not easily got. Going to sleep beneath a walnut tree was once said to bring dreams of the year to come. In art, a walnut may represent Christ, as St. Augustine explained: the nut's green outer husk is Christ's mortal flesh, the shell the wood of the cross and the kernel his divinity. The seeker after Christ may be represented as a small bird or squirrel attempting to prise open a walnut (right).

CHILI & TOMATO

Several foodstuffs native to the Americas have been spread worldwide. In India chilis (right) are displayed with limes in vehicles and houses to avert malign spirits and the evil eye. The first cultivated tomatoes were probably produced by the Aztecs. Called *tomatl*, they were small and yellow, which is why when they arrived in Italy tomatoes were given the name *pomodoro*, or golden apple. The Pueblo peoples of the American Southwest used tomato seeds in divination rituals.

CHERRY

In Christian tradition cherries are the "fruit of paradise". In paintings of the Madonna and Child, the infant Jesus may be depicted holding cherries in his hand, symbolizing heaven and the rewards of virtue.

LIME

In India lime wards off evil spirits, perhaps because of its sharpness. In the eighteenth-century British navy a daily lime ration was found to prevent scurvy; hence the nickname "Limeys" for Britons in general.

MANDARIN

Oranges in Far Eastern symbolism are usually the mandarin or tangerine rather than the larger varieties called simply "oranges" in the West. They represent good fortune because of their gold color and perfection owing to their round shape.

POMELO

This large yellow fruit features at Chinese New Year as an emblem of wealth and prosperity, because its color is associated with gold and because its name (*you*) sounds the same as "to have" or "to possess".

QUINCE

"They dined on mince / And slices of quince", wrote Edward Lear of his newlywed Owl and Pussycat; and the quince is an ancient symbol of marriage, sacred to Aphrodite (Venus) and Dionysus (Bacchus).

WATERMELON

In Mexican art associated with the Day of the Dead, watermelon is often depicted as the food of the dead. In Chinese *zi* means both "seed" and "children"; hence watermelons and other seed-filled fruits signify the hope for many progeny.

flowers & plants

Flowers, and plants in general, are universal decorative motifs (left, inlaid marble decor in India) and the symbolism connected with them is almost inexhaustible. Meanings can often be traced to their form (three-petaled flowers are associated with the Holy Trinity) or color (yellow blooms often attract solar symbolism). Much vegetal symbolism has roots in the ancient idea of "correspondences" in the natural world, of which humankind was the focal point. Thus, the shape or color of a plant might be understood as a "signature", or symbol, of its appropriate medical uses: for example, a herb with red blossom would be used to treat scarlet fever or ailments of the blood, and a root shaped like a foot could be used to cure the gout.

Flowers collectively are emblems of spring and early summer, when most bloom. They also represent the brevity of existence: a human being, in the words of *The Book of Common Prayer*, "cometh up, and is cut down, like a flower". It was a trope of Renaissance poets to urge the beloved to awaken to love, before youth and beauty faded to become, as Shakespeare wrote, "the violet past prime".

No flower has attracted more use as a symbol than the rose (see opposite). Christian tradition alone furnishes a rich treasury of rose symbolism. God created the rose thornless, it was said, but the rose acquired its thorns at the fall of Adam and Eve to symbolize the loss of innocence. The sinless Virgin Mary was the "rose without thorns". The red rose is also an emblem of martyrdom; it was said to have acquired its hue from drops of Christ's blood.

LILY

Betokening purity and virginity, the white lily is a flower of the Virgin Mary, the "Heavenly Lily", and of other virgin saints. The archangel Gabriel often holds a lily in depictions of the Annunciation, where the flower represents Mary's miraculous conception by the Holy Spirit. In other traditions, the lily is linked to fertility and sex, perhaps from the phallic shape of its unopened blossoms. The heraldic fleur-de-lys (lily or iris) was the royal badge of France; its three petals represented the Holy Trinity.

CHRYSANTHEMUM

The chrysanthemum, whose name means "golden flower", blooms long past summer and into winter, and hence in Far Eastern tradition represents longevity. In China it is also a symbol of perfection and intellectual accomplishment, since the words for "chrysanthemum" and "whole" or "complete" sound the same (*ju*). In Japan the chrysanthemum is the national heraldic flower. It represents the sun. The "Chrysanthemum Throne" refers to Japan's monarchy.

THE LANGUAGE OF FLOWERS

In Victorian times it became popular for lovers and close friends to communicate in code through **TUSSIE MUSSIES**, small **POSIES** or **NOSEGAYS**. In an era when more explicit expressions of intimacy were often socially difficult or unacceptable, this could be more than a quaint pastime. Much of the "language of flowers" derived from traditional flower symbolism: thus, **PANSIES** would convey that the friend or beloved was in one's thoughts. Different shades of **ROSE** expressed different degrees of love: a **WHITE ROSE** meant innocence and chastity; a **YELLOW ROSE** devoted friendship; and a **RED OR SCARLET ROSE** intense passion. The art of flower arranging tends now to be based upon aesthetic concerns, but may still refer to traditional flower symbolism. **WHITE FLOWERS**, symbolizing virgin purity, are still traditional for weddings.

A similar floral code exists in Japan, called **HANA KOTOBA** ("flower-language") but it was not confined to lovers: samurai frequently adopted flowers as their heraldic emblems (**MON**). In modern times *hana kotoba* has embraced much of western flower symbolism.

NARCISSUS
In Greek myth Narcissus spurned the nymph Echo, who pined away in anguish. The gods punished the youth by making him fall in love with his own reflection, but when he too pined away and died, they took pity on him and turned him into the little narcissus flower, which is a symbol of dying young.

ANEMONE
Meaning "of the wind", this briefly flowering bloom represents life's transience and fragility. An ancient tradition associated anemones with dying and resurrecting gods: they grew on the spot where Adonis, the lover of the goddess Aphrodite, perished, and they appear in depictions of the Crucifixion.

HEARTSEASE
The wild relative of the garden pansy has two names: heartsease, owing to its medicinal uses, and pansy (French *pensée*, thought) from its habit during August of nodding forward as if in contemplation. It symbolizes thought and fond remembrance.

DAFFODIL
A daffodil was once an emblem of bad luck; if brought into an English house it meant poultry would be barren. The name derives from asphodel, the flower of the Greek underworld.

VIOLET
The tiny violet symbolizes humility and is linked with the child Jesus, whose wisdom astonished the Temple teachers but who remained obedient to his parents (Luke 2.51). The flower's hue, resembling the imperial purple, hints at Christ's status as the King of Kings and also, as a color of mourning, his death on the cross.

DANDELION
Named "lion's tooth" (*dent de lion*) from its jagged leaves, this common flower is a Christian symbol of grief and mourning, no doubt due to its bitterness. Blowing the dried seedhead is a traditional means of love divination.

DAISY

The daisy—literally the "day's eye"—is a symbol of the sun, opening when the sun rises and closing when it sets. As such it is potent against magic: daisy chains were once believed to protect children from being stolen by fairies.

ROSE
Roses represent the cosmic center, the mystic heart. White roses represent perfection, purity and innocence, in contrast to the red, which stand for the passionate heart and sexual desire. A red rose was an attribute of the love-goddess Aphrodite (Venus), its thorns representing the pangs of love.

CARNATION
Carnations, or pinks, share some of the symbolism of roses, purity (when white) and passion (when red). As emblems of motherhood and maternal love they are associated with the Virgin Mary. The flowers denote betrothal and marriage in Netherlandish art of the 1400s and 1500s. The symbolism of motherhood and marriage are both present in Raphael's *Madonna of the Pinks*, where the flowers allude to Mary as both the Virgin Mother of God and the Bride of Christ.

PEONY
The ancients wore the seeds of this striking flower to ward off evil. It takes its name from Paion or Paeon, a deity who healed the gods' wounds in the Trojan War. Appreciated for its bold color, in China the peony was a flower of the emperors and symbolized royalty, honor, nobility, wealth and the joys of springtime.

SUNFLOWER
Standing with its face turned toward the sun, the sunflower is both a solar emblem and a traditional symbol of devotion, particularly of a loyal subject to a monarch, or of a Christian believer to the Church. It is also a symbol of fecundity, potential and renewal, owing to its great seedhead, densely packed with seeds. Kansas in the USA is the "Sunflower State".

HAIL THE SPIRIT OF THE LOTUS

sprouting in mud at the bottom of a pond or lake, then rising through the murky water to bloom in sunlight on the surface, the **LOTUS** or **WATER LILY** is a widespread symbol of the process of creation and spiritual ascent. In ancient Egypt, the flower represented the creation, when the first god came into existence on a mound that arose from **NUN**, the primordial sea. It was also the heraldic plant of upper Egypt, the southern part of the pharaoh's "Two Lands". In Hindu tradition, the lotus grew from the navel of **VISHNU** as he rested between cycles of creation on a cosmic **SERPENT** in the waters of chaos. From the lotus sprang the god **BRAHMA**, who acted as demiurge to bring forth the world at the start of the next cycle. Lotuses with differing numbers of petals symbolize the principal **CHAKRAS**, or energy centers of the body (see pages 100—101).

The lotus is a central motif in Buddhism. The **BUDDHA** (shown above holding a lotus bud) used the plant's life-cycle as a metaphor for the path from ignorance (the muddy depths) to the clear mind of enlightenment, and the flower is ubiquitous in Buddhist art. The Buddha and other enlightened beings often sit on lotus **THRONES**, or have a **NIMBUS** of lotus petals. The most popular sacred mantra of Tibetan Buddhism, *om mani padme hum*, hails the precious teachings of the Buddha as the jewel (*mani*) in the lotus (*padme*).

IVY
In some traditions, holly and ivy denoted male and female respectively, and both were evergreen symbols of continuing life in the depths of winter. But as a Christmas decoration toxic ivy had to stay outside, lest it bring bad luck. On the other hand, a Scottish girl who placed an ivy leaf in her bosom would soon meet her future husband.

MISTLETOE
Producing yellow flowers and white berries in midwinter, the mistletoe plant represents the continued potency and fertility of nature. It was sacred to the ancient Druids, the priestly caste of the Celts, who only cut the parasitic plant from oak trees, using a golden sickle. According to Pliny, they used it in fertility potions.

香祖
沈振麟

ORCHID

(*left*) In the Far East the orchid is a flower of elegance, prized for its delicate scent. It symbolizes love and feminine beauty on the one hand, and gentlemanly refinement on the other. However, the orchid was also believed to offer protection against barrenness, and is strongly associated with fertility. This association is also found in the West: the flower's name derives from the Greek (*orkhis*) meaning "testicle". By contrast, the beauty of the flower also links it to spirituality and purity.

POPPY

Sacred to the Greek earth goddess Demeter, the poppy symbolized the oblivion between death and rebirth, probably from its narcotic properties. The poppy's use as a token of war remembrance (above) derives from John MacRae's 1915 poem opening: "In Flanders fields the poppies grow, / Between the crosses, row on row."

CAMELLIA

In China the evergreen camellia represents beauty and endurance, since it flowers at the start of winter, and its auspicious red blooms are common New Year decorations. In Japan, though, camellias betoken unexpected death.

HELIOTROPE

The heliotrope is a solar emblem because it "turns to the sun", the meaning of its name. Clytie, abandoned by the sun god Apollo, became a heliotrope. It adorned the crowns of Roman emperors and in Christian art it denotes devotion to God.

HYACINTH

A youth loved by the god Apollo, Hyacinthus was accidentally struck by a discus and died; the hyacinth sprang from the spot where his blood fell. Hence the flower is a symbol of the spring, when the sun (Apollo) brings forth new life.

JASMINE

In Arabic the name of the fragrant jasmine means "God's gift", and in both East and West it is linked with feminine grace and beauty. The flower is associated with the Virgin Mary in Christian tradition and is a symbol of motherhood in Thailand.

SHAMROCK & CLOVER

A heraldic plant of Ireland, the shamrock is said to have been used by St. Patrick to instruct the Irish on the Holy Trinity, the "Three-In-One". Four-leafed clovers were reputed to be powerful protectors against fairy enchantment.

WISTERIA

This flower is called *fuji* in Japan and is celebrated in April and May in various *fuji matsuri* or "wisteria festivals". It can connote sorrow, in the sense of a love lost but the heart enduring.

MARIGOLD

With its bright orange or yellow heads, the marigold is a solar flower, sacred to the gods in India, where marigolds abound at ceremonies and festivals. In China it is called the "flower of ten thousand years", a symbol of longevity that featured on imperial robes. In Christian tradition it symbolizes the Virgin, hence its name ("Mary gold").

ROSICRUCIANISM

Rosicrucianism is a name given to beliefs and practices of esoteric and occult societies that trace their descent from a figure named "Christian Rosenkreuz". The name is symbolic: "Rosenkreuz" means "Rosy Cross" and the cross is, of course, the central emblem of Christianity, while the rose is an important Christian and alchemical motif. The existence of this mysterious secret Christian society, whose members included philosophers and alchemists, was first announced in an anonymous work entitled *Fama Fraternitatis Roseae Crucis (Report of the Fraternity of the Rosy Cross)*, which was published in Germany in 1614. It describes, in highly symbolic and metaphorical language, how "Christian Rosenkreuz" discovered ancient wisdom and magical knowledge. The work was followed by the *Confessio Fraternitatis* (1615) and the *Chemical Wedding of Christian Rosenkreuz* (1616), the last an alchemical allegory that describes a progression of mystic rites.

The search for spiritual and physical transformation was based on the notion that humanity became impure at the Fall, but can reclaim its purity by ascending, through a series of initiations, to the enlightened plane, where one may learn the mysteries of the universe and gain insight into the heart of the divine itself, symbolized by the rose and cross (left). The rosy cross is a complex symbol, but put most simply it denotes the quest for physical and spiritual purity, and also the purity of life that was essential for those hoping to progress in that quest.

Rosicrucianism was like the Great Work of alchemy and attracted many alchemists, so it is no surprise that Rosicrucians drew heavily on alchemical symbolism. The engraving opposite comes from a German work of 1785 entitled *The Secret Symbols of the Rosicrucians from the 16th and 17th Centuries*, and depicts the process of spiritual ascent as the symbolic *Mons Philosophorum*, or "Mount of the Philosophers".

LAUNDRY BARREL Outer purification by the power of the heavens, denoted by the sun and moon. In it a senior adept plants the tree of spiritual success.

BLACK CROW In alchemy it symbolizes *nigredo* or blackening: the beginning of transformation.

WINGED DRAGON Emerging from the inner darkness, this denotes earthly matter beginning to take spiritual form.

PHILOSOPHER The philosopher is the gatekeeper of the mountain cave, the guardian of knowledge.

INITIATES The three figures may represent body, soul and spirit: all must collaborate to achieve the goal.

MICROCOSMIC MAN
Supported by angels, the Rosicrucian microcosmic human has its feet in the earthly realm and its head, seat of wisdom, in celestial light. The six-pointed star denotes the Hermetic axiom: "As above, so below."

ROSY HEART
The cross and rose are sometimes found with the heart. As explained in Rosicrucian texts, the heart of the true initiate is closed at the bottom, so that earthly influence may not enter, and open at the top, to divine influences only.

ORB & CROWN The domain of the divine and goal of the quest. The crown is God the Father, the orb Christ; below is the mystic "House of the Holy Spirit". Red alludes to the alchemical *rubedo* (see page 61).

TRINITY TREE The three stars refer to the sacred mystery of the Holy Trinity, source of all truth.

FURNACE The refiner's fire of inner purification. Like the laundry barrel, this is a biblical image (Malachi 3.2).

WHITE EAGLE The alchemical *albedo*, or whitening, that follows *nigredo*: the point of transformation is near.

LION Guardian of the Royal Castle and the final stages of ascent, this represents truth, power, strength and spiritual vigilance.

HEN The brooding hen symbolizes the seeker's patient contemplation of subtle mysteries.

HARE The art of alchemy, delving into sacred truths; and the quick intellect of the spiritual seeker.

THE GOLDEN DAWN

Rosicrucianism influenced the rites of a number of societies devoted to CEREMONIAL MAGIC—the use of magical symbols, rites and ceremonies in the quest for mystical and supernatural knowledge. The most influential of these occult societies was the HERMETIC ORDER OF THE GOLDEN DAWN, founded in Britain in 1888, with adherents including W.B. Yeats and Aleister Crowley. The Golden Dawn initiate rose through ten grades based on the SEFIROT of the KABBALISTIC TREE (see pages 38–39). However, the idea of ascending stages reflects Rosicrucian practice. Rosicrucianism also influenced the rituals of the first seven grades, which constituted the "Order of the RED ROSE and CROSS OF GOLD". The developed WILL is the key: without it success on any path is unlikely. Through will, the magician controls supernatural forces invoked in magical rites. The German engraving below shows how the will (*wille*) can be a force for good (*wohl*) or ill (*wehe*).

GARDENS

The first recorded gardens were those of ancient Egypt, depicted in tombs some 3,500 years old, with trees, flowers and fish-filled ponds. The earliest formal planted spaces, though, were probably created in the Neolithic era, when people began to cultivate plants for food. From those times gardens have represented settled humanity in contrast to the wilderness of the nomads and hunters. In gardens nature is controlled, restrained and contained, and hence they symbolize peace, tranquility, order, freedom from anxiety and the conscious mind—as well as being an enduringly popular decorative motif, from weavings to ceramics (Ottoman tile, right)—in the same way that the wild forests or deserts beyond the walls or fences of the garden represent chaos and disorder, unpredictability and hidden terrors. In psychological terms, gardens represent the conscious and wilderness the subconscious.

Gardens are often planted as places of retreat from the cares of the world. They may symbolize a romantic ideal of nature, as in aristocratic English gardens, or an ideal of order and regularity, as in their French counterparts (see page 52). Or, as in the Christian and Buddhist monastic traditions, gardens may be designed expressly as places of profound contemplation. They may be representations of paradise, as in the Near East and Islamic world, evoking the places where humans once lived in primordial bliss; or they may represent the heavenly regions to which the blessed are assigned after death, the abode of gods and immortals.

PARADISE GARDENS

(*left*) The ancient Near Eastern idea of paradise was of a blissful realm fed by four streams, like the four rivers that flow from Eden. These divide the garden into four parts, reflected in the Islamic Firdous (Paradise) of the Quran. The traditional oasis-like gardens cultivated in Iran, filled with fragrant flowers, fruit trees and spices, are designed to represent this paradise on Earth. The words "paradise" and "Firdous" both derive ultimately from the ancient Iranian *pairi-daeza*, meaning "enclosure". A paradisal four-part garden can be found at the mausoleum of Mumtaz Mahal, the Taj Mahal, at Agra (left).

FLORA

The Roman deity of springtime and flowers, Flora (the equivalent of the Greek Chloris) dwelled with her consort Zephyr, the west wind, in a garden of myriad fruit and flowers where spring reigned perpetually. She was celebrated at the exuberant, flower-filled Roman spring festival of Floralia. Botticelli famously depicted Flora in his painting *Primavera* (detail, left).

GETHSEMANE

The "garden" of Gethsemane was an olive grove where, on the eve of the Crucifixion, Christ suffered mental agonies during hours of solitary vigil and prayer while his disciples slept. Gethsemane represents the spiritual seeker's "dark night of the soul", the often painful transition to insight and self-awareness.

WESTERN PARADISE

The popular Chinese goddess Xi Wang Mu, the "Queen Mother of the West", resides in a paradise in the Kunlun Mountains of the far west, the abode of the celestial immortals. She tends beautiful gardens whose central feature is a tree bearing the peaches of eternal life, from which the gods and goddesses replenish their immortality.

THE VIRGIN IN THE GARDEN

The ENCLOSED GARDEN (Latin HORTUS CONCLUSUS)—a wall or fence containing fruitfulness—is a traditional symbol of the VIRGIN MARY, an idea derived from the biblical song of songs (4.12). In art, for example in depictions of the ANNUNCIATION or MADONNA AND CHILD (above), the virgin may be shown within an ideal garden that serves as a symbol of her virginity and of the IMMACULATE CONCEPTION (her own conception free of original sin—her womb is the pure garden in which Christ grows). Mary in the garden echoes ADAM AND EVE in their primordial state of purity in EDEN. Variations on the enclosed garden may show the virgin in a ROSE BOWER (Mary is the "rose without thorns") and she may also be depicted in a garden with a UNICORN, a symbol of chastity and purity.

EDEN

According to the Book of Genesis, God placed **ADAM AND EVE**, the first man and woman, in the earthly **PARADISE** of **EDEN**, a garden where they lived in harmony with nature and in a state of blissful innocence, free from craving, anxiety, pain, need or death. The garden represents the ideal human relationship with God, which was broken when, tempted by **SATAN** in the form of a **SERPENT**, Adam and Eve disobeyed God's command not to eat the fruit of the **TREE OF KNOWLEDGE** of good and evil (above). In Judaism, this act set a precedent for humankind's inclination to stray from obedience to God. For Christians, it made humankind inherently sinful until the coming of Christ brought the possibility of redemption. For their disobedience Adam and Eve were expelled from Eden without eating from the **TREE OF LIFE**, which would have bestowed immortality. The story of Eden sought to explain the human condition of inevitable death and propensity to evil. Eden remains a symbol of paradise lost, and of an unattainable state of perfection and bliss.

ENGLISH GARDENS

At the aristocratic country houses of eighteenth-century England a new style of garden emerged that symbolized the Enlightenment ideal of nature and reason in perfect harmony. Such "English gardens" were very carefully planned and planted, but were designed to look asymmetrical, informal and "natural", typically with sweeping areas of grass dotted with artificial lakes or ponds set against woodland. A Romantic element was sometimes introduced in the form of fake Classical ruins, evoking Roman antiquity and the idea that "all things must pass".

FRENCH GARDENS

With their highly symmetrical designs centered on a palace or mansion, their formal plantings, elegant parterres, clipped topiary, trim lawns and broad, radiating walks and avenues, the French gardens of the seventeenth and eighteenth centuries were designed as microcosms. They symbolized the perfectly ordered society of which the monarch or lord was the pinnacle—just as the mansion of God was the center of a perfectly ordered universe.

ZOOLOGICAL GARDENS

What we now call a zoo has its roots in the medieval outdoor menagerie, a garden that included exotic animals as well as plants and flowers. King Henry I of England (ruled 1100–1135) is recorded as keeping lions, leopards, lynxes, camels and porcupines, which served as a symbol of his power and reach. Aztec gardens were a similar mix of plants and animals. Moctezuma (ruled 1502–1520), the last king of the Aztecs, had pleasure gardens that symbolized his domains, containing plants from all over the Aztec empire.

ORCHARDS

Enclosures of fruit trees share the fertility and fruitfulness symbolism of gardens, a variation on the *hortus conclusus*. A theme popular in Renaissance art was the nymph Pomona, the goddess of fruit trees, being wooed in her orchard by the disguised god Vertumnus.

FOUNTAINS

Often forming the focus of a formal garden, a fountain represents the source of life, the spring that flows in paradise from the roots of the Tree of Life, as described in the Book of Genesis. In art it may represent the fountain that bestows youth or immortality.

ZEN GARDENS

With asymmetrical yet carefully harmonious arrangements of rocks, mosses, shrubs and ponds or meticulously raked gravel evoking the sea of *samsara* (the cycle of life, death and rebirth), Zen gardens are designed as ideal places for meditation. They represent in landscape form the Zen Buddhist aesthetic and spiritual ideal of *wabi-sabi*, the "quiet and simple elegance" that evolved from the discipline required to attain *satori* (enlightenment).

CHINESE GARDENS

In China, gardens ranged from large and spacious imperial pleasure gardens to more intimate temple and private ones. Even in a small urban garden, the intention was to create the illusion of being immersed in nature, which one contemplated from carefully positioned pavilions or shelters. Gardens symbolized the cosmos, with the attendant balance of *yin* and *yang* elements such as dark and light plants, shade and sunshine, and water and hills.

the elements

The ancient cosmological and alchemical traditions of the West acknowledge a fourfold cosmos with four cardinal directions (north, south, east and west) and elements (earth, air, fire and water; see illustration, left). These are categories of matter and spirit which, in infinite combinations, account for all phenomena of the universe. Related to this fourfold concept were the seasons, for which the symbolism remained remarkably consistent from the Classical age to the Baroque. Spring was often a young woman, perhaps the goddess Flora or Venus (Aphrodite), with flowers and a hoe or spade. A wheatsheaf, fruit and a sickle were the usual attributes of Summer, often personified as the earth goddess Ceres (Demeter). Grapevines are attributes of Autumn, who may be depicted as Bacchus (Dionysus), the god of wine and revelry. Cloaked against the chill, Winter is often an old man by a fire, sometimes with the god Boreas, the north wind, or Vulcan (Hephaistos), the god of fire.

Chinese cosmology recognizes five elements or "phases" (*wu xing*): wood, fire, earth, metal and water. These are essentially types of energy, so spring, east and wind are "wood"; summer, south and heat are "fire"; the center and thunder are "earth"; autumn, west and cold are "metal"; and winter, north and rain are "water".

CHAC & TLALOC

The Maya personified the frequent tropical rains as the god Chac (right), lord of water and lightning and guardian of agriculture, who brought the first corn (maize). His Aztec counterpart Tlaloc was an ambivalent god, bringing gentle fertilizing rains but also disastrous storms.

WIND

In the Book of Genesis, the first stirrings of creation are represented by God moving a wind on the face of the primal waters. The wind is personified in Classical myth by deities such as Zephyrus or Zephyr, the gentle west wind of spring, and Boreas, the bitter north wind of winter. The master of the winds was Aeolus, who gave the wandering Odysseus a bag holding all the unfavorable winds—which a crewman foolishly opened.

FLOOD

Flood myths are found worldwide and many share the idea of a cataclysmic destruction—often at the instigation of a deity, like Noah's flood—from which the world emerges anew. Chinese philosophers spoke of the "flood-like *qi*", the universal force that can be cultivated so that one "flows" toward the good, just as a river always flows downhill. In Buddhism being overwhelmed by water symbolizes the loss of self.

EARTH

Earth, like water, is viewed in traditional Western cosmology as female and passive. It is the realm of mortals in contrast to the heavenly and divine sphere, and the place of creation, symbolized by the many myths of a deity forming the first people from soil, or of creation beginning when an expanse of earth rises up from the primordial waters.

WATER

Passive and female, water is nonetheless capable of immense transforming force: either rapid and violent like an ocean storm, or subtle and slow like a river that cuts a valley through a mountain. Many traditions, such as those of the Bible and ancient Egypt, describe the world before creation as a watery void, replete with potential.

FIRE

An active and male element, fire symbolizes the dynamic process of spiritual and material transformation. At a domestic level, the fire for cooking, warmth and light was a symbol of the shared values and ties that bind a family. It was the traditional heart of the human household, as reflected in the Latin word *focus*, which simply means "hearth".

AIR

Traditionally viewed as male and active, air represents the region between Earth and the heavens, the realm of spirit or "ether". In Hindu tradition air is associated with Brahman, the breath of life, and in China with *qi*, the invisible life-force. Clouds may be manifestations or vehicles of the divine, and as rain-bringers often represent fertility.

ELEMENTALS

In Western esotericism "elementals" are spirit-beings that embody the four elements: goblins and gnomes (earth); sylphs (air); mermaids and undines (water); and salamanders (fire).

RAINBOW

In Africa the rainbow represents the Cosmic Serpent, mother of all things. In central and southern Africa she is Chinawezi, who divided the world with her husband Nkuba, the Lightning. The rainbow serpent is also found in Aboriginal traditions.

WHIRLWIND

The "twister" or tornado features in Native American myth as a symbol of the sheer power of the Great Spirit. Among the Iroquois, the whirlwind Hadu'i was a primal being of disease and death. In the Bible, the whirlwind is a vehicle of divine majesty, linking Earth and heaven.

THUNDER & LIGHTNING

In many Native American traditions, THUNDER was the beating of the wings of the THUNDERBIRD, while LIGHTNING was the flashing of its eyes. This mighty elemental deity was often represented as a great EAGLE (right). Among the Nootka of northwest North America, lightning was personified as a SNAKE called HAIETLIK, the lord of ill winds. For the Greeks, thunderstorms were manifestations of the wrath of ZEUS, the god of sky and weather, who hurled THUNDERBOLTS in his rage. In pre-Christian northern Europe, thunderclaps were the beatings of the hammer of the thunder-god THOR, striking against his ANVIL and emitting sparks of lightning. In Indian tradition a similar role was played by the sky-god INDRA, who wields a VAJRA or thunderbolt. In Buddhist tradition the "diamond thunderbolt" symbolizes the total clarity and sharpness of the enlightened mind.

metals & stones

Metals, stones and rocks represent durability, strength and eternity—immunity from death and decay, as in the gold mask of Tutankhamun (right)—in contrast to the impermanence of organic matter. Rocks were seen by the Greeks as the bones of the primal earth mother, Gaia. The Chinese tradition of *feng shui* has a similar understanding of rocks—as the bones of dragons whose bodies constitute the landscape. In the Psalms, God is the rock that gives refuge in times of anguish, and Peter (Greek *Petros*) is the rock (*petra*) on which Christ builds his church.

Raw stone is ambivalence, asexuality and passivity. It is also potential: the transition from rough rock to dressed or polished ashlars is the central metaphor of Freemasonry (see page 158), symbolizing the journey from the impure, unenlightened state to spiritual maturity and wisdom. Similarly, the refining of ore into the pure metal represents the purging of sin by God, the "smelter and purifier of silver" and "refiner's fire" of the prophet Malachi (3.3, 13.9). In Western alchemy, the physical quest to transmute lead into gold, the supreme solar metal, symbolizes the parallel quest to attain the purity of the soul. The alchemical hierarchy of metals, from gold down to lead, reflects the astrological hierarchy of the planets, from the sun to Saturn, and each metal shares a symbol with its corresponding planet. Precious and semiprecious gems are seen similarly, with "birth stones" associated with each astrological sign.

"Metal" is one of the five elements, or cosmic energies, of Chinese tradition (see page 54). As a force it is understood as *yin*, and its energy is that of decline and withdrawal, perhaps from the fact that the raw ore must be reduced in order to extract the metal. Hence metal is linked with the west, where the sun sets, and with the autumn, the decline of the year.

GOLD

A universal symbol of the sun, gold is associated with supreme solar deities. The Qoricancha, the temple of the Inca sun god Inti, was encased entirely in sheets of gold. The Egyptians believed the sun god had flesh of gold and bones of silver, and in Hindu tradition gold represents petrified sunbeams. It is linked with the heart by the notion of correspondences: just as gold corresponds to the sun in the earthly sphere, the heart is the sun in man. Gold represents spiritual perfection and the inner light of mystical illumination, which is why statues of the Buddha are often gilded. Like the Golden Fleece of Greek myth or the gold of the alchemists, it is the goal of the great quest, whether physical or, in symbolic terms, spiritual. Gold is the metal of royalty and kingship par excellence, fashioned into crowns and other traditional emblems of royal power, the sceptre and orb (see page 150).

THE AGES OF MAN

The Greeks believed that humankind had passed—and steadily degenerated—through successive ages of GOLD, SILVER and BRONZE, and into that of IRON. In Ovid's version, the Age of Gold was the primal age when humans lived free from sickness, labor and old age, and died as if merely falling asleep. ZEUS created a new race to inaugurate the Age of Silver: they lived for a century, but were violent, arrogant and dominated by their mothers. Zeus destroyed them and created a third human race, of the Age of Bronze, that discovered metal and founded civilization, but ended up killing each other with bronze weapons. Zeus then made a final race, inaugurating the Age of Iron. This race—modern humankind —achieved a kind of balance in which good and evil were combined.

BRONZE & BRASS

Combining copper with tin (bronze) or zinc (brass), these alloys denote the union of opposites: copper is linked with the sun and white metals with the moon. Harder than iron, bronze represents strength and celestial power. Bells and sacred instruments are made from it, and the brazen serpent set up by Moses cured snakebite. The Egyptians believed the firmament was made of bronze.

MERCURY

A liquid metal also known as quicksilver, or "living silver", Mercury represents the planet of the same name and also the Roman god (Hermes to the Greeks), the swift deity of transitions and exchange. In Daoist alchemy, mercury was linked with immortality and was combined with other metals in elixirs to promote longevity —sometimes with fatal consequences.

COPPER

The metal is linked with the planet and goddess Venus (Aphrodite). She was born on Cyprus, where copper was mined in Classical times: the island gave the metal its name (Latin *cyprium* or *cuprum*). Copper was once the most versatile of all metals, especially when alloyed to make bronze (see above).

SILVER

Silver is widely linked to the moon and female lunar deities such as Artemis (Diana), as well as with maternal figures such as the Virgin Mary (left) and with queenship. As a metal associated with darkness it was ambivalent: it was linked with wisdom and eloquence (the "silver tongue"), but also with shady deeds and betrayal (Judas Iscariot's "thirty pieces of silver").

IRON

Hierarchically inferior to gold, silver or copper (bronze), iron symbolizes Mars, the god and planet of war. Perhaps because of its use in weaponry, its use in the construction of Solomon's temple was forbidden. As a martial metal, it also represents courage: the Iron Cross, the Prussian and later German award for bravery in battle (right), was based on the cross insignia of the medieval Teutonic Knights.

LEAD

The heavy, brooding character of the god and planet Saturn is reflected in lead, their corresponding metal. In alchemy it represents base humanity, the point from which transcendence begins.

TIN

Tin was equated with the god and planet Jupiter. The flag of Cornwall, where tin was mined in antiquity, is a white cross on black, sometimes said to be the colors of tin and its ore.

JADE

(*left*) Green nephrite jade has been highly prized in China for more than 6,000 years. For Confucius (551–479BCE), its warm glow, purity, pleasant ringing, hardness and durability symbolized respectively humanity, moral integrity, wisdom, justice and perseverance. Jade was believed to preserve the body and hence was associated with immortality. The supreme deity, the king of heaven, was the "Jade Emperor" and a jade disk (the circle of heaven) with a square hole, known as a *bi*, was the "Gate of Heaven".

TURQUOISE

(*below*) In Native American traditions turquoise is a stone of the gods. This Aztec double-headed snake figure is a pectoral, carved out of wood and inlaid with turquoise mosaic and other materials, such as spondylus shell (the red areas). The fire god of the Aztecs was Xiuhtecuhtli, "Turquoise Lord". Turquoise Boy was a protector deity of the Navajo.

EMERALD

(*right*) The color of this stone connects it with spring growth, fertility and regeneration: Ireland is traditionally the "Emerald Isle". It is a Christian symbol of faith, hope and eternal life and is a wedding anniversary stone. Reputedly fashioned by the gods, Thailand's sacred gold-clad "Emerald Buddha" (right) is a potent national symbol.

DIAMOND

A universal symbol of durability and eternity, and the most popular stone for engagement and wedding rings, a diamond symbolizes the hope for lasting love. In Buddhism, it represents the total clarity of the enlightenment state, the "diamond thunderbolt" (*vajra*) that cuts through ignorance. The Tantric Buddhism of Tibet is also known as Vajrayana, the "Way of the Diamond Thunderbolt".

THE HEALING POWER OF STONES

Following the ancient principle of cosmic correspondences, the Sumerians associated certain minerals with the planets: DIAMOND (the SUN), SELENITE (MOON), AGATE (MERCURY), EMERALD (VENUS), RUBY (MARS), JACINTH (JUPITER) and SAPPHIRE (SATURN). The earliest record of the curative use of crystals is the Ebers Papyrus (ca. 1550BCE), the world's second oldest medical text. Present-day crystal lore ascribes special curative, protective and psychospiritual properties and symbolism to a wide range of stones. Some of these characteristics derive from traditional associations and from perceived natural correspondences linked to color or appearance. Red GARNET, for example, is said to be good to treat disorders of the blood and heart. Rose AMETHYST or "love stone" is said to assist the release of negative emotions and promote love of oneself and others. OPALS are sacred to Native American and Australian shamans and are associated, owing to their translucence, with the MOON and WATER; they are said to enhance psychic awareness.

AETITE

Known as a "pregnant stone", an aetite—a stone with a smaller stone rattling inside it—was worn for protection by children and women in childbirth. It was also said to detect thieves.

BENBEN

In ancient Egypt, pyramidal structures symbolized the Benben, the primordial stone at Heliopolis that was revered as the place where the sun god came into being in the form of the Benu bird —the first act of creation.

FLINT

Prehistoric flint arrowheads and speartips were once called "thunderstones", due to a belief that they were the tips of lightning bolts. In ancient Europe they were widely worn as talismans.

"GAIA'S BONES"

In Greek myth, the gods destroyed the world in a flood. But Deucalion and Pyrrha survived and managed to re-create humankind by throwing "Gaia's bones" —stones from the ground —over their shoulders. Deucalion's stones became men and Pyrrha's stones became women.

LAPIS LAZULI

Mined in Afghanistan, lapis lazuli was a cosmic and celestial stone in the ancient Near East, Egypt and China, often associated with supreme and solar deities. In China it was the stone of Heaven (*Tian*).

LINGAM

Smooth polished pillars represent the *lingam*, the phallus of the Hindu god Shiva, the divine procreator. They are revered emblems of fertility and re-creation. A stone ring around the base represents the *yoni* or vulva, symbolizing the union of male and female forces.

LITERATI STONES

Chinese scholar-gentlemen prized rocks and stones with unusual hues, shapes and textures as objects of contemplation and symbols of the amorphous *qi* that pervaded nature.

METEORITE

Rocks from the heavens were venerated as divine gifts and credited with extraordinary powers. The ancient black stone in the Kaba shrine at Mecca is probably a meteorite, a physical symbol of the primordial bond between God and humankind.

OMPHALOS

Sacred both to the earth goddess Gaia and the solar god Apollo, Delphi was revered by the Greeks as the center of the world, symbolized by a sacred stone: the *omphalos*, or "navel" of Gaia.

PEARL

Pearls are linked with the moon and female fertility. Growing mysteriously (as was thought) in the body of a shellfish, the pearl was understood in East and West as a symbol of secret or esoteric wisdom. In Christian tradition it represents Christ in the womb of Mary.

RUBY

Red rubies denote love, passion and zeal. Popular for wedding rings, rubies were once believed to grow paler as love declined. In antiquity they were held to counter sorrow and poison. As royal gems they adorned crowns and regalia.

SAPPHIRE

Because of its color, sapphire has long been linked with the heavens, and symbolizes celestial peace, truth and harmony; in *chakra* lore it is linked with the third eye, insight and devotion to the divine.

SISYPHUS

King Sisyphus of Corinth tried to cheat death and was condemned to spend eternity pushing a rock up a hill, only for it to roll down just before the top every time. The rock symbolizes futility and the limits of human free will when we seek to defy nature.

ALCHEMY

Alchemy has been decribed as the art of transformation. The task, or "Great Work," of the alchemist was to transform a raw and unrefined base material or First Substance (Prima Materia)—either the human soul or, physically, a mysterious metallic substance that was rarely identified—into something pure and perfect. It involved the discovery of a powerful essence named the Philosopher's Stone, also known as the Elixir or Tincture, that could turn base metal lead into superior gold or silver. Many alchemists sought the physical Stone in laboratories, but others regarded alchemy as a more profound internal transformation: the refinement and perfection of human nature.

The base matter had to pass through distinct phases of transmutation that were represented by a wealth of symbols (see below). There was no standard repertory, and while alchemists often used the same symbols, many employed identical symbols to mean different things, even in the same manuscripts. Hence the *nigredo* or "blackening" phase may be represented by a black toad (left) or black bird, as in the main image (right)—from a sixteenth-century German alchemical manuscript entitled *Splendor Solis* (*The Splendor of the Sun*), which is famous for its beautiful and richly symbolic illustrations.

TREE OF LIFE
The tree symbolizes the process of ascent from base matter (the earth in which the tree is rooted) to transcendent purity (the sky).

MAN ON LADDER
The man climbing the ladder represents the adept who has begun along the upward path to spiritual perfection—the "fruit" he will gather in his basket. He is also the physical Prima Materia at the *nigredo* (blackening) stage.

PHILOSOPHERS
The "Adept" (red robe) and his "Senior"(white robe) represent the final phases of the Great Work, the *albedo* and *rubedo* (see box, right).

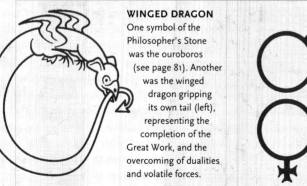

WINGED DRAGON
One symbol of the Philosopher's Stone was the ouroboros (see page 81). Another was the winged dragon gripping its own tail (left), representing the completion of the Great Work, and the overcoming of dualities and volatile forces.

PLANETARY METALS
Each of the seven major alchemical metals is a microcosmic reflection of the cosmos and is symbolized by the sigil, or sign, of the heavenly body that is held to influence it. These signs (left) represent Mars (top), which rules iron, and Venus (bottom), which rules copper.

BIRDS Symbols of the purified soul, soaring free of earthly constraints. They are successively lighter in color, reflecting progress from the initial *nigredo*, represented by the black crow.

GOLDEN CROWN The crown around the Tree of Life represents the Great Work, the attainment of the perfection (denoted by the crown as circle) in the form of gold or spiritual perfection.

FLOWERS The flowers represent the Red Tincture or Philosopher's Stone, the "golden flower" of the Great Work.

THE GREAT WORK

Each phase of alchemical transformation is marked by a color and a range of symbols. The first was NIGREDO, or blackening (CROW, RAVEN or TOAD), reducing the BASE MATTER to a black substance in order to release its "male" and "female" elements (KING AND QUEEN or SUN AND MOON. These are reunited (MARRIAGE OF THE KING AND QUEEN) in the ALBEDO, or whitening phase (SWAN, WHITE EAGLE or SKELETON); next is VIRIDITAS, yellowing or greening (GREEN LION), followed by an iridescence (PEACOCK'S TAIL, RAINBOW). Success at this stage brings forth the WHITE STONE, or WHITE TINCTURE (UNICORN, MOON, WHITE ROSE), which can transmute LEAD into SILVER. The next phase, RUBEDO, or reddening (ROOSTER, RED ROSE, PELICAN) leads to the final transformation (SUN, PHOENIX reborn in fire) that brings forth the RED TINCTURE or PHILOSOPHER'S STONE, which can change matter to GOLD. The GREAT WORK is then complete.

GREEN LION DEVOURING THE SUN

The green lion was a potent symbol that stood for the vital force that must be distilled from the base matter. At a physical level, it represented acids such as vitriol (sulphuric acid) and nitric acid, which were strong enough to dissolve even gold (symbolized by the sun).

mammals

Animals are central to symbolism. They have figured in the human imagination since the earliest known human art was created, ca. 34,000 years ago, in the cave of Chauvet-Pont-d'Arc in southeast France. From their discovery it was recognized that these and later Palaeolithic depictions of big cats, bears, horses, bison, mammoths and rhinoceroses were unlikely to have been created as a mere pastime. Although the cave art chiefly depicts only those animals with which humans had direct physical contact, either as hunters or hunted, it seems clear that the creatures were also potent symbols, perhaps involving a kind of sympathetic magic aimed at controlling those that were strong, fast and dangerous—and perhaps also at acquiring these very same powers, much as happens to this day in traditional shamanistic cultures.

What is certain is that animals became central to human life—from domesticated ruminants to working horses (left)—and to symbolism, whether from their physical forms or colors, their habits or dwellings, or from their actual or imputed characteristics, like swiftness, agility, slowness, bravery, cunning, persistence, treachery and protectiveness. In fact, virtually every human physical or psychic trait has its own potent animal symbol, and the animal kingdom as a whole is thus a mirror of humankind—both of our conscious selves and of our deepest, untamed subconscious and unconscious instincts: the "beast within", or what Carl Jung called the "animal soul".

WOLF
(below) A near-universal symbol of savage predation, the wolf represents the enemies of Christ (the Lamb). Its fearlessness also made the wolf a badge of warriors. It is a symbol of the might of Rome, from the legend that a she-wolf suckled the city's founders, Romulus and Remus.

FOX
The cunning trickster of the Old World, the fox has a reputation for guile and untrustworthiness; it represents the wiles and hypocrisy of Satan, Prince of Darkness. In Chinese legend foxes become beautiful women to lead men astray, but in Japan they are messengers of Inari, god of rice and prosperity.

COYOTE
(left) Famed as a trickster, the coyote is a byword for gluttony and resourcefulness. A mixed blessing to humans, it outwits monsters but also provokes their wrath. In Navajo myth, Coyote helped humans ascend into this world, but thwarted their attempt to become immortal.

JAGUAR
Jaguars were emblems of royalty, power and fertility among the peoples of Mesoamerica. At home on land, in water or up trees, and hunting by day or night, the jaguar was Lord of Animals, the elements and secret wisdom.

TIGER
The largest of the big cats, the tiger is more solitary and elusive than the lion, rarely emerging from the forest save to breed. Hence, as well as being symbols of ferocity and bravery, tigers are also widely credited with mysterious and supernatural powers. In China they are tomb protectors and soul guardians, while the celestial White Tiger represents the west and autumn: the seed of *yang* and regrowth that lies within the time of rising *yin* and withdrawal.

PUMA
Ranging across the mountains of the Americas from Canada to Chile, pumas are also known as cougars, mountain lions and panthers. As emblems of royalty and imperial might they were of great heraldic importance to the Inca people, who conceived of their Andean empire as a great puma and called their capital, Cusco, the "Big Puma".
The puma's head was the temple-fortress of Sacsahuaman and its tail was an area of the city that is still known today as Pumachapan—the "Puma's Tail".

LEOPARD
The leopard has a reputation for vigilance owing to the "eyes" that adorn its coat, and this is often what the leopard denotes in European heraldry (see page 79). Like the lion (below), the animal stands for bravery and ferocity, but also for cunning, from its method of hunting —alone and at night, when it kills in sudden deadly forays. In some parts of Africa evil spirits may take the form of a leopard; elsewhere, though, the "droplets" on its pelt symbolize rain, linking the leopard with the fertility of the land.

LIONS: FIERCE PROTECTORS

The most widespread of the great cats, the LION has been a symbol of bravery, power and kingship since ancient times. In ancient Sumeria it was a protective symbol of the war god NERGAL, and Assyrian palaces and temples were guarded by fierce hybrids of lion, bull and man (below, center). Tombs of Greek warriors often portrayed lions to ward off evil spirits. In Christian art, the jaws of HELL were often depicted as a lion's mouth; on the other hand, CHRIST as Messiah is the "Lion of Judah", while a winged lion is the emblem of ST. MARK, symbolizing Christ's physical and spiritual power. A lion is the mount of the Hindu goddess DURGA, the destroyer of evil (below, right).

Much symbolism is attached to the male lion, owing to its strikingly majestic appearance. However, the ferocity of the lioness—who does most of the hunting—is acknowledged in the Egyptian lioness-goddess SEKHMET (below, left), daughter of the sun god RA, bringer of plagues and scourge of Egypt's foes. The lioness as protector is reflected in Sekhmet's role as a goddess of healing.

COUSINS OF HUMANKIND: PRIMATES

The human-like habits, appearance, mimicry and dexterity of **APES** and **MONKEYS** have earned them a special place in animal symbolism. For many cultures they embody the baser aspects of humankind, such as greed and unbridled sexuality, and their curiosity and intelligence have often been understood as cunning and duplicity. **SUN WUKONG**, or the **MONKEY KING** of the sixteenth-century Chinese novel *Journey to the West*, is typically mischievous; not even the gods can prevent him from stealing their peaches of immortality. After being punished he accompanies a pious pilgrim on a quest for Buddhist texts and is later deified. This hints at the duality inherent in primate symbolism.

In India monkeys are regarded as mischievous too, but they are also sacred and inviolable creatures of **HANUMAN**, the popular monkey god (right). The son of the wind god, Hanuman is a loyal, brave and fearless shapeshifter, who utilizes his cunning to aid the divine hero **RAMA** against **RAVANA**, the evil king of Lanka. In Egypt, the baboon-god **THOTH** was the creator of hieroglyphic writing and keeper of secret wisdom and magic; similarly, the Maya of central America revered the monkey as the inventor of art, hieroglyphic writing and mathematics.

BULL

A potent symbol of masculine strength and virility but also of humankind's powerful baser urges and instincts. The Persian god Mithras was often shown slaying a great bull, symbolizing victory over our animal nature; initiates in the god's all-male cult were baptized in bull's blood. The bull was the totemic royal beast of ancient Crete, which is the setting for several Greek bull myths with a strong strand of sexual transgression, such as the story of the abduction of the maiden Europa by Zeus in the form of a bull and, most famously, the Minotaur born to Queen Pasiphae of Crete. The hero Theseus eventually killed the bull–man monster (see page 125). The bull that fathered the Minotaur was captured by Herakles as one of his twelve labors.

POLAR BEAR

Arctic traditions fear and respect the bear for its strength, patience and human-like cleverness—it can creep up on a sleeping walrus and kill it with a block of ice; wait patiently for hours by an ice hole to catch its prey; and build a nest of snow in which to give birth. It is the foremost shamanic animal among Arctic peoples, and because of its color is linked with the moon: the Moon Man, the patron being of Inuit hunters, wore a polar bear pelt.

HORSE

The horse embodied swiftness, strength, nobility and energy for Old World cultures, and acquired a similar status among Native peoples after the Spanish reintroduced the animal to America. It was the royal beast of the ancient Celts, and for the Norse it understood the wisdom of the gods; Odin himself rode an eight-legged stallion. In China too horses symbolized status and military power, and were the bearers of spiritual and worldly gifts.

DEER

Stags are widespread symbols of fertility and regrowth, as embodied in the antlered Celtic deity Cernunnos, the "Horned God", and lord of animals. From their swiftness and sharp ears, deer also represent hearing in depictions of the five senses. In Buddhist art, deer allude to the deer park where the Buddha first taught; they symbolize the humility and alertness of the ideal pupil. A hart by a stream represents the soul yearning for God (Psalm 42.11).

BEAR

Bears sometimes stand and walk upright like people, and among Native American and other shamanistic traditions they are revered as kindred beings and guardian spirits with powers of metamorphosis, magic and healing. European tradition held that bear cubs were born formless until "licked into shape" by their mothers, and hence bears were symbols of creation. In Greece the bear (*arktos*) was sacred to Artemis, goddess of hunting and childbirth.

KANGAROO

The kangaroo features in Aboriginal stories of the Dreaming, a primordial epoch when ancestral creator heroes traveled across the landscape, shaping its features as they went. Malu the Red Kangaroo journeyed for hundreds of miles from the Kimberleys to the center of the continent, leaving sacred landmarks such as creeks, caves and rocks infused with his creative spirit.

COW

Famously sacred and protected in Hinduism, cows are widely revered as beasts of nurture. In ancient Egypt the benign but powerful cow-goddess Hathor was the protector of women and the dead, and the goddess of fertility, sexual love, music and dance, as well as a symbolic divine mother of the pharaoh. In Norse myth Audhumla was a great cow whose four streams of milk nourished Ymir, the king of the Ice Giants, from whose body the world was created.

ELEPHANT

(*left*) Despite their size, elephants are gentle beasts that will come to one another's aid and gather to comfort a dying member of the herd. This partly accounts for the ancient belief in an elephant's sagacity: the Greeks revered its wisdom and Thais whisper their intimate problems into an elephant's ear. In India, before any enterprise many Hindus will pray to the elephant-headed Ganesha, god of wisdom and Remover of Obstacles. An elephant is also the mount of Indra.

SWINE

(*above*) Dangerous, swift and aggressive, boars were ambivalent symbols of forceful rulership and destructive tyranny. In ancient Greece there were several chthonic myths relating to epic boar hunts. Boars are also clever, and the Celts regarded them as sacred and prophetic animals with magical protective properties. Pigs may be symbols of fertility, as in Egyptian images of the sky goddess Nut suckling her piglets (the stars). But elsewhere in the Near East swine were generally viewed as unclean scavengers and the prohibition on eating their flesh remains in Judaism and Islam.

GOATS & SHEEP

(*left*) Rams and male goats are ancient symbols of male fertility and lust, owing to their phallic horns and vigorous mating. As a symbol of generative power the ram was revered in Egypt and linked with the creator deities Amun and Khnum, who were often depicted with ram's heads. Ovine symbolism abounds in Christianity. Christ is the Good Shepherd of his flock; the innocent Lamb of God sacrificed at Passover; and the scapegoat of Leviticus 16.22, laden with the sins of humanity. The Shepherd separates the sheep (the faithful) from the goats (sinners). The goat is the beast of the Devil, who is typically depicted with cloven hooves, goaty beard and horns—an image likely derived from the lustful Classical goat-god Pan, lord of nature, and his goat-man acolytes, the satyrs.

BUFFALO

In North America, before their decimation by hunters in the nineteenth century, buffalo (bison) swarmed across the Plains from Canada to Mexico in their unstoppable millions, a staggering manifestation of animal power and vitality, and a respected source of sustenance for Native American peoples. Bison appear in prehistoric cave paintings in Europe, where their symbolism as a beast of great spiritual might was perhaps similar. In Tantric Buddhism, the fierce protector deities Mahakala and Yamantaka are each depicted with a buffalo's head, symbolizing their power over evil forces.

HARE & RABBIT

The alertness and swiftness of hares and rabbits lie behind their widespread role as tricksters in Asia, Europe, Africa and the Americas. Many traditions discern a hare or rabbit in the face of the moon; in China, a lunar hare pounds the elixir of eternal life. As famously fast breeders, they are associated with promiscuity and fertility. In British folklore a rabbit's foot was held to be lucky and a cure for cramp and rheumatism; but it was unlucky to meet a hare, or to mention hares or rabbits at sea. Both superstitions may be an echo of the ancient Celts belief that the creatures were powerful spirits.

CATS & DOGS

cats and dogs are our most familiar animal companions. Little changed from their wild ancestors, **CATS** retain a contradictory symbolism, appreciative of human attentions but also strongly independent and often with a secret life beyond the home, especially at night. This accounts for the suspicion that cats were the familiars of demons and malign witches. But the ambivalence of cats already existed in ancient Egypt, where they were sacred to **BASTET** (*right*), a benign goddess who was also a ferocious avenger: in the form of a cat she nightly beheaded the serpent **APEP**, the enemy of the sun god.

science suggests that all **DOGS** descend from **WOLVES** tamed in china ca. 14000BCE. Natural pack animals, dogs symbolize loyalty and helpfulness. Their acute sensory powers link them with the spirit world: in Japan dogs were believed to detect ghosts, while the Maya buried dogs with their masters as guides to the spirit world. Dogs may also be fierce guardians, like **CERBERUS**, the three-headed watchdog of **HADES**. (This roman mosaic, above, is a "beware of the dog" sign.) In china, the "Dogs of Fo" guard the Dharma.

JUDAISM

Judaism developed from the religion of Judah, the ancient Israelite kingdom that fell in 586BCE. Its basic elements are God, his Law, and his people, Israel. Jews believe in one universal and eternal deity, the creator and lord of all. This deity entered into a covenant (*brith*) with the Israelites, choosing them as "a light to the nations" (Isaiah 49.6), to bring all peoples to the worship of God. In return for God's patronage and protection, Jews follow the commandments (*mitzvot*) and rules of God's Law (Torah), set out in the first five books (the Five Books of Moses, or Pentateuch) of the Hebrew Bible, Judaism's holy scripture.

Many Jewish symbols refer to the relationship between God and Israel. The Star of David (see box, below) may be the most familiar to a modern observer, but a more ancient symbol is the seven-branched ritual candlestick, or *menorah*. A great *menorah* stood in the Jerusalem Temple, founded by King Solomon and the focus of Jewish worship and pilgrimage until its destruction by the Romans in 70CE. Most Jewish households have a *menorah* to light on the sabbath and religious holidays. A nine-branched *menorah* is lit during the festival of Hanukkah (Rededication), which celebrates the rededication of the Temple in 164BCE after the defeat of Greek conquerors who had defiled it. In medieval Spain, depictions of the sacred furnishings of the Temple sometimes adorned Jewish Bibles: the example opposite (right) is from an Aragonese Bible of ca. 1299.

Most Jewish homes have a *mezuzah*, a small box that holds the Shema Yisrael prayer (Deut. 6.4), fixed to a doorpost. It shows that the home too is a holy space, dedicated to God and sacred values. Other symbols include the *hamesh* amulet (left), or "Hand of Miriam". It is worn to invoke God's protection against the "evil eye" and other malign influences.

THE ARK OF THE COVENANT God was believed to reside in the Temple within the sacred Ark holding the tablets of the Ten Commandments, whose opening words are given. It is guarded by two cherubim.

INCENSE PANS These two pans were for burning frankincense during Temple rites.

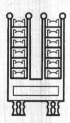

SHOWBREADS The showbreads were loaves displayed on a special table in the Temple as a permanent offering to God. There is one loaf for each of Israel's twelve tribes.

THE STAR OF DAVID

The most widely used Jewish symbol is the Magen David, or **STAR OF DAVID**, which appears in synagogues (right) and on the flag of Israel. The use of the six-pointed star is relatively modern, originating in medieval Prague. It has its origins in the mystical and Hermetic **SEAL OF SOLOMON**, a **HEXAGRAM** formed of two interlocking triangles. In the mystical **KABBALAH** the seal symbolizes the interrelatedness of earth and heaven and the inextricable bond between God and humankind.

The seal has been explained as a representation of the **FOUR ELEMENTS**. The **DOWNWARD-POINTING TRIANGLE** symbolizes **WATER**, and the **UPWARD-POINTING TRIANGLE** denotes **FIRE**. When the two are superimposed, a horizontal line bisects the upward triangle near its apex, making a symbol for **AIR**; and the downward triangle, similarly bisected, is a symbol for **EARTH**. Through such correspondences the hexagram represents both the unity and complexity of God's creation.

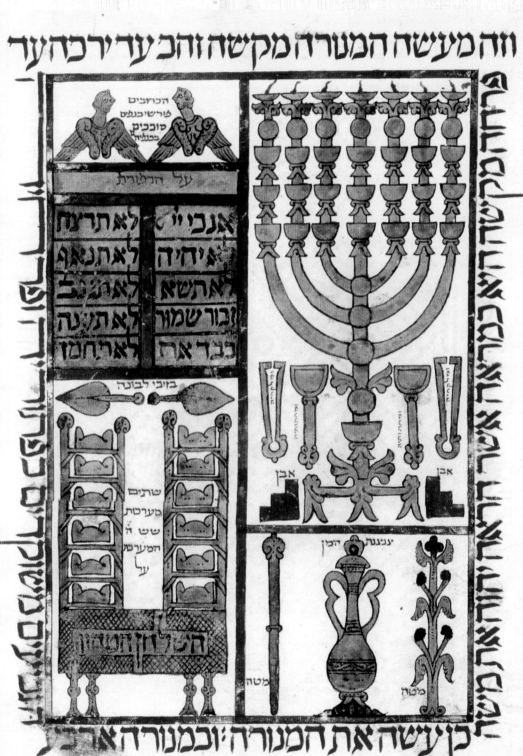

MENORAH The golden candlestick is historically the commonest Jewish symbol. The seven branches may represent the six days of creation plus the sabbath, or the seven planets known to ancient peoples.

SNUFFERS & TONGS These instruments were used for tending and extinguishing the candles in the Temple *menorah*.

AARON'S STAFFS The staffs symbolize Aaron's (Moses' brother) role as priest: one of them miraculously sprouted buds. They flank a vessel containing the manna that sustained the Israelites in the wilderness after the Exodus from Egypt.

water creatures

Creatures that dwell in seas, rivers and lakes share to a great extent the symbolic and mystical associations of water. Our planet is two-thirds water, and water affects humankind both as a commodity that is essential to life and crop fertility, and in the form of cataclysmic floods. Many mythologies conceive the cosmos before the beginning of time as vast primordial waters of chaos—a limitless expanse of pure force and potential. This is sometimes represented as a vast sea creature, such as the biblical Leviathan (see page 73). From the association with the waters of the womb, aquatic creatures are often fertility symbols in general, or more specifically phallic; they may also be emblems of resurrection and cosmic regeneration.

Water is widely connected with ritual cleansing and purification, and is one of the most ancient of Christian symbols (left, a fourth-century floor mosaic with the fish as the Christian races of people). Dark waters are linked with profound and esoteric knowledge; sea creatures symbolize the ability to penetrate the depths of wisdom, and in many traditions water creatures are intermediaries between the earthly and divine or spirit realms. Ancient deities were sometimes represented in fishlike form, such as the Phoenician Dagon or the Mesopotamian Oannes (Adapa), the bringer of knowledge. In psychoanalytical terms, water creatures represent the active subconscious, working away unseen beneath the conscious mind.

CONCH
The conch is a Hindu and Buddhist ritual instrument, perhaps because its note suggests the primordial sound *Om*. In Buddhism a conch is also one of the Eight Auspicious Emblems. It grows in a clockwise direction and hence is symbolic of "turning to the right" in the sense of truth, embodied in the Dharma, the Buddha's teachings.

SCALLOP
A scallop shell is an emblem of the goddess Aphrodite (Venus for the Romans), who was born from the sea or, in some accounts, from the shell itself. Scallops were worn by pilgrims to the shrine of St. James at Compostela in Spain, and hence became a symbol of the saint as well as of pilgrimage in general.

CRAB
The erratic gait of the crab explains why it is a symbol of deviousness: its Latin name, *cancer*, was given to the ravaging disease that spread unpredictably. The constellation Cancer is said to represent a crab sent by the goddess Hera against the hero Herakles. He crushed the crab, but Hera set it in the stars.

TWO FISHES
A pair of fishes represents the constellation Pisces. When the fishes are represented in an oval or circular form they are also a symbol of the vagina or *yoni*—"origin of life" in Sanskrit. In China two fishes symbolize sexual intercourse. However, they also symbolize a happy and prosperous marriage.

THE OCEAN WOLF

The great predator of the seas, gliding silently from the dark depths to attack its prey with swift and efficient ferocity, the **SHARK** embodies brute savagery and the universal fear of hidden danger. Unsurprisingly, sharks feature greatly in South Pacific traditions. The Hawaiian shark god **KAMOHOALI'I** was revered as the inventor of surfing, and the **'AUMAKUA** were ancestral spirits in the form of sharks. The theme of shapeshifting is also seen in the Fijian god **DEKUWAQA**, who manifested as a basking shark that guided warriors' canoes on night raids. In the Trobriand Islands, a rite of passage for young men is to set off alone in a canoe and catch a shark. In the Solomon Islands, skulls of the deceased were placed inside reliquaries carved in the form of a shark.

The Tlingit of Alaska were among Native American peoples for whom the shark was often a totem clan ancestor, and in Aboriginal Australian traditions sharks feature as ancestor beings of the primordial **DREAMTIME**.

The "great fish" that swallowed Jonah in the biblical story is sometimes held to be a shark rather than, as more traditionally, a **WHALE**.

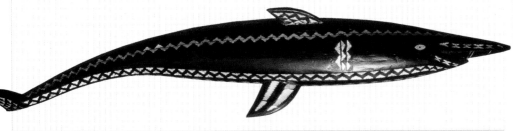

CARP

A carp can live for up to fifty years and hence in Chinese tradition it is a symbol of longevity. It is also a symbol of perseverance and military valor, because it naturally swims against the current. In Japan the *koi* carp is a love symbol, since *koi* is also an old Japanese word for "love". (See also page 72.)

THREE FISHES

Three fishes with a single head in the center is a form of symbol known as a *trinacria*, and represents the power of threes in a number of traditions. The fish is an ancient Christian symbol (see page 73) and three fishes in a triangular arrangement symbolize the Holy Trinity, the three-in-one of Father, Son and Holy Spirit.

SALMON

The epic lifecycle of this fish, which swims across thousands of miles of ocean and back up the river of its own birth in order to spawn, has made it a totemic creature in many societies, representing death and rebirth, fecundity, wisdom and foresight. In Irish myth, a single taste of the flesh of a magical salmon gave the hero Finn unbounded powers of prophecy.

SEAL

Seals figure in some cultures as primordial ancestors, able to take on human shape—a tradition reflected in Scottish legends of selkies, seal-women who removed their pelts on land and could not return to the sea without them. For some Native Americans of the Pacific Northwest, seals bestow the skills of swimming and fishing.

DOLPHIN

(*above*) For Native Americans these intelligent mammals were messengers of the spirit world. The Greeks linked them with love, salvation and spiritual rebirth, owing to the association of *delphis* (dolphin) and *delphys* (womb). Dolphins were symbols of the sea gods Poseidon and Oceanus, and also Dionysus, the god of altered states.

OCTOPUS & SQUID

(*right*) The Hydra, the many-headed monster fought by the hero Herakles, is often depicted on Greek vases as a giant squid or octopus. These creatures may have inspired the legendary sea monster known as the kraken (see page 73). The octopus also represents inconstancy, from its ability to change color when in peril.

FISH OF ABUNDANCE

In china and japan, fishes are symbols of wealth and prosperity, since the chinese word for fish (*yu*) also means abundance and affluence. carp (see page 71) and their more domesticated variety, goldfish, are kept in ponds and at times displayed in jars. the chinese name for the goldfish, *jinyu*, also means "abundance of gold", which explains the fish's traditional popularity in china and japan. goldfish, and fish in general, are often found as decorative motifs. a fish (*yu*) and lotus (*lian*) are a pun on the phrase *yu lian nian*, "perpetual wealth." *yu* also means "wish", and fish dishes are often eaten at festivals to convey felicitations. at chinese new year a fish is served complete with head and tail, conveying a wish for prosperity all the year through. in ancient china, people ate the flesh and offered the heads as a sacrifice to the god of wealth.

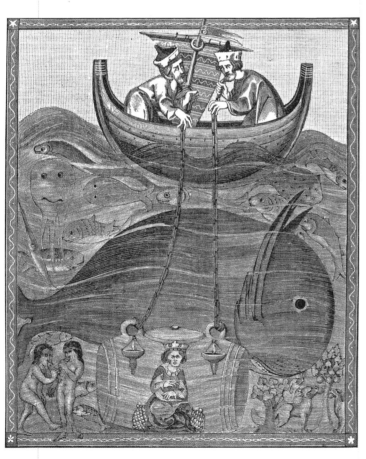

WHALE

Societies that traditionally depend on the whale (left) for their livelihoods accord it great respect. In Japan, the coastal Koganji temple is a shrine to the spirits of whales killed in hunts, and Alaskan Inuit shamans invoke whale spirits in traditional rites. For the Kwakiutl of Vancouver Island, the whale bestows long life and prosperity.

In Western tradition the most famous story about a whale is in the biblical Book of Jonah. Seeking to evade God's command to prophesy the destruction of Nineveh to its citizens, Jonah flees on a ship. But God causes a storm and the fearful crew throw Jonah overboard. He is swallowed by a "great fish", usually depicted as a whale but sometimes as a large dolphin or even a shark. Jonah remains inside the creature for three days until he repents and is freed. The episode became a popular Christian allegory because Jesus compared Jonah's experience to his own coming death, followed three days later by his resurrection (Matt. 12.40). The whale symbolizes the intermediate state between death and rebirth and, in the water rite of baptism, the spiritual transition from "death" to "rebirth" in Christ.

TIAMAT & APSU

Babylonian myth symbolized the primal salt water and sweet water oceans as two sea beasts, respectively named Tiamat (above) and Apsu. They coupled to produce many gods, including Ea, who killed Apsu. In revenge, Tiamat unleashed a mighty war, but was slain and cut in two, one part becoming the sky and the other the Earth. Tiamat symbolized the forces of chaos, which must be defeated before the ordered cosmos can come in to being.

MAKARA

A mount of the god Vishnu is Makara, a common water creature in Hindu myth. Resembling a fish with the legs and head of a mammal, it represents the divine powers of the waters.

LEVIATHAN

The biblical sea-monster (Job 41) may derive from the Babylonian Tiamat. Its mouth could represent the jaws of hell; for the philosopher Hobbes, Leviathan represented the autocratic state.

CHRIST THE FISH

In early christianity, the faith was often symbolized as a **FISH**, which is found as an emblem on the walls of catacombs and on the sarcophagi of believers, as well as on seals and lamps. It is one of the earliest christian symbols, and until the fourth century ᴄᴇ it was far more common than the **CROSS**.

The use of fish symbolism (above, Raphael with Tobit) derives from several episodes in the gospels that center on fish and fishing, a principal livelihood for those living on the shores of Lake Galilee. These episodes include the calling of the first two disciples, the fishermen brothers Andrew and Peter; the miraculous feedings of huge crowds with a small number of **LOAVES AND FISHES**; the miraculous draught of fishes, which symbolizes the growing church; and the miracle of finding a **COIN** inside a fish to pay the temple tax.

Given these associations, it is hardly surprising that christ should often be represented as the "fisher of souls", and the fish became a symbol of christ himself, since the Greek for fish, **ICHTHUS**, was understood as an acronym of *Iesous christos, Theou uius, soter* ("Jesus christ, son of god, savior"). Initiated in water through the sacrament of baptism, christians are christ's "little fishes" (*pisciculi* in Latin) and the **FONT** in which they are baptized (originally by full immersion, as in some present-day churches) is literally the "fishpond" (Latin *piscina*). The fish is also a symbol of **ST. PETER**, designated by christ as the "fisher of men", and of **ST. ANTHONY OF PADUA**, who is said to have preached to the fishes. (see also page 70.)

MERMAID & MERMAN

Tales have been told since ancient times of merpeople, sea-beings with human upper bodies and fishes' tails. For mariners, the mermaid—perhaps derived from dimly discerned seals or walruses, or nursing dugong or manatees—embodied a yearning for the fleshly pleasures of home. In more recent times, the idea of the mermaid has been interpreted as symbolizing the outer world and the inner depths of the subconscious, that part of our nature which lies submerged.

KRAKEN

The kraken of Scandinavian legend was said to dwell in the North Atlantic between Iceland and Norway and is variously described as resembling a giant squid, octopus or crab. Huge shoals of fish fled before it, which was a boon for fishermen—unless they sailed too near the monster. When the creature surfaced it is said to have resembled an island, and when it dived beneath the water it caused a whirlpool so violent that ships could be sucked to destruction.

sky creatures

Most cultures have seen birds as intermediaries between the heavenly and human worlds, a fact acknowledged in mythical hybrids like the Hindu and Tibetan Garuda, which is part eagle and part human. Birds are invoked as protectors and healers during the shaman's trance-flight, and for the Egyptians the soul flitted between this world and the next in the form of the *ba*, a bird with the head of the deceased. For the Navajo the soul became an owl.

The Romans interpreted the flight or sounds of birds as clues to the future, and the Egyptian god Thoth is often shown as an ibis, its curved bill suggesting a scribe's pen (see page 174). With its strutting display the peacock (left) is a common symbol of vanity and pride. But in Hinduism it is the mount of Kama, god of love, and in Greece it was the bird of the goddess Hera (Juno to the Romans), the "eyes" of its tail having come from Argos, a hundred-eyed giant. The bird's flesh was believed to be incorruptible, hence it became a symbol of immortality and of Christ's resurrection. In Buddhism it symbolizes the universal vigilance of Avalokiteshvara, deity of compassion.

FALCON

(*right*) In ancient Egypt the soaring falcon was the king of the birds and the bird of kings. It was identified with the great god Horus, the "Distant One"—who is depicted as a falcon or, most often, as a hawk-headed man. Horus in turn was identified with the pharaoh while he was alive: he bore the titles "Son of Ra", the sun god, and "Living Horus", the god in human form. The "Eye of Horus" symbol takes the form of a human eye with a falcon's distinctive cheek-markings below it (see pages 174–175).

VULTURE

The powerful Egyptian vulture goddess Nekhbet symbolized the pharaoh's rule in the south of his kingdom (Upper Egypt), just as the cobra represented his rule in the north (Lower Egypt). Nekhbet's protective image sometimes adorned the pharaoh's headdress, and she was painted on his bedroom ceiling to keep watch over the sleeping monarch at night. With wings outspread, Nekhbet sometimes bears the hieroglyph for "eternity" in her talons.

CROW

Crows, rooks and ravens are the largest birds of the crow family and are linked with darkness and ill omen: in Christianity they are associated with the Devil and in Celtic myth with war and death. But for the Romans crows were symbols of hope, because their caw sounded like the Latin word *cras* ("tomorrow"), and in China a crow is the soul of the sun. In Aboriginal traditions, a figure named Crow helps mold human culture, while Crow, like Raven, is a widespread Native American culture hero and trickster.

CUCKOO

The cuckoo is famed as the herald of spring, but also, less positively, as the symbol of marital infidelity. The female cuckoo lays its single egg in another bird's nest, and the deceived host raises the hatchling, which ruthlessly expels the host bird's own chicks as it grows. Strictly speaking the "cuckold"—an old word for cuckoo—is the adulterous interloper in a marriage, but this term has transferred itself to the deceived husband, the one who has been cuckolded or "cuckooed".

LORD OF THE SKIES: THE EAGLE

soaring high on huge wings, possessing keen eyesight, sharp talons and an apparently fierce stare, eagles are emblems of power, supremacy in their (aerial) domain and all-seeing authority. The eagle's image was borne on the standards of the roman legions (who called it "the bird of Jove"), and a two-headed eagle denoted the might and extent of the roman and Byzantine empires (see page 79). The eagle was also the imperial bird of the Aztecs, while the Native American Thunderbird, lord of storms and rain, was envisioned as a giant eagle (see page 55).

The bald eagle is the heraldic bird of the united states, an emblem of sovereignty and independence.

Eagles can be agents of revenge: for stealing fire, Prometheus was tortured by one sent by Zeus (see page 95).

As the lord of the heavens, the eagle embodies spiritual wisdom. An eagle devouring a serpent occurs worldwide as an emblem of the triumph of the spirit over brute force, or more simply of good over evil. The eagle is also a symbol of St. John the Evangelist, owing to the elevated and "spiritual" nature of his gospel.

OWL
With its inscrutable stare, deadly and silent flight and nocturnal habits, the owl has attracted sometimes sinister associations of supernatural and occult powers. Among many peoples it is a bird of wisdom and prophecy. The owl was famously sacred to Athene, Greek goddess of wisdom, and was depicted on the coins of her city, Athens. It was a bird of death in Egypt, India, East Asia and some Native American traditions, although in others it was a sacred protector.

MAGPIE
The bird's pied plumage, part black—though also beautifully iridescent—and part white, makes this the most ambivalent member of the crow family. As the old rhyme goes, one magpie portends sorrow, but two mean joy. The magpie is also an emblem of theft, from its attraction to shining objects, which it pilfers to line its nest. In China, however, the magpie (*xi*) is altogether more auspicious. It is traditionally a bird of good omen, since the Chinese word for "happiness" is also *xi*.

BAT
In many traditions bats are agents of darkness and evil, linked with underworld spirits, and in eastern European folklore with the bloodsucking vampire. Their habit of darting about silently at dusk in a seemingly erratic and unpredictable manner (in fact they are hunting for insects) makes them widespread symbols of nightmarish chaos. However, in China bats are positive symbols, because the word for bat (*fu*) sounds like the word for luck, good fortune, blessings and fulfillment.

DOVE OR PIGEON
In the Bible the dove is a divine messenger and a symbol of peace, returning to Noah with an olive branch to signal God's reconciliation with humankind. In Christian art a white dove is the Holy Spirit, as at the Annunciation or Christ's baptism. Doves and pigeons are popular Chinese emblems of longevity and marital fidelity.

HUMMINGBIRD
The only bird that can fly backward, the tiny but often splendidly plumed hummingbird was thought to be a messenger of the gods. For the Aztecs, the bird's aggressive behavior toward creatures often many times its own size linked it with their god of war, Huitzilopochtli, "the Hummingbird of the South".

ROC
Derived in part from the Iranian Simurgh (see right), the giant roc of Arabian myth and fable was said to be so enormous that it was able to carry off an elephant in its claws, and in "The Fifth Voyage of Sindbad" a roc drops a stone large enough to sink Sindbad's ship. Thunderclaps were said to be the beating of the great bird's wings.

SIMURGH
Resembling a giant peacock with leonine forepaws and a canine head, the Simurgh or Senmurv of Iranian tradition represents the combined powers of heaven and Earth. Fierce but benevolent, it bestowed fertility on the land and possessed the world's wisdom. It lived for centuries and, like the Classical phoenix, perished in flames.

RAVEN THE TRICKSTER

Among the Inuit and Native American traditions of Alaska and the Pacific Northwest, the **RAVEN** is an important creator, **CULTURE HERO** and **TRICKSTER**, and a clan emblem (left). Reflecting the nature of this large and intelligent member of the crow family, the partly anthropomorphized Raven is a character of great resourcefulness. By some accounts he was born by magical means, of a woman who swallowed a **FEATHER** or a **STONE**. After the waters of the primordial **FLOOD** receded, runs one Haida story, Raven found a giant **CLAM** full of little animals too scared to move. He persuaded them to leave their shelter and explore the world: they became the first humans.

The creator and trickster aspects of Raven are often present simultaneously. The Tsimshian recount how Raven stole fire from the gods to give to humans. As a punishment Raven, who was originally a white bird, was scorched black by the gods. Other myths tell of Raven stealing the **SUN** and other heavenly bodies from a greedy chief and hurling them into the sky; and bringing humankind the first **SALMON**, berries, and other gifts. Raven is the principal deity of the Alaskan Inuit.

CRANE

In Chinese tradition only the mythical *feng huang* (see opposite) is more auspicious than the crane. Reputed to live for centuries, the crane is a common symbol of longevity and also of filial duty, because its young echo the song of their parent. The bird's high flight represents wisdom and success: a white crane was the rank badge of the emperor's highest officials. The crane bears souls to the afterlife, and its image adorns coffins at traditional Chinese funerals. In India, however, the crane denoted treachery, and in Celtic lore it was at times a bird of ill omen.

SWAN

The themes of soul-flight and transformation are widespread in swan symbolism. In Greek myth, Zeus changed himself into a swan to seduce the beautiful Leda (above), and in Celtic tradition the souls of the dead took the form of swans to fly to and from the Otherworld. In the story of the god Oenghus, his lover Caer is a maiden who turns into a swan every other year, and swan-maidens also feature in the folklore of Russia and elsewhere. The myth that mute swans sing only before death lies behind the idea of the "swan song", a person's poignant final creative utterance.

THE SPIRIT OF FIRE: THE PHOENIX

The **PHOENIX** of classical myth was a fabulous bird of beautiful plumage that lived in the Arabian desert or Ethiopia. According to one account, the bird lived for five centuries before building itself a funeral pyre of aromatic twigs on an altar and then burning up in its own heat. Miraculously, the phoenix emerged rejuvenated from its own ashes. The creature came to symbolize resurrection and life after death, as well as divine wisdom and the element of **FIRE**. In medieval Christian art the phoenix commonly represented the resurrection of Christ, and the phoenix and **PELICAN** could symbolize his divine and human natures respectively. The phoenix also represents **CHASTITY**, since it reproduced without sexual intercourse.

The creature's origins lie at least partly in the Egyptian **BENU** bird (see below), and it shares features with the Persian **SIMURGH** (see page 75). The name "phoenix" is also given to the Chinese **FENG HUANG** bird (see below; this illustration, right, is a Thai temple detail).

STORK
A herald of spring and, in Christian tradition, of Christ's coming. In Greece the stork was sacred to Hera, queen of the gods; her role as a goddess of childbirth may be related to the legend that storks bring babies. In Europe it is thought lucky if a stork nests on your roof. The bird never forgets its own nest, and hence is a symbol of constancy. Like the crane it is a Chinese symbol of long life and filial devotion.

COCK & HEN
The cockerel or rooster is a symbol of vigilance and wakefulness, and also of masculinity, especially the vain and strutting kind. Its early morning cry is a call to prayer in Shintoism, and in Islamic belief Muhammad saw a giant cock in the first heaven that cried "There is no god but Allah". Hens are symbols of cowardice from their timidity, but also of new life and nurturing motherhood.

ROBIN
The robin is especially visible in winter, when the leaves are scant and many other birds have fled south. It is thus a symbol of endurance and, from its remarkable lack of fear, of boldness. It is the bird of Christmas, its red breast traditionally a reminder that Christ was born to shed his blood for humankind. In English folklore, the bird was stained with blood when it plucked a thorn from Christ's brow.

WREN
The tiny wren has one of the loudest songs, and the mother will flutter aggressively around a would-be predator. It is thus a symbol of great courage and maternal protectiveness. Associated with the Virgin Mary, the wren was sometimes called "Our Lady's hen".

BENU
At the sun temple in Heliopolis, the Egyptians revered the mythical Benu bird as the first deity, a manifestation of the creator sun god. Depicted as a grey heron, the shining bird brought light into the darkness of chaos, and uttered a cry that was the first ever sound.

FENG HUANG
The *feng huang*, or Chinese phoenix, is the most sacred bird in Chinese tradition. Often resembling a peacock or a golden pheasant, it was perhaps a wind deity in origin, and it was revered as the guardian of the south and therefore a symbol of the sun, summer warmth and harvest. The *feng huang* was the particular emblem of the empress, as the *lung* dragon was of the emperor, and the dragon and phoenix together symbolize marital bliss. The bird is associated with flattery, since it was said to appear only during the reign of a just emperor, and poets could flatter the ruler by proclaiming the *feng huang*'s arrival.

QUETZAL
The brilliantly plumed quetzal is prized in American traditions as an emblem of fertility and spring vegetation. The Aztecs associated it with their great god Quetzalcoatl, the "Green-Feathered Serpent". It is a national emblem of Guatemala.

GOOSE
In one Egyptian myth, the first sound was the honking of the sun god in the form of goose. The bird was sacred to the Roman god Mars and a symbol of vigilance after cackling geese alerted troops to a nighttime attack on the Capitol in Rome in 390BCE. Hamsa, a goose or swan, is the mount and emblem of the Hindu god Brahma.

ROYALTY & HERALDRY

The practice of adopting special signs and symbols as a means of identifying a person or group is very ancient. The European traditions of heraldry began in the Middle Ages with the need of knights, often clad in full armor, to identify friend and foe in the heat of battle. Gold (or yellow), silver (or white), red, green and blue were common colors, and a great many individual symbols were used, such as lions, boars, eagles and other creatures associated with ferocity and bravery. Crusaders often included the cross, but generally avoided green so as not to be mistaken for Muslim warriors.

Devices were originally borne on the shield, but came to be displayed as emblems of prowess and dynastic pride in other, peaceful contexts. Some became highly elaborate, with the escutcheon (shield) flanked by "supporters" (see below), topped by a "crest" (usually a helmet), and accompanied by a family motto or inscription. Many rulers set up specialist bodies to regulate the granting of "arms" and avoid confusion and disputes. Special rules were developed to denote children (legitimate or otherwise) and other descendants. Arms were also granted to cities and other civic bodies.

The Anglo–French heraldic tradition, also used in the US and other English-speaking countries, has its own distinct symbols and a precise, specialized vocabulary largely derived from medieval French. For example, gold (or yellow), silver (or white), red, green and blue are called respectively *or*, *argent*, *gules*, *vert* and *azure*. The emblem of the French city of Amiens, shown on the stamp below, is described as follows: "Gules an ivy branch covering the field argent, on a chief France ancient." The clinging ivy on a red "field" (background) symbolizes the city's loyalty to the crown, represented in the "chief" (top band) by "France ancient", the old French royal symbol of the fleur-de-lis.

The arms of Christopher Columbus (right) were granted by King Ferdinand and Queen Isabella of Spain in 1493. They are "quartered", allowing a wide range of symbols.

GOLDEN CASTLE
A royal emblem, denoting Isabella's kingdom of Castile. Her marriage to Ferdinand united their two realms. The three towers refer to the Holy Trinity, proclaiming the kingdom as a bastion of the Christian faith.

ISLANDS & WAVES To the original "few islands and ocean waves" of the original arms, Columbus subsequently added a continental landmass.

LION & UNICORN
Many coats of arms are flanked by additional symbolic elements called "supporters". The royal arms of Great Britain are supported by the lion of England and the unicorn of Scotland, symbolizing the union of the two kingdoms.

STARS & STRIPES
Dating from the twelfth century, the ancestral arms of the Washington family bear two red bars and three mullets (stars). The arms are said to have inspired the US flag and are today the emblem of the District of Columbia.

LION RAMPANT
The royal emblem of León, Ferdinand's kingdom. "Rampant" is a heraldic term meaning "rearing up" defiantly. Lions are among the most frequently used heraldic symbols (see box, right).

ANCHORS
Columbus added the five golden anchors "in fess" (horizontal) to his arms to denote the Genoa-born discoverer's status as a Castilian "Admiral of the Ocean Sea".

COLUMBUS FAMILY ARMS
The fifth part of the shield bears, according to the original decree, the customary arms of the Columbus family. Columbus moved them here after adding the admiral's anchors.

HERALDIC BEASTS

The heraldic LION is an emblem of courage, power and justice. The badge of monarchs, it appears often in heraldic forms such as the LION RAMPANT (rearing up; see left), LION PASSANT (striding past) and LION REGARDANT (staring out). Apart from its spots the heraldic LEOPARD, denoting swiftness and vigilance, differs little from the lion. The fierce EAGLE, looking down from on high, is another common regal emblem. The DOUBLE-HEADED EAGLE originated in the Roman and Byzantine empires, its two heads signifying domains east and west. The symbol was inherited by the Holy Roman Emperors and the tsars of Russia. The Austrian emperors retained the symbol after the Holy Roman Empire was abolished in 1806.

Other beasts include the GRYPHON (see page 89), the LYON-POISSON (denoting prowess on land and sea) and the WYVERN (signifying fortitude against pestilence and war.

RUSSIAN EAGLE

The arms of imperial Russia (top) show a black double-headed eagle holding an orb (for Christianity) and scepter (for sovereignty). It bears an escutcheon with St. George and the dragon and is surmounted by the crowns of "All the Russias"—Russia, White Russia (Belarus) and Little Russia (Ukraine). The arms were readopted in 1992 after seventy-five years, retaining the crowns but changing the imperial black to gold.

snakes & reptiles

There is no animal symbol more widespread and complex than the snake, which appears all over the world in a great range of forms and has inspired more sacred mysteries and cults than any other creature. Snakes dwell underground and hence symbolize the forces of the earth and the underworld. They are also associated with hidden and secret knowledge and with dark and sinister powers. A snake's venom may cause harm or even death, and it is the incarnation of lurking hostility and duplicity—the familiar beast of Satan, who is "the great serpent" in Judeo-Christian tradition. In parts of England, as late as the twentieth century some people would kill the first snake they encountered in spring in the belief that doing so would keep all enemies at bay for a year.

Yet alongside these negative associations the snake is also the embodiment of the powers of the earth, and the familiar of powerful earth goddesses such as the Greek Gaia and the Aztec Coatlicue, and as such linked with creation, fertility, protection and healing. This aspect derives from what must always have seemed the most remarkable habit of snakes: the regular shedding of their skins, which in many traditions was understood as the animal being miraculously rejuvenated, or literally dying and being reborn. The snake was thus credited with extraordinary powers of transformation, healing and magic, and the creature's flesh, venom or sloughed skin were used in traditional healing in many societies.

Serpents are often connected with the forces of cosmic creation, as in the Hindu myth that recounts how divine beings coiled Vasuki, a gigantic *naga* or snake-deity, around a mountain and then, pulling on the serpent's head and tail, turned the mountain like a butter-churn. It vigorously agitated the primordial ocean of milk and in so doing initiated the creation of the cosmos. According to Hindu cosmology the cosmos is repeatedly created, destroyed and created anew in great cycles, and between these cycles the great creator god Vishnu rests on the coils of a cosmic serpent, Ananta.

SERPENTS OF THE WATERS

often deadly poisonous, WATER SNAKES embody the unseen dangers of the dark depths and have inspired fearsome mythological SEA SERPENTS, especially among seafaring peoples. Greek myth has the nine-headed HYDRA defeated by Herakles (see left and page 178), the sea serpents that slew LAOCOÖN and his sons, and the six-headed sea monster SCYLLA, which snatched sailors from ships. In Norse myth, the NIDHOGG serpent lay at the bottom of the sea, gnawing the roots of the cosmic tree YGGDRASIL and representing the inevitability of change and destruction. But water serpents can also be powerful creators. For the Rio Indians of the Amazon, the ANACONDA represents a mythical ancestor who swam up the great river and regurgitated the first people onto the land. African and Australian beliefs tell of a great creator RAINBOW SERPENT that dwells in the watery underworld but appears in the sky as the RAINBOW.

SERPENT MOUND

The Great Serpent Mound in Adams County, Ohio, is a monumental earthwork more than 400m (1,400ft) long, created by Native peoples ca. 1,000 years ago and depicting a giant snake apparently devouring an egg. The "head" points to the sunset on the summer solstice, so the effigy may symbolize the sun (the "egg") being swallowed by the cosmic serpent at midsummer, the turning of the year. The snake is a potent symbol for many Native American peoples.

PYTHON

In Greek myth the primal earth goddess Gaia set the giant serpent Python to guard her sanctuary at Delphi, which was believed to be the very center, or navel, of the world. Python embodied the sacred energy and oracular powers of the earth, which were vouchsafed to the Pythia, the priestess of the Delphic oracle. According to myth, Python was slain by the solar god Apollo, who made Delphi his own chief shrine.

WADJET

The hooded cobra was revered by the Egyptians as a manifestation of Wadjet, or Udjet, the cobra-goddess of Lower Egypt, the region of the Nile delta. Wadjet's image adorned the pharaoh's crown in the form of the golden uraeus, rearing up to spit venom into the eyes of pharaoh's enemies. Her counterpart was Nekhbet, the vulture goddess of the south, Upper Egypt (see also page 175).

NAGA

Appearing frequently in Indian traditions are the *naga*s, serpent deities usually depicted as cobras. They symbolize the connection between Earth and heaven and hidden forces such as earthquakes. In Buddhist legend the seven-headed *naga* Muchalinda sheltered the meditating Buddha under his seven hoods in a storm. Emerging from dark into light, snakes are also symbols of enlightenment.

COATLICUE

The name of the Aztec earth goddess Coatlicue means "Serpent Skirt", and she has been described as the being through which spirit becomes matter, symbolized by the serpent (*coatl*): a serpent with a head at each end of its body is probably one of her emblems. Coatlicue was the mother of Quetzalcoatl, the Green Feathered Serpent (see page 77), and also of the sun god Huitzilipochtli.

CADUCEUS

(*right*) The badge of physicians since antiquity, the caduceus consists of two serpents intertwined around a winged staff and was the emblem of Asklepios, the Greek god of healing (Aesculapius to the Romans). Those seeking cures would sleep among snakes in the god's temple. The emblem represents the duality of the serpent as a force of harm and good, a poisoner but also the child of Gaia, the Earth, and bearer of healing earth-magic. The god Hermes (Mercury) also bore the caduceus as his messenger's staff, an emblem of peace and protection.

OUROBOROS

The ouroboros, or uroboros, is a very ancient symbol in the form of a snake devouring—or disgorging—itself. It represents the eternal cycles of the cosmos, the transcendence of duality, and the union of opposites. In origin it may have symbolized the daily renewal of the Egyptian sun god after his nightly journey through the darkness of the underworld.

VISION SERPENT

For the Maya, snakes symbolized the spirit of life. It was believed that sacred ancestors appeared as snakes in order to mark the accession of a new Mayan ruler. In sacrificial bloodletting rites, paper was soaked in the perpetrator's blood and ritually burned to release a "vision serpent", a manifestation of a spirit in the form of smoke. The spirit was depicted in Mayan art in the form of a writhing, coiling serpent being (above).

ROD OF MOSES

According to the Bible, God instructed Moses to erect a bronze snake as a means of healing snakebites (Numbers 21.9). The image of the brazen serpent was understood by Christians to prefigure the cross of Christ, by whose death the sins of humankind were healed. A snake nailed to a cross occurs in medieval art as a symbol of resurrection and the sublimation of the spiritual over the corporeal realm.

BASILISK

In old bestiaries the basilisk, or cockatrice, was a monster with a cockerel's body and wings, a serpent's tail and a stare that killed anyone unfortunate enough to catch the creature's eye. In earlier Greek sources it was simply a serpent with a crown-like protrusion on its head, hence its name (*basiliskos*, "royal"); it was perhaps derived from the cobra. In Christian tradition the creature symbolized lust.

MEDUSA

(*right*) The Gorgons were three monstrous sisters who had writhing snakes instead of hair and a gaze that turned living beings to stone. To avoid her stare, the hero Perseus took the precaution of looking at the Gorgon Medusa (right) in a polished shield as he cut off her head. He later used the snake-fringed head to turn his enemies to stone. Drops of blood from Medusa's severed head turned into the monster amphisbaena, a serpent with a head at each end. Symbolically the amphisbaena represents duality and disunity, and also unpredictability, since it was able to attack from either head.

CROCODILE

(*below*) Symbols of deceit and the perils of the waters, crocodiles were sacred to the Egyptian god Sobek (right), who was shown as a man with a crocodile's head. Elsewhere in Africa, the crocodile is a revered ancestor spirit and linked to fertility as the lord of water.

SATAN THE SERPENT

(*left*) In Christian lore, Satan took the form of a serpent to tempt Adam and Eve to eat the forbidden fruit in Eden (left), thus bringing about humanity's loss of innocence. God then punished the serpent by making it crawl forever after on its belly.

SALAMANDER

(*below*) Greek fable claimed that the salamander was born in fire and impervious to flames; the Romans believed that asbestos was the creature's discarded wool. In Christianity the salamander symbolized resistance to the fires of lust and passion, and in alchemy it was a symbol of fire itself and of sulphur. It is also an emblem of courage.

THE COSMIC TURTLE

Found in many traditions is the idea that the world rests on a great TURTLE or TORTOISE, a universal symbol of strength or permanence. In Native American EARTH DIVER myths, the world begins as an infinite watery chaos, far beneath the sky world where all creatures live. One animal, such as a MUSKRAT, a BEETLE or a COOT, leaves the sky and descends to the bottom of the waters to retrieve a handful of mud. There is nowhere to put the mud, so a turtle takes it on its back. Bit by bit, the creature brings up enough mud to create dry land, a new world where life can flourish. In Chinese myth, the creator goddess NÜ GUA uses the legs of a giant tortoise to hold up the heavens, and in Hindu tradition, the mountain that churns the ocean (see page 80) rests on the back of KURMA, a giant turtle that is an avatar of VISHNU.

THREE POISONS

In Buddhist tradition the snake is a symbol of enlightenment (see page 81) but also of hatred. Hatred, desire (represented by a pig) and ignorance or delusion (a rooster) are the "Three Poisons" that fuel negative actions and keep beings trapped within the "endless ocean" of birth, death and rebirth. The creatures are depicted in the center of images of the "Wheel of Life" (see page 161).

APEP

Every night, the Egyptian sun god sailed through the waters of Duat, the underworld, where his defenders fought off the attacks of the forces of darkness, symbolized by the great underworld serpent Apep (Apophis). The serpent was often shown being speared by the fierce god Seth, representing the nightly triumph of the sun and of order over chaos.

TURTLE & TORTOISE

Their slow movements on land, their relative safety from predators within their shells, and their long lives make turtles and tortoises widespread symbols of stability and longevity. A turtle produces up to 200 eggs at a time, hence they are also fertility symbols in many traditions. The Maya, for example, linked them with their god, Chac, the lord of the rains and fertile soil. Turtles and tortoises are involved in the creation or maintenance of the cosmos, commonly seen as holding up the heavens or the earth on their backs (see box, above). Together with the White Tiger, the Azure Dragon and the Red Bird, the Black Turtle is one of Chinese tradition's Four Sacred Creatures. A tortoise is said to have brought secrets of creation to the primal being Fuxi.

FROG & TOAD

Frogs and toads are symbols of abundance and fertility, probably because of the profusion of their spawn. The Egyptian frog goddess Heket was a protector of pregnant women and newborn babies, and the title "Servant of Heket" probably meant a midwife. The toad secretes poison and is often a more sinister emblem than the frog, the familiar of black witches. Its lively mating habits make it a symbol of lust and it was sacred to the love-goddess Aphrodite. In Chinese folklore a three-legged toad in the moon spits out gold and silver coins. It is an emblem of wealth, immortality, the moon—and also avarice, because the words for "toad" and "greed" sound the same (*chan*).

insects & arachnids

Insects and spiders often embody positive qualities such as fortitude, industry and cooperation. Sometimes the symbolism has a cosmic dimension: butterflies, which turn from earthbound caterpillars or into often spectacular creatures of the air, are widespread symbols of regeneration, rebirth and resurrection. The scarab, or dung beetle, lays its eggs in a ball of dung which it rolls along: the dung nurtures the larvae when they eventually hatch. The Egyptians depicted Khepri, the sun god at dawn, as a cosmic scarab that rolled the sun up from the underworld, its life-giving powers renewed (left).

However, insects and arachnids also attract negative symbolism from their stings and their habit of creeping silently in and out of dark places. Spiders are supremely ambivalent. Widely admired for their diligence, patience and marvelous weaving skills, they feature as creators and culture heroes like the Great Weaver of the Maya who spins the web of life, or Spider Woman, the protector ancestor of the Navaho and Zuni. A famous Scottish legend recounts how King Robert Bruce, in hiding after six failed attempts to defeat the English, was inspired by a spider's persistence in building its web to try one more time: he eventually drove the English from Scotland.

But spiders, which were once reputed to be venomous (few are), set unseen traps for unwary prey that are doomed to become more entangled the more they struggle. This makes them widespread symbols of treachery, ruthlessness and the "tangled web" of deceit.

BUTTERFLY

(*left*) In many traditions the apparently miraculous life cycle of caterpillar-chrysalis-butterfly represents the journey of the soul from life through death to heaven and, ultimately, resurrection. However, their brief lives and flitting habits also make butterflies symbols of inconstancy, superficiality and vanity.

MOTH

(*above*) The "night butterfly" that dies in the flame to which it is drawn symbolizes the suffering lover or the devotee seeking to be consumed by the flames of the divine—or simply recklessness. With its skull-like marking, the so-called death's head moth (above) is an omen of death.

THE INDUSTRIOUS BEE

Bees play an important role in many societies as providers of HONEY, a chief source of sugar, and beeswax for CANDLES. As harbingers of SUMMER they are symbolically associated with light and the SUN, born according to Egyptian myth from the tears of the sun god. Once erroneously believed to reproduce without sex, bees were symbols of CHASTITY and, in christian tradition, the VIRGIN MARY.

Presided over by a QUEEN BEE, a (sometimes humorous) symbol of female power, the teeming HIVE (below) represents DILIGENCE and an ordered, efficient society. It is a symbol of the poet or orator, vessel of honeyed words. MEAD, honey liqor, is linked with wisdom and inspiration, like the magic MEAD of the Norse gods. Gathering honey carries the risk of being stung, and in christian tradition this is an allegory for following christ at the risk of martyrdom. However, through christ the believer will overcome the "sting" of death (1 corinthians 15.55) and gather the "honey" of resurrection and salvation.

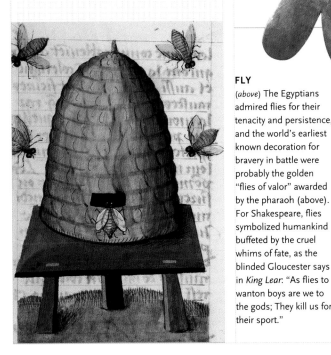

ANT

A universal symbol of industry and creative cooperation, and also of wise foresight, owing to the belief that ants laid up a store of wheat or barley for the winter. In fact, the "grains" that ants are often seen to carry are usually the larvae of the ant colony. In parts of West Africa, ants and termites are associated with fertility: the anthill or termite mound symbolizes the sexual organ of the earth when it mated with the sky at the beginning of time, thus creating the world.

CATERPILLAR

Caterpillars have been widely linked with rebirth and resurrection, from their apparently miraculous metamorphosis into moths and butterflies. They were even credited with healing powers: in parts of England, as late as the 1950s, a hairy caterpillar was worn round the neck as a cure for whooping cough.

CENTIPEDE

In China, the centipede is one of a group known as the Five Poisonous Creatures (centipedes, lizards, scorpions, toads and vipers). To this day they are woven and embroidered on a wide range of artifacts —particularly children's clothing—as a charm that works on the principle of like repelling like, to ward off the Five Poisonous Creatures and other perils.

LADYBIRD

Also called ladybug, ladyfly, ladycow, maybug and marygold, this familiar, bright red beetle was sacred to the Virgin Mary (Our Lady), its black spots held to represent the tears that she shed over the bloodied body of Christ. Earlier, though, it was a creature of Freyja, the Norse goddess of love, and in European folklore it was said to land on those who would soon find a sweetheart.

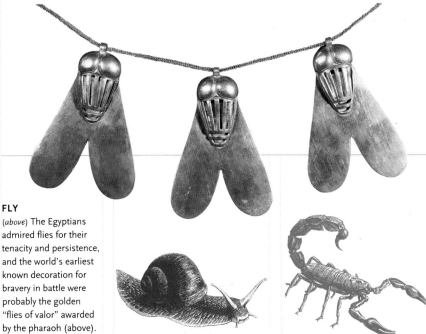

FLY

(*above*) The Egyptians admired flies for their tenacity and persistence, and the world's earliest known decoration for bravery in battle were probably the golden "flies of valor" awarded by the pharaoh (above). For Shakespeare, flies symbolized humankind buffeted by the cruel whims of fate, as the blinded Gloucester says in *King Lear*: "As flies to wanton boys are we to the gods; They kill us for their sport."

SNAIL & SLUG

The snail is a symbol of the moon from the shape of its shell and its ability to "wax" and "wane" from within it. Resembling the aroused sex organs of woman (their underside and mucus) and man (their horns), snails and slugs are linked with sexuality and fertility.

SCORPION

Widely linked with destruction and death, in Egypt the scorpion was a symbol of Seth, god of chaos, who became a scorpion to attack his rival Horus. The constellation Scorpio is said to be a scorpion sent by the goddess Artemis (Diana) to kill the boastful hunter Orion.

fabulous beasts

The human imagination has extended the symbolic capacity of the animal kingdom by adding many beasts of its own. These may be fabulous examples of existing species, like the Thunderbird or the three-headed dog Cerberus, or fantastical hybrids such as the man-horse centaur or the lion-eagle gryphon. These creatures are typically wild and untamed, destroyers or protectors, or both, and often possess special powers. They embody the elemental forces of the universe, symbols of both cosmic order and disorder.

The most prominent of all fabulous beasts is the dragon. Often depicted as a great winged reptile (above), the dragon—also called a "serpent" or "worm"—is to be found in most cultures as a source of fascination, fear or reverence. The four elements of earth, air, fire and water were conjoined in the dragon, which lives in the earth or the waters, flies in the air, and often breathes fire. Many peoples interpreted rainbows as the body of a giant cosmic serpent or dragon that divided the ordered world from the unseen heaven or chaos beyond. For psychologists, the essential dualism of dragons may represent inner conflict in the human mind, the interaction of light (the conscious) with the dark (the subconscious and the Shadow archetype, our sinister alter ego).

Some fabulous animals very likely arose from travelers' reports of real creatures seen in distant lands, but many more are undoubtedly the products of a human imagination untrammeled by a scientific awareness of the limits of nature.

THE CHINESE DRAGON

In chinese tradition, the dragon is a fierce but usually benevolent protector, and the blue-green celestial dragon symbolizes the east, the sun and the fertility of the land; it also guards the heavenly mansion of the gods. The dragon's energy holds together all the phenomena of nature, and is the source of benevolent rains as well as hurricanes, which are said to be caused by sea dragons. According to the chinese system of geomancy (*feng shui*), dragons determine the form of the landscape, and the feng shui master places buildings and furniture in accordance with "dragon lines", powerful currents of dragon energy that run through the earth. Yu the Great, the mythical founder of china's quasi-historical xia dynasty, was a dragon-being. All emperors were said to be Yu's incarnation, and the five-clawed dragon, long (shown below), became the emblem par excellence of the emperor—his wife's remained the phoenix—and unauthorized use of the image by commoners was punishable by death.

MANG DRAGON

(*right*) The ordinary, non-imperial dragon was depicted with four claws. Dragons are often shown clutching a fiery ball, which is in fact a pearl that they have disgorged. The dragon was said to exude an essence that was the distillation of the moon, which took the form of a pearl.

QILIN

(*below*) Of Chinese origin, the *qilin* is an auspicious creature known throughout East Asia. It has the body of a deer, the tail of an ox, the hooves of a horse and a small horn. It is often depicted with multicolored hair or scales and flames. A *qilin* appears only during the rule of a just leader.

THE DRAGON & THE TIGER

(*above*) The Japanese dragon derives from early Chinese examples that were depicted with three claws. According to Japanese myth, the dragon Tatsu, the embodiment of the spirit of nature, is in permanent conflict with the tiger, the embodiment of physical nature. This conflict can bring about earthquakes, thunderstorms and other natural phenomena.

ST. MICHAEL & THE DRAGON

In Christianity the dragon is evil. According to Revelation 12, the archangel Michael, leader of the heavenly host, defeated a seven-headed dragon that was the embodiment of Satan; the heads were held to symbolize the seven deadly sins. Satan is said to have become a dragon to devour Margaret of Antioch, a third-century martyr; but she burst from its belly by making the sign of the cross.

GRYPHON

(*right*) The gryphon (griffin, griffon) is a magnificent hybrid of the lion and eagle (here in stylized form, right). It appears in legend as a fierce and virtuous guardian of treasure, embodying vigilance and the capacity for vengeance (being sacred to Nemesis in Greece).

DRAGON OF OSIRIS

(*below*) Depicted as a winged serpent, the imperial dragon of Egypt represented the god Osiris, ruler of the dead, king of the underworld and lord of fertility. The dragon was believed to cause the Nile's annual flood, which replenished the fields with water and a rich alluvial soil.

EGYPTIAN SPHINX

(*above*) Recumbent lion temple guardians with, in some accounts, an eagle's wings symbolized the divine spirit of the sun god in the person of the pharaoh, whom the sphinx protected. Often given a human head (though many at Thebes have a ram's head), a sphinx may bear the image of a particular king, such as the Great Sphinx of Giza, which portrays the pharaoh Khephren (ca. 2600BCE), builder of the nearby pyramid. A Greek sphinx has the head of a woman and was given to issuing riddles. Jung saw her as a symbol of the devouring mother.

CELTIC DRAGON

(*left*) Celtic Welsh legend recounts that the roar of two fighting dragons was so loud that women became infertile. In another tale, the warrior Uther dreamed of a red dragon, so named himself Pendragon ("chief dragon"). The red dragon became the badge of Uther and his son, Arthur, and for centuries it has been the emblem of Wales.

CHIMERA

So outlandish was the terrifying, fire-breathing Chimera that it came to symbolize anything fantastical, unproven or nonexistent. It had a lion's upper body, a serpent's lower half or tail, and a goat's head on its back. It was slain by the hero Bellerophon, astride his steed Pegasus (far right).

PERSEUS & ANDROMEDA

(*below*) In Greek myth, King Cepheus chained his daughter Andromeda to a rock near Joppa (Jaffa) to placate a sea dragon, Ceto, that was ravaging his kingdom. Mounted on the winged horse Pegasus, the hero Perseus slew the dragon and rescued Andromeda. A symbolic tale of divine, celestial power overcoming the forces of darkness and chaos, the story may be the origin of the Christian legend of St. George.

UNICORN

Often depicted like a white horse but with a single, twisting horn and cloven hooves like a deer, the unicorn was a symbol of chastity, purity and femininity. The creature was said to avoid human company, except that of a virgin maiden, in whose lap it would lay its head. It became a symbol of Christ, and the unicorn with its head or horn in Mary's lap represented the Annunciation. The horn was said to detect poison and make it harmless.

CENTAUR

Combining a human torso and a horse's body, the centaur embodied brutishness and licentiousness, and it symbolized the inner turmoil of man in conflict with his sensual impulses. However, the centaur Chiron was wise, kind and learned—a friend of Apollo and the tutor of Achilles and other heroes.

ECHIDNA & TYPHON

In Greek myth Gaia, the Earth, coupled with her brother Tartaros, the darkness, to produce Echidna and Typhon, who symbolized dark cosmic forces and the dangers of transgressing taboos. Echidna had a maiden's torso and the lower parts of a repulsive serpent; Typhon was a hundred-headed giant. They too coupled incestuously to produce the Nemean Lion, the Lernean Hydra (see pages 146–147), Cerberus, Orthrus, the Chimera, the Greek Sphinx, and other famous beasts.

PEGASUS

In Greek myth, Pegasus is the winged horse that resulted from the union of Poseidon and Medusa. Everywhere Pegasus trod, a spring erupted. While drinking at one such spring, Bellerophon captured Pegasus, then rode him to victory over the fire-breathing Chimera.

CERBERUS & ORTHRUS

Two monstrous guard dogs: the three heads of Cerberus, at the gates of Hades, symbolized life, death and the afterlife; the two heads of Orthrus, watchdog of Geryon, denoted supernatural vigilance. Herakles overcame both beasts (see page 179).

AMAMET

Also known as Ammit and Amut, this terrifying creature was the devourer of Egyptian souls in the underworld, acting to enforce divine retribution. It took the hybrid form of three real-life dangers lurking in the Nile, combining the jaw of a crocodile with the head and mane of a lion on the body of a hippopotamus.

DAOISM

The term "Daoism" (also written Taoism) is the name given to a host of traditional Chinese religious beliefs and practices. These are underpinned by an ancient view that the cosmos and everything in it is made up of a force or essence named *qi* (*ch'i*). This comprises two opposing but complementary forces, *yin* and *yang*, which originally meant the sunny (*yang*) and shaded (*yin*) side of a hill. *Yang* refers to all that is masculine, bright, hard, dry, warm and active, while *yin* is feminine, dark, moist, cold and inactive. Most crucially, all things contain both *yin* and *yang*, and whenever *yang* dominates it inevitably contains within it the seed of *yin*, and vice versa. Thus summer, the season of greatest *yang*, must transmute into winter, the season of greatest *yin*. The entire principle of *yin* and *yang* is summarized in the symbol known as the *taiji* (*tai chi*), which shows *yin* and *yang* in balance, each containing a dot that is the seed of the other (see illustration, page 13).

The *yin–yang* system operates together with the Five Elements, or Phases, metaphysical forces of transformation named "fire", "wood", "metal", "water" and "earth". The first two are *yang*, the last two *yin*, and metal is neutral, the point of balance. Everything in the cosmos and all transformations can be categorized according to these five and the flow of *yin* and *yang*. The term Daoism refers to the Way (*Dao*): the principle whereby *qi* is endlessly created and dissolved, giving rise to all the phenomena of the universe.

Daoism is also, more specifically, a religious philosophy and ritual practice. In this sense it is based on *wu wei*, "non-interference", learning to perceive the Dao but not to interfere with it—literally "going with the flow" of *qi* in order to achieve harmony and order in one's life. One goal of Daoist practice is the attainment of long life, and Daoist alchemists have long aspired to immortality, with a special place in the Daoist pantheon reserved for the Eight Immortals.

Symbolism is everywhere in Daoism. This temple incense burner (left) has three legs and three tiers, representing the Chinese trinity of heaven, earth and humankind, and an auspicious eight sides (eight = five + three). Daoist priests wear robes such as this nineteenth-century example (opposite), replete with symbolism.

CRANE Reputed to live for 600 years, the white crane provides the aerial means of transport for immortals on their journeys between worlds.

TRIGRAMS Eight combinations of three lines are used in Chinese divination: broken lines are *yin*, unbroken *yang*. The two trigrams here represent west/water (left) and east/fire (right).

BUTTERFLY & CHRYSANTHEMUM A butterfly symbolizes summer and a chrysanthemum autumn; together they are *yang* and *yin* and the transition of the seasons.

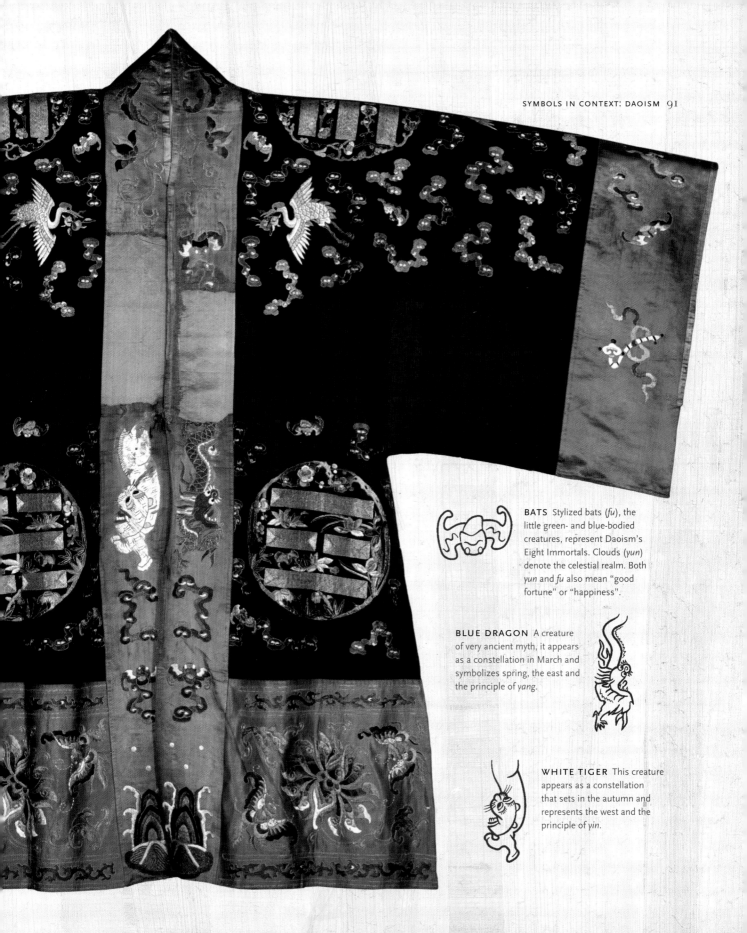

BATS Stylized bats (*fu*), the little green- and blue-bodied creatures, represent Daoism's Eight Immortals. Clouds (*yun*) denote the celestial realm. Both *yun* and *fu* also mean "good fortune" or "happiness".

BLUE DRAGON A creature of very ancient myth, it appears as a constellation in March and symbolizes spring, the east and the principle of *yang*.

WHITE TIGER This creature appears as a constellation that sets in the autumn and represents the west and the principle of *yin*.

HUMANKIND

MOST PEOPLES RECOGNIZE THREE DISTINCT PHASES OF LIFE: CHILDHOOD, ADULTHOOD AND OLD AGE. THE HUMAN STORY HAS BEEN SEEN AS A DECLINE FROM INNOCENCE AND PHYSICAL PERFECTION TO OUR PRESENT STATE OF MORTALITY, MORAL UNCERTAINTY AND SUBJECTION TO THE WHIMS OF FATE.

life & destiny

Pervading all human history, mythology and psychology is humankind's awareness of its own mortality: our knowledge that infancy and youth must pass and that the ultimate destiny of all living creatures is the same.

FATHER TIME

Time has often been portrayed as an old man, whose wings are a reminder that "Time flies". He carries an hour-glass and like Death, the Grim Reaper, a scythe. The figure derives partly from Cronos (Saturn), a primal god linked with agriculture (hence the scythe), whose name was confused with Greek *chronos*, "time".

MEMENTO MORI

A common motif in the Renaissance and Baroque was the *memento mori*— literally "remember to die" in Latin— a reminder that life can be cut short at any moment and that youth and beauty will inevitably decay. A rose, which blooms for a short time before its petals wither and fall away, was one frequent image.

GRAVES & TOMBS

Graves are primarily monuments that enable the dead to live on in memory; they also, in most instances, bear witness to the religious tradition of the deceased. However, tombs and graves have often been regarded as literally homes for the dead, where the soul dwells after death, and portals to the afterlife. Tombs and graves from China and Egypt to Mesoamerica were supplied with the same goods that the deceased required in life, from food and domestic artefacts to weaponry and, in the cases of the elite, even servants and warriors.

THE KNIGHT'S DREAM

El Sueño del Caballero by Antonio de Pereda Salgado (ca. 1655) includes a skull and other symbols of worldly vanity, such as a clock, roses, riches and the mask of youth. The knight dreams of an angel whose banner is a reminder of Death: "Eternally it stings, swiftly it flies and slays."

first men & women

The origins of humankind have fascinated most cultures, and almost every tradition has its own distinctive account of the appearance of the first people. Often the earliest humans are a couple, with the first man usually appearing before a woman—no doubt reflecting (and serving to justify) the patriarchal structure of many societies. Women's inferior standing was further entrenched by accounts relating how women brought about many of humankind's ills, as in the Judeo-Christian tradition of Adam and Eve (see below).

But Maori and many Native American traditions feature a woman as the first ancestor. In Maori tradition Hine-Hau-On, the Earth-Created Maiden, was formed from the sands of an island, and this echoes a widespread theme of humans being created from earth or clay. The idea of a deity breathing life into clay creations is well known from the Bible, which actually has two accounts of human creation. One simply states that God formed humans, man and woman, in his image (Genesis 1.27); in the other (2.21) God forms the man from clay and then makes the woman from one of his ribs. There are many parallels to the latter version in other cultures, such as a Central African story in which the first woman is created from the first man's left knee.

ADAM & EVE

(left) In the Bible, Adam and Eve (left) are the First Parents and archetypal symbols of primordial innocence, but also of corruption, disobedience and sin. Their story accounts for the origin of human shame, mortality, sickness and pain—in short, the human condition (see also page 52).

NÜ GUA & FUXI

Some of China's oldest myths involve Nü Gua and Fuxi. Revered as humankind's creator and protector, the goddess Nü Gua dipped a vine in mud and flicked it in all directions, each muddy droplet becoming a human being. The god Fuxi taught humans skills such as fishing, farming, music and writing. The pair may be shown with intertwined serpents' tails (above), symbolizing the creative powers of the earth and the union of male and female forces.

CAVES OF EMERGENCE

American peoples often revere caves as places out of which humans first emerged into the world from within the earth. These humans may have been forced to ascend owing to their own transgression, so that the emergence cave is also a symbol of moral growth from baseness to wisdom. As humans ascend to their point of emergence, they are often led by a figure such as Corn Mother (above) or Spider Woman, deities that symbolize the earth and its powers.

CULTURE HEROES

Many origin myths involve **CULTURE HEROES**, supernatural figures who bring essentials of life and culture such as fire or farming skills. Many are also **TRICKSTERS**, such as the **RAVEN** and **COYOTE** of Native American tradition, who may rob, trick or deceive superior beings into giving up jealously guarded knowledge. The theft of **FIRE** from the gods is a common theme, from the classical Greek **PROMETHEUS** (see below) or the Aztec **TEZCATLIPOCA** ("one-foot", right) to the Micronesian hero **BUE** of Kiribati, who snared the sun, and the humble Native American Cherokee **WATER SPIDER**. Culture heroes symbolize humanity's link with the divine realm but also our separation from it through acts of disobedience and defiance. As such they represent the freedom of the human spirit, and humankind's unrelenting assumption of the quasi-divine role of forming the world for itself.

PROMETHEUS

In Classical myth, the god Prometheus created the first man from clay and stole fire from heaven for humankind. For this Zeus had him bound to a rock, where an eagle daily tore out his liver, only for it to grow back and the torture to resume (above). In some accounts, Prometheus used the fire to animate his clay creations: he thus symbolized the "divine spark" of intelligence and creativity that separates humans from beasts. In Christian tradition he prefigured Christ, interceding for humanity and suffering torments.

FIRST WOMAN

For the Navajo, the first human was a woman and this idea is found elsewhere in Native American traditions. According to the Huron and Iroquois of the Northeast, the first ancestor was Ataentsic, the earth goddess and offspring of the Sky People. For many Native American peoples, corn (maize, above) features as a central motif in accounts of the creation of the first people, for example Mother Corn is the creator of the Arikara while the Cherokee tell of the first woman named Selu ("Corn").

KHNUM THE POTTER

Depicted as a man with a ram's head, the creator god Khnum was linked with the fertile soil and the annual Nile flood. In the Egyptian creation account, he is said to have formed humans from clay on a potter's wheel. He symbolized the source of life, because the Egyptian for ram (*ba*) meant the same as "soul" or "spiritual essence". The divine potter appears widely in creation mythology elsewhere in Africa. In Rwanda, for example, women leave water by the bed at night so that God may form the child of clay in their womb.

PANDORA

To punish humans for the sins of Prometheus (see left), the god Zeus created the first woman, Pandora, as a gift for Epimetheus, the slow-witted brother of Prometheus. Pandora came with a mysterious "box" (actually a jar): when she opened it she released evil and sickness into the world. All that remained in the jar was hope.

DREAMTIME

Australia is crisscrossed by sacred routes of the Dreamtime, a primordial epoch in which ancestral heroes in the form of humans, kangaroos, wallabies, lizards, birds or snakes journeyed through the landscape, creating rocks, creeks, caves and other features.

the body & mind

In the Western cosmological tradition, the human body was once understood as a microcosm (Greek *mikros kosmos*, "small world"), with every aspect of the body corresponding to a part of God's universe, the macrocosm (*makros kosmos*, "great world"). The eyes, for example, corresponded to the sun and moon, the flesh to the earth and the intellect to the celestial "ether". This assumption is one basis of astrology, which holds that the workings and motions of the stars and planets have corresponding effects on individuals. Adam Kadmon, the perfect archetypal human in the Jewish mystical tradition of the Kabbalah (see pages 38–39), reflects the image of God, and is the link between humankind and its creator.

Broadly speaking, each individual part of the body possesses a symbolism which encompasses its known or—as with the heart and other internal organs—traditionally assumed range of functions. No physical features have greater symbolic significance than the eyes, the "portals of the soul". They are the focus of human facial expressions, which in art, together with bodily postures, constitute a near-inexhaustible symbol system in themselves. Widespread and ancient is the belief in the "Evil Eye", the mere glance that transmits misfortune. The Evil Eye often works only by direct eye contact with the victim, an idea probably related to the notion of the eyes as openings to the soul. Thus Perseus was able to kill the Gorgon Medusa, whose glance turned creatures to stone, only by looking at her in a mirror; the similarly lethal-eyed cockatrice or basilisk could be slain likewise. The Evil Eye may also be "outstared" by its own image. An eye depicted on a raised hand is a common amulet in the Mediterranean and Near East, where mariners may also ward off danger by painting eyes on the prows of their vessels.

THE EYE OF POWER

The **EYES** denote authoritarian vigilance, the "all-seeing" eye of a deity or ruler that is both fearsome and protective: hence the deliberately enlarged eyes of Late Roman and Byzantine statues and religious icons. In ancient Egypt, the **SUN** and **MOON** were respectively the right and left eyes of the god **HORUS**. His rival **SETH** ripped them out, but they were restored by **ISIS**, Horus' mother and defender. The **WADJET** amulet, or **EYE OF HORUS**, represented divine healing and protection. Also common are the ideas of the **EVIL EYE** (see main text) and the **THIRD EYE**, the hidden organ of "second sight" in the center of the brow. The **BUDDHA'S EYES** look down in compassion from temples in Nepal and Tibet (above).

HEAD

For the ancient Greeks the crown of the head represented the celestial sphere. More widely, the head is a symbol of the mind and the life of the spirit. The highest yogic *chakras* are in the head and represent insight and wisdom (see pages 100–101). For many the head was the seat of the soul, and the ancient Celts and Maya kept the heads of defeated enemies as potent talismans.

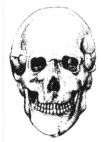

SKULL

A common emblem of death and the transience of earthly life. Crowned with laurels, it proclaims that a person's reputation will long outlive them. A skull also denotes old age and the melancholy temperament. A skull at the foot of Christ's cross refers to Golgotha or Calvary, literally the "Place of the Skull", but it is also the skull of Adam, reputedly buried at the same spot.

HAIR

In the Bible, Samson's hair is the source of his supernatural strength, which ebbs when it is cut by Delilah. Long hair may also be a sign of maturity, holiness or obedience to God. Hindus shave the head as a sign of mourning, and in ancient Egypt a shaven scalp denoted priesthood. For women, loose hair may denote sexual innocence, but letting hair down is also a sexual signal, as in the tale of Rapunzel, whose locks are used as a rope literally to draw her lover to her. Among Native American peoples, the scalp of an enemy was once a prized trophy.

MOUTH

The mouth is a symbol of speech, but also of eating and gluttony. In Egypt, the soul entered the body through the mouth: the "Opening of the Mouth" ritual (above), performed on a mummy before burial, aimed to reanimate the deceased's speech and other senses to prepare for the afterlife. In Christian symbolism, the entrance to Hell may be a gaping mouth, perhaps because of an association of the mouth's inner redness with the infernal flames.

TEETH

Bared teeth can express ferocity and hostility but also fear. Monsters and demons are depicted with prominent or exaggerated teeth, often sharply pointed, as a symbol of their wild and terrifying nature—especially in the case of quasi-human creatures such as vampires and werewolves, which may be represented in normal human form except for their beast-like fangs. But teeth bared in a grin or smile can also be a sign of happiness.

TONGUE

A symbol of speech and the sense of taste, though a protruding tongue may denote ferocity, as in the *haka* war-dance of the New Zealand Maori people (above) and depictions of the Gorgon Medusa and the Hindu goddess Kali. The tongue is also associated with eloquence, wisdom and, from its form and color, with flame. The "tongues as of fire" that descended on Christ's disciples at Pentecost (Acts 2.3) symbolize the gift of the Holy Spirit.

EAR

Egyptian "Hearing Ear" shrines bore ears that were believed to channel prayers directly to the deity. In folklore, an itching, ringing or burning ear means that you are being spoken of out of earshot.

NOSE

The symbol of smell, the nose is seen as a person's foremost point: to "follow your nose" is to go straight ahead; something obvious is "under your nose"; and to show disdain is to "look down your nose" at someone. In the Far East it is common to point to the nose to denote "I" or "myself".

BREATH

(*above*) Breath is the divine life-force: many traditions describe a deity making humans from clay and animating them by his or her breath (see page 94). In Latin, *spiritus* means both "spirit" and "breath", and hence *inspiration* is literally "breathing in" the creative spirit; the life-force is taken away when we *expire*, or "breathe out" for the last time.

THE FOUR HUMORS

Medieval physiology (above) held that the body was comprised of four "HUMORS", substances that corresponded to the four elements: CHOLER or BILE (FIRE), BLOOD (AIR), MELANCHOLIA or BLACK BILE (EARTH), and PHLEGM (WATER). The ideal state of body and mind was a perfect balance of the humors, but in most people one or other predominated. Thus one might be classed as "choleric" (quick to anger, hasty, prone to pride); "sanguine" (from the Latin *sanguis*, blood: cheerful, energetic, courageous, even unruly); "phlegmatic"; or "melancholic". Moods and sickness were ascribed to shifts in the balance of the humors owing to the heavens, weather, diet, location and many other variables.

BLOOD

Blood is widely believed to contain the cosmic spirit of a creator deity, or to represent the owner's life-force. The mixing of bloods may seal an unbreakable pact or bond. Due to its color, blood was linked with heat and the sun: the Aztecs held that the sun god required human blood to rise each day (above). For Roman Catholics, the Eucharist wine becomes literally and miraculously the blood of Christ; for Protestants it is usually symbolic.

HEART

The seat of love and passion, of courage and the spirit in many traditions. For the Egyptians, the heart and not the head was the seat of wisdom, knowledge, memory and emotions. It was the only organ left in the body after death, to be weighed by the god Anubis to test its owners virtue. In Roman Catholic tradition, the Sacred Heart or Bleeding Heart (above) represents the sufferings and compassion of the Virgin Mary.

HANDS

The ability to use the **HANDS** played a crucial part in our evolution, marking the step from an **APE**-like primate to the first human-like creature, **HOMO HABILIS**, the "handy" or "skilled man". The hand is the wielder of strength and power, the performer of actions, the transmitter of commands and the defender against evil.

In Islam, the **HAND OF FATIMA**, said to represent the hand of the prophet's daughter, is a common amulet against the **EVIL EYE** (see box, page 96). In Christian art, the hands of **CHRIST** or a saint may be depicted in any of a range of symbolic gestures, for example the right hand raised with two **FINGERS** pointing upward is the usual sign of blessing, while laying a hand on the **HEAD** of a sick person is an act of healing. **GOD** may be represented simply as a hand emerging from the **SKY. MUDRAS**, distinctive hand and finger gestures with a wide range of symbolic meanings, are common in Hindu and Buddhist iconography. The illustration below shows the hand of the **BUDDHA** in **VITARKA MUDRA**, the gesture of debate or teaching.

ARM

The arms raised or held out in front indicate supplication or prayer, an act of submission to the gods and simultaneously of receptivity to divine power. In ancient Egypt, a pair of raised arms was the hieroglyph of the *ka*, the creative life-force of the individual. The finger of command is usually at the end of a raised, extended arm that has expressed leadership and authority since Classical times (left). An arm raised in salute honors a person superior in rank, or an elevated principle.

BELLY & NAVEL

In Egyptian art, a large belly denoted prosperity and education. In China and Japan the abdomen was the seat of life, and elsewhere it is the home of instinct and "gut feeling". The yogic third *chakra* resides in the belly: this may relate to the widespread symbolism of the navel or belly button as the source of life, as when the Hindu creator god Brahma emerges from a lotus growing from the navel of Vishnu.

FINGER

Fingers represent the sense of touch. One finger pointing in the distance is a gesture of command (see above); in portraits, a finger may casually indicate an achievement of the sitter, such as a military victory, book or building. Holy figures raise their first two fingers in blessing. In a V-shape, palm forward, these two fingers denote "Victory", the salute of Winston Churchill; but with knuckles forward it is a gross insult—as are many other gestures worldwide that exploit the phallic symbolism of the raised finger.

FOOT

Feet are often associated with divinity coming to Earth, and going barefoot is a sign of humility. Early Buddhist art denoted the Buddha by his footprints, which in various places are said to be miraculously preserved in rock. Christ showed his humility by washing the disciples' feet, and a female "sinner"—traditionally Mary Magdalene —expressed her devotion to Jesus by washing and anointing his feet. Feet are also linked with spreading the gospel, as St. Paul said, citing Isaiah: "How beautiful are the feet of those that bring good news?" (Romans 10.15).

SKELETON

Skeletons appear widely as symbols of death. Death itself may be an animated skeleton, like the Grim Reaper of Western tradition. In Tibet, skeleton beings called *chitipati*, "lords of the funeral pyre", attend Yama, the god of death. They dance and wield thunderbolt standards that symbolize enlightenment, through which one learns that death is merely a necessary transition.

THE CHAKRAS

According to traditional Indian physiology, vital cosmic energy travels along the spinal axis of the human body through channels called *nadi*s. This energy, or "subtle body", condenses at seven main points (and a number of minor ones) along the axis . They are symbolized either as lotus flowers (*padma*s) or, more commonly, as spinning vortices or wheels (*chakra*s).

Whether or not we are aware of them, these centers are said to be always active, and each *chakra* corresponds to a different level of consciousness. Different states of mind arise as energy travels through the *chakra*s, from the base or root *chakra* at the perineum (the seat of basic animal survival), to the crown of the head (the seat of supreme consciousness and enlightenment). Indian philosophers linked these changes with the five elements (*tattvas*): earth, air, fire, water and "ether" (*akasha*). In modern times they have been related to the operation of the endocrine glands; the different parts of the brain (thus the root *chakra* relates to the brain stem or "lower brain"); and psychophysiology, the study of physical causes behind psychological states such as fear or joy (for instance, why a sense of unease may be accompanied by a "gut reaction", in the third *chakra*). But the *chakra*s are not fully explicable in physiological or material terms.

For most people, most of the time, it is the five lower *chakra*s that dominate the subtle body's energy. The aim of Tantric yoga is to cultivate the subtle body so that energy rises to activate the two highest *chakra*s.

As shown in charts such as the one opposite, each *chakra* is depicted as having a certain number of petals, and is linked with a color, element, planet and deity, as well as with other symbols.

SEVENTH CHAKRA
Sahasrara chakra (crown area) relates to enlightenment and transcendence of self. Petals: 1,000. Elements: None (transcends the material plane). Planet: Ketu. Deity: The "inner Guru".

SIXTH CHAKRA
Ajna chakra (brow area) relates to conscience, insight, the power of the mind. Petals: two, luminescent. Elements: all. Planet: Saturn. Deity: Shiva–Shakti, the androgyne, uniting polarities.

KUNDALINI

The practice of cultivating the CHAKRAS (see main text) is visualized as arousing a potent mass of dormant energy that is symbolized by a sleeping SERPENT coiled at the ROOT CHAKRA at the base of the spine. This is called KUNDALINI, from the sanskrit *kundal*(coil), and practitioners aim to induce the "serpent" to rise up the body through the *chakra*s to the CROWN CHAKRA in order to attain perfect physical and psycho-spiritual balance.

Kundalini ascends through NADIS— invisible "subtle body" channels as well as visible ones such as nerves and blood vessels. There are fourteen main *nadi*s, but the most important are the SHUSHUMNA (spinal cord) and two channels that interweave around it, the PINGALA (red) and IDA (white). The *pingala* is solar and masculine and is symbolized by the SUN or the RIGHT EYE. *ida* is lunar and female and its symbol is the MOON or LEFT EYE.

SOMA CHAKRA
As well as the seven main *chakra*s there are a number of minor ones. The twelve-petaled *soma* (nectar) *chakra* lies in the forehead area, between the sixth and seventh *chakra*s, and is associated with higher consciousness, mental clarity and states of bliss.

CHAKRA ANIMALS
Most *chakra*s are linked to a symbolic creature: first *chakra* is the elephant Airavata (left); second *chakra* is Makara, the crocodile; third *chakra* is the ram of Agni; fourth *chakra* is the deer or antelope; fifth *chakra* is the elephant Gaja; and *soma chakra* is the hybrid beast Kamadhenu.

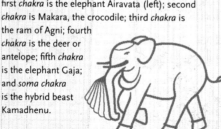

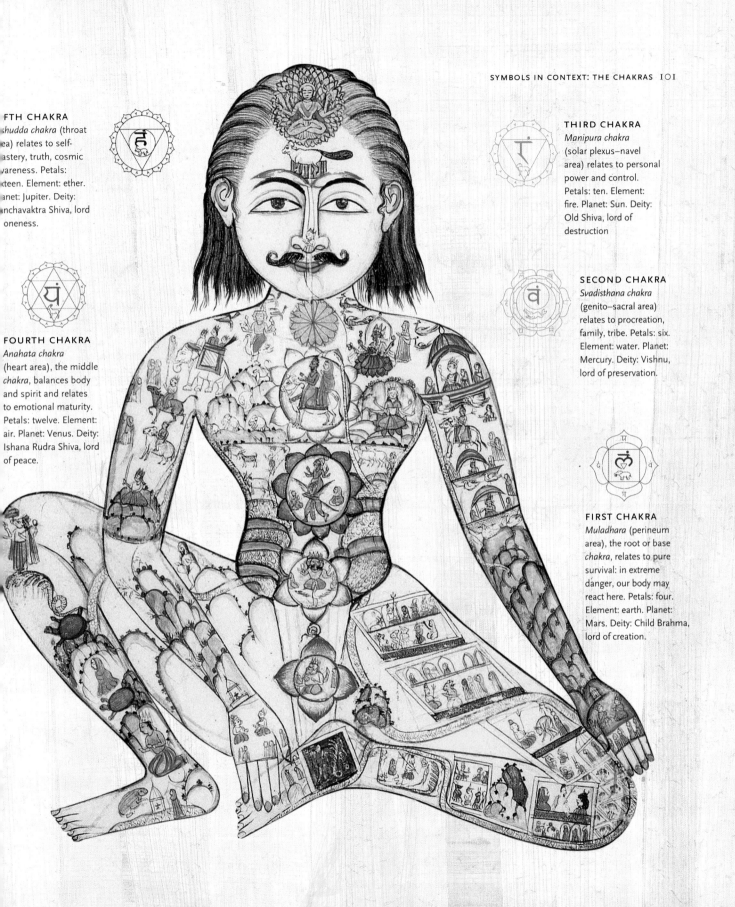

FTH CHAKRA
shudda chakra (throat
ea) relates to self-
astery, truth, cosmic
wareness. Petals:
xteen. Element: ether.
anet: Jupiter. Deity:
*nchavaktra Shiva, lord
*oneness.

FOURTH CHAKRA
Anahata chakra
(heart area), the middle
chakra, balances body
and spirit and relates
to emotional maturity.
Petals: twelve. Element:
air. Planet: Venus. Deity:
Ishana Rudra Shiva, lord
of peace.

THIRD CHAKRA
Manipura chakra
(solar plexus–navel
area) relates to personal
power and control.
Petals: ten. Element:
fire. Planet: Sun. Deity:
Old Shiva, lord of
destruction

SECOND CHAKRA
Svadisthana chakra
(genito–sacral area)
relates to procreation,
family, tribe. Petals: six.
Element: water. Planet:
Mercury. Deity: Vishnu,
lord of preservation.

FIRST CHAKRA
Muladhara (perineum
area), the root or base
chakra, relates to pure
survival: in extreme
danger, our body may
react here. Petals: four.
Element: earth. Planet:
Mars. Deity: Child Brahma,
lord of creation.

sex & fertility

Male and female are widely seen as the two fundamental principles around which the cosmos is organized. They are opposing but complementary forces, each containing within itself the seed and potential of the other, as strikingly expressed in the *taiji*, the Daoist emblem of *yin* and *yang* (see page 13). This sense of simultaneous cosmic opposition and integration underlies much of traditional symbolism associated with human sexuality, since in premodern physiology the human body was regarded as a microcosm of the universe (see page 96).

Similarly, the Earth itself offered a wide range of sexual correspondences: in some cultures, for example, caves represented the vaginas of female earth deities, while trees and other prominences were associated with rampant and often ithyphallic male gods such as the Greek Pan and his followers, the satyrs. It was once widely believed that brain, bone marrow and semen were all the same substance, and that the male seed resided in the head. This partly accounts for the widespread occurrence of horns or antlers as a symbol of male fertility deities, as the Gaulish Cernunnos and other horned gods of ancient and tribal societies.

The female sexual organ perhaps appears symbolically in the stylized forms of the lozenge and the mandorla, or *vesica piscis*, the almond-shaped nimbus. It has also been suggested that the symmetrical heart symbol traditionally associated with love is in fact a stylized representation of the spread vulva. As such, it is claimed, it was a profoundly sexual symbol of female power and fertility.

INCUBUS & SUCCUBUS

(*above*) In medieval Europe, the lowest order of Satan's demons were said to be the succubi and incubi. The female succubus seduced sleeping men in order to breed demons; her male counterpart, the incubus, attempted the same on sleeping women (above). For Freud, such demons arose in part to explain nocturnal arousal and dreams of forbidden sexual desires.

VENUS FIGURINES

(*left*) The palaeolithic hunter's concern with fertility is shown by the female images in stone, wood, bone or ivory known as "Venuses" and discovered in various parts of Eurasia. The "Venus of Willendorf" found in Austria and dated to ca. 23,000BCE (left), is typical of these personifications of fecundity in its exaggerated sexual characteristics.

YONI

(*below*) In Hinduism the *yoni*, or vulva, is the supreme symbol of female sexuality as the phallus, or *lingam*, is of the male. The *yoni* can be represented as a ring or rings around the base of a *lingam*. In Tantric Buddhism the two arcs of the stylized *yoni* represent the gateway to rebirth.

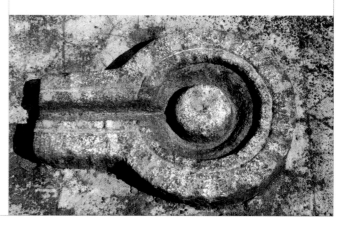

YANTRA
In Hindu Tantra, the creative cosmic energy transmitted by the sexual play of the divine couple Shiva and Shakti are represented in the diagrammatic form of the *yantra*. A cosmogram (a pattern of colors and lines symbolizing the cosmos), the *yantra* is used as an aid to meditation in order to assist internal physical and psychospiritual transformation.

YAB-YUM
In the Tantric Buddhism of Tibet, an image of two deities in sexual embrace represents the inseparability of wisdom (the goddess) and compassion (the god). Known as the *yab-yum*, literally "father-mother", the image symbolizes both the spiritual path (the cultivation of wisdom and compassion) and its goal (wisdom and compassion united in perfect knowledge).

NUTS & SEEDS

The **ACORN** is both **EGG**-like and (in its cup, left) phallic, and so an apt symbol of fertility. As the **SEED** of the mighty **OAK** it denotes powerful potential. Acorns and other **NUTS**, such as **HAZELNUTS**, were widely used in folk-charms to divine clues to the identity of a future spouse. To confer fertility on newlyweds, nuts or seeds might be thrown at the bridal pair or baked in seedcakes: this is the origin of confetti and wedding cakes. The poet Robert Burns (1759–1796) records how, in parts of Scotland, sweethearts set two hazelnuts in a fire side by side: if the nuts stayed burning together the couple were to marry, but if they sprang apart it was not to be.

Seeds and grains were employed in divinatory incantations or counting-rhymes in a similar way; so too were the soft seedheads of various grasses or the pips and stones of **FRUIT**. One old English rhyme, popular among children to this day, was a means of divining your or your spouse's occupation: "Tinker, tailor, soldier, sailor, rich man, poor man, beggarman, thief". In America the rhyme may go on: "Doctor, lawyer, merchant, chief". It is spoken while counting off fruit pips or stones (especially **CHERRY** stones).

In Chinese tradition fruit containing many seeds, such as **WATERMELONS** and **POMEGRANATES**, were symbols of the blessing of many offspring.

MAYPOLE
Raised on village greens since pagan times, the maypole is a strikingly phallic symbol of joy and fertility. It is the focus of dances held around May 1, the old Celtic festival of Beltane ("Bright Fire"), to celebrate the beginning of summer fruitfulness and the rising light.

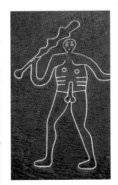

PRIAPUS
The Cerne Abbas Giant, an ithyphallic figure cut into the chalk downs of Dorset, England, was first recorded in the late 1600s but is reputed to date to Saxon times or earlier. It probably depicts the hero Herakles with his club.

SHEELA-NA-GIG
Known in Ireland as the "sheela-na-gig", the stone image of a female holding open an enormous vulva occurs on some churches and other buildings in the British Isles. She may be either an old fertility goddess or a grotesque image of female lust.

DIVINITY

SINCE THE DAWN OF CONSCIOUSNESS, HUMANKIND HAS BEEN AWED BY THE MYSTERIES OF THE COSMOS, THE NATURAL WORLD AND LIFE ITSELF. THIS FASCINATION GAVE RISE TO THE IDEA OF DIVINITY, A POWER BEYOND NATURE THAT SHAPES AND CONTROLS THE UNIVERSE AND HUMAN DESTINY.

GODS & GODDESSES

Supernatural forces came to be embodied as gods and goddesses, each with a special domain such as the sea, the sky, storms, fertility, love, war or justice. They were often represented in familiar forms: male and female, animal and human.

FATHER GODS
In many cultures the head of the pantheon is a male god, often understood as the cosmic creator and embodying the heavens, like the thunderbolt-wielding Greek god Zeus (above). As with Ra in ancient Egypt, the sun symbolizes the supreme male creator in many civilizations.

MOTHER GODDESSES
Goddesses such as the Hindu Parvati (left) are personifications of feminine power and fertility. Like the primal Gaia in ancient Greece or the Mother Earth of Native American peoples, they may be embodiments of the Earth itself, giving life to plants, beasts and humans.

PANTHEONS
Deities may be systematized as a pantheon in the form of an extended family or clan. These may reflect ties and generational rivalries typical of humankind. In Greek myth, Cronos overthrew his father, Ouranos, but was in turn overthrown by his own son Zeus. Egyptian myth has a struggle between Seth, god of chaos, and his nephew Horus, god of order. Headed by the Jade Emperor, the Chinese pantheon was unusual in being a vast heavenly bureaucracy that mirrored the imperial government on Earth. Pantheons often have a special abode (see page 108).

(see page 108).

DIVINE OFFERINGS
This Egyptian tomb painting shows the female pharaoh Hapshepsut (depicted as male, as convention required) making an offering to the god Ra-Harakhte, a form of the gods Ra and Horus.

MOON DEITIES

(*left*) The moon is widely seen as feminine, in contrast to the male sun. As Queen of Heaven it is linked with powerful figures such as the Virgin Mary and the Greek goddess Artemis of Ephesus (left). Lunar deities preside over the cycle of birth, death and rebirth. In some traditions, though, the moon is associated with male gods and linked with masculine fertilizing power.

EARTH & SUN DEITIES

(*below*) With notable exceptions, such as Geb in Egypt, ancient deities embodying the Earth were female, from the Greek goddess Gaia to the Native American Mother Earth and the Maori goddess Papa. They were archetypes of life-giving forces,

fertility and sustenance. Most sun deities are male, with the sun's brightness a potent symbol of the light of intellect. Sun gods often became identified with universal fatherhood. However, in Japan the emperors once claimed descent from a female, the sun goddess Amaterasu (below).

SKY DEITIES

(*above*) Most sky deities are male, such as the Greek Zeus and the Native American Father Sky. An exception is Nut, the Egyptian sky goddess, who is depicted arching over the Earth. Nut coupled with Geb, the Earth, until they were separated by Shu, the god of air (above).

THUNDER GODS

(*above*) As lord of storms, the Greek sky god Zeus (the Roman Jupiter) wields a thunderbolt, as does the Vedic Indra. The Norse god Thor (above) has a magic hammer that can both destroy and heal. The Thunderbird in North America has a similar dual nature.

DEITIES OF ARTS & CRAFTS

Creative skills are the preserve of deities like the Greek smith god Hephaistos (the Roman Vulcan), or goddesses like Athene (Minerva), who invented magic weaponry as well as the olive tree for food, fuel and lamplight. The Greek god of the arts was Apollo, whose symbol is the lyre. As a sun god he signified the light of inspiration. Gods such as the Celtic Lugh and Germanic Wodan were skilled in many arts, including war.

DEITIES OF DANCE

In their flowing movements and gestures, dancing deities often symbolize the creative rhythm of life. In some cultures they denote rites of passage, such as the coming of adulthood. As Nataraja, or Lord of the Dance, the Hindu god Shiva has four arms to indicate the constant dynamism of the forces of nature.

DEITIES OF RAIN & STORMS

Like many storm gods—they are almost always male—the Japanese Susano is an aggressive bringer of chaos. But Baal, the ancient Canaanite storm god, was also lord of fertility as the controller of rain. The Mayan rain god Chac and his Aztec counterpart Tlaloc had a similar beneficent role as guardians of agriculture. (See also **THUNDER GODS**, opposite.)

DEITIES OF REVELRY

Altered states such as drunkenness and acting were ascribed by the Greeks to Dionysus (the Roman Bacchus), god of wine. Imbibing wine at sacred Dionysiac revelries produced ecstatic release associated with spiritual enlightenment.

DEITIES OF THE SEA

Sea divinities are associated with the primal power and changeability of the sea. Poseidon (the Roman Neptune), brother of Zeus and the mightiest of several Greek sea gods, wields a fisherman's trident as the god of sea tempests. The Inuit Sea Spirit is a woman who presides over all the sea creatures that are eaten by humans.

FERTILITY DEITIES

Fertility deities were generally female, like the Greek Earth goddess Gaia (above) and her offspring Cronos. His Roman counterpart, Saturn, was an ancient agricultural deity who wields a scythe. The daughter of Cronos was Demeter ("Earth Mother"), sister of Zeus. The Hindu goddess of fertility is Shri, consort of the creator Vishnu. Such deities oversee soil productivity and protect crops, but if angered they can cause drought and famine.

DEITIES OF SEX & LOVE

The Greek love goddess Aphrodite (the Roman Venus) was born from the primeval ocean in a miraculous renewal of life: she was engendered by the foam that marked where the genitals of Uranus, castrated by his son Cronos, had fallen from the heavens into the waves. The Hindu goddess Lakshmi (above, with Vishnu) also arose from the waters, and is symbolized by the lotus that represents radiant beauty,

purity, procreation and spiritual strength. However, sexual desire is often personified as a male deity, such as the Greek Eros (the Roman Cupid). In art he is often depicted winged, blindfolded and with a bow and arrow to symbolize the blindness of love, which may strike anywhere. In Baroque art Cupid became *putti* or cupids, winged infants often conflated with angelic beings called cherubs.

ONE GOD OR MANY GODS?

The Egyptian god **AMUN**, whose name means "All", came close to being an all-embracing divine power, especially after he was merged with the sun god as **AMUN-RA**. For Hindu philosophers the many deities are all aspects of **BRAHMAN**, the one ultimate reality (not to be confused with the god **BRAHMA**, right). The Bible refers to **YAHWEH** and **ELOHIM**, two traditions of the divine, and **GOD'S** words "let *us* make humankind" (Genesis 1.26) hint at a prebiblical polytheism. The God of **ABRAHAM**, **ISAAC** and **JACOB** was seen as one among many rival national gods. However, from around the sixth century BCE, prophets such as Jeremiah ceased to recognize that other gods existed: there was only one, universal god. This divine entity became the triune god of Christianity and **ALLAH** (Al-Illah, The God) of Islam.

PROTECTOR DEITIES

Gods that protected the home and its occupants were common in ancient cultures, such as the Egyptian Bes and the Roman domestic spirits known as Lares. Offerings were made to these deities on special occasions such as births and weddings. For Tibetan Buddhists, the enlightened being Avalokiteshvara is the protector of Tibet and the deity of universal lovingkindness, denoted by the many arms with which he dispenses compassion (left). Every Dalai Lama is said to be his incarnation.

DEITIES OF HEALTH

The Greek demigod of medicine Asklepios, son of Apollo, was usually depicted with a snake, whose skin-shedding symbolizes regeneration and healing. The Mayan Ix Chel, "Lady Rainbow", oversaw healing and also childbirth, a dangerous time for women that often had its own specific goddess like Heket (Egypt, left) and Eileithyia (Greece), who fixed the length of labor and the moment of delivery. Birth also came under the general protection of goddesses such as Isis and Artemis.

SPIRITS OF PLACE

features of the natural world, such as oddly shaped rocks, old trees, springs, wells, mountains and woodlands may all possess what the Romans called a **GENIUS LOCI** or **"SPIRIT OF PLACE"**. such beings may be benign, malevolent or merely mischievous. In Japanese tradition every region, village and home has its own resident spirit, while in many parts of Africa, oceania and Australia special respect is paid to spirits of place. Australian Aborigines believe that their **DREAMTIME** ancestors left their spirits at places such as **ULURU** (below). For the Greeks, Mount olympus was the abode of the gods, and the chinese traditionally revere mountains as emblems of power and stability. Rivers suggest a perpetual outpouring of creative spirit: Hindus personify the Ganges as a great goddess, **GANGA**, and rivers were similarly revered as goddesses in celtic Europe. Holy wells may provide water with miraculous healing powers, like the spring celebrated at Lourdes by Roman catholics. The ancient Greeks believed that woods and streams were inhabited by female nymphs called **DRYADS** and **NAIADS** respectively, as well as male **SATYRS** led by **PAN**, the god who embodied the spirit of nature. Evergreen trees may be revered as potent symbols of eternal life, like the germanic fir tree of **WODEN**, or of spiritual awakening, such as the **BODHI TREE** under which the Buddha attained enlightenment.

DEITIES OF WAR

(below) Symbolically war is the battle between forces of good and evil, between order and chaos, and hence many deities of war occupy a high place in their pantheons, sometimes as controllers of death. The Egyptian Seth, lord of chaos, was also invoked as a national protector, and several pharaohs (such as Sety I) took his name. The Greeks admired Athene, patron of Athens and the mentor of Greek heroes such as Perseus, rather more than their violent war-god Ares. But the Romans gave Ares' equivalent, Mars (below), much greater respect as the patron of Roman military and imperial prowess. The great Babylonian goddess of love and fertility, Ishtar, was also a warrior.

DEITIES OF THE UNDERWORLD

(left) The dead may go to an underworld that often has its own presiding deity, like the Egyptian Osiris, the Greek Hades, or the skeletal Aztec god of the dead, Mictlantecuhtli (left). Some deities, such as the Canaanite Mot (Death), could be outwitted, thus enabling the dead to return to Earth.

AVATARS & INCARNATIONS

(right) In Hinduism, Vishnu has ten earthly forms or avatars ("descents"), in which he intervenes to preserve the world. One of the most famous of these avatars is Rama (right). As God's incarnation on Earth, Jesus Christ represents a unique divine intervention in world history.

SOUL GUIDES

The Greek god Hermes was called psychopomp, or "soul-bearer", for his role in escorting deceased souls to the underworld. Hermes (the Roman Mercury) was identified with Thoth, the ibis-headed Egyptian god, who performed a similar role. Huitzilopochtli, the Aztec national god, was linked with the souls of fallen warriors, symbolized as hummingbirds. In Norse myth slain warriors were escorted by the female Valkyries to Valhalla, the feasting hall of the dead.

DEMONS

The biblical Satan gained increasing severity, moving from "the accuser" (ha-satan) of Job to become a hostile spirit, then the prince of demons and angel of death. His chief assistant was Beelzebub (properly Beelzebul, "Lord of the Flies"). Some cultures have spirits that may be either good or evil, such as the jinn of Arabian tradition. Hindu "antigods" (asuras) are not evil but rather powerful base instincts that bind people to earthly existence.

RESURRECTING DEITIES

A god or goddess who dies (or descends to the underworld) then returns to the land of the living is a common mythological theme. Such accounts may symbolize the seasonal cycle of winter to spring, barrenness to fertility, and the beings involved are often fertility deities such as the Babylonian Ishtar, the Greek Persephone and the Aztec Quetzalcoatl. The resurrection of Christ is a symbol of universal renewal and salvation.

divine messengers

A belief in the existence of supernatural intermediaries is common to many cultures and faiths. Beings called "angels" appear often in the Bible, but it is not always clear what the term means. The word itself simply means "messenger"—divine or otherwise—but in fact "angels" have a wide range of functions. As well as angels there are also archangels, or "chief angels", like Gabriel and Michael, the only two angels named in the Bible. Two other archangels, Raphael and Uriel, appear in apocryphal books. The cherubim who guard the gates of the Garden of Eden with flaming swords are also understood as types of angel. Guardian angels are said to protect individuals and sacred places. Christian tradition includes a whole array of other angelic beings (see box, opposite).

Divine messages conveyed by angels may take the form of blessings, warnings or prophecies. For some, angels are metaphors for the channels through which God "speaks" to mortals, or symbolic embodiments of what today we might term intuition. Receiving angelic messages in dreams or hearing angel "voices" are sometimes seen as the unconscious workings of the mind coming to the fore, or as possible signs of mental illness.

Celestial beings with similar roles to angels occur in other traditions, from ancient Mesopotamia to Islam. For the Egyptians the divine messenger was Thoth, the god of wisdom, whom the Greeks identified with Hermes in the form Hermes Trismegistus, "Thrice-Great Hermes", legendary author of *The Emerald Tablet*, one of the texts responsible for the Western occult tradition.

ST. MICHAEL
(*left*) Messenger of God's judgment, standard bearer and head of the angelic host, the archangel Michael (left) led the expulsion of Satan and his rebel angels from heaven (see opposite). Many hilltop churches are dedicated to him, often on sites once sacred to the Classical god Apollo. As leader of the heavenly host, Michael is symbolized by his standard and armor, and is the patron of soldiers and protector of all Christians.

BODHISATTVAS
Many Buddhists believe either literally or symbolically in transcendant beings called *bodhisattva*s, who have gained enlightenment and manifest in various forms in order to help others reach salvation. The most popular is Avalokiteshvara, the embodiment of compassion (see page 108). In the Far East, this male being became the popular goddess of mercy, named Guanyin in China and Kannon in Japan.

AQUINAS'S HIERARCHY OF ANGELS

st. thomas aquinas (1225—1274) drew up a description of the host of heaven that consists of nine angelic "choirs", or orders, orbiting the throne of GOD. (this thirteenth-century illustration shows angels and archangels turning around god.) the nine divide into three hierarchies. the first contains SERAPHS, CHERUBS and THRONES. seraphs, or seraphim, are visualized as pure FIRE and represent the most ardent love for the divine because they see god most clearly. cherubs, or cherubim, are linked with knowledge of the divine and the primal creative power of god. thrones are associated with divine judgment.

the second hierarchy contains angels called DOMINIONS, VIRTUES and POWERS, who oversee the workings of the cosmos and defend it from the powers of evil. the third hierarchy consists of PRINCIPALITIES, ARCHANGELS and ANGELS. they are concerned directly with human affairs. the principalities guide the

rulers of nations to govern righteously. Archangels pronounce news of major divine interventions and lead the heavenly host. The lowest order are personal GUARDIAN ANGELS, who protect, guide and comfort individuals throughout their lives, from birth to death, and guide them toward salvation.

ISLAMIC ANGELS

Belief in angels (*malaikah*) is an article of faith for Muslims. At the top of the hierarchy are Hamalat al-'Arsh, God's four throne bearers; next come the Karibuyin (Cherubim), who perpetually praise Allah. Earthly affairs are the province of the archangels Jibril, Mikhail, Asrail (or Israil) and Israfil. Angels are innumerable, as the Quran indicates: "Every raindrop is accompanied by an angel, for even a raindrop is a manifestation of being."

FALLEN ANGELS

Ancient Jewish and Christian legend claims that part of the heavenly host were cast out of heaven for refusing God's command to bow to Adam. The leader of these rebel angels was Satan. They were expelled by the archangel Michael and his host and cast into the deepest depths, whence they caused evil on Earth. As Christianity spread, so all malevolent spirits, as well as pagan deities, were labeled demons, fallen angels or agents of the devil.

ANGEL OF THE LORD

In the Bible, the heavenly being that counseled Abraham, Isaac and Jacob was described as the "Angel of the Lord". Not always benign, it became the Angel of Death during the Passover.

ANGIRIS

In Hinduism, celestial messengers between God and humans. In particular they advise on the correct conduct of sacrificial rites.

ARCHANGEL GABRIEL

Messenger of divine mercy, Gabriel is symbolized by a lily representing his role in the Annunciation and his association with the Virgin Mary. Muslims revere him as Jibril, the angel who conducted Muhammad on a visit to heaven.

ARCHANGEL RAPHAEL

Messenger of divine healing, in which role Raphael appears in the apocryphal Book of Tobit, helping the hero Tobias to cure the blindness of his father Tobit. Raphael is symbolized by the caduceus wand or sometimes by a pilgrim's staff.

ARCHANGEL URIEL

Messenger of divine wisdom, Uriel appears in the apocryphal Book of Esdras. He is symbolized by a book, and also by a sheaf of ripened wheat.

DAEMONS

In Greek myth *daemons* were supernatural agents that presided over public and family life. They could have good or evil intent, acting as guardian angels or possessing a person in order to deliver a prophecy.

HERMES

Hermes was the Greek god of transfer, transaction and exchange. He was a bringer of good luck and the overseer of trade. Like Thoth, he guided souls to the afterlife and was the wing-footed messenger of the gods, symbolized by the caduceus.

KARIBU

The Assyrian *karibu* were protector beings depicted as winged creatures, half-beast, half-human. They guard temples, homes and other special buildings, as well as people. The word is the likely origin of "cherub", the first angelic being mentioned in the Bible.

VALKYRIES

"Choosers of the Slain", the Valkyries were Norse female spirits who selected which warriors would die in battle, then escorted them to Valhalla, the "Feasting Hall of the Slain", in Asgard, the domain of the gods. The Valkyries were also protectors, instructing young warriors and watching over them in battle.

BUDDHISM

Buddhism is named after the Buddha (Enlightened One), who was born Prince Siddhartha Gautama ca. 500BCE in southern Nepal. Many Buddhists simply refer to their religion as "the Dharma", which specifically means the teachings of the Buddha, who came to his insights when he attained enlightenment or "awakening" (*bodhi*) after sitting in meditation at Bodh Gaya for forty-nine days. His key insight was that human existence is fraught with *duhkha* (suffering or dissatisfaction) caused by craving. Through the workings of *karma*, this leads to negative actions (*punya*) that propel the soul to rebirth, and so on in an endless tragic cycle.

One of the most universal Buddhist symbols is the Dharmachakra, or Dharma wheel. It represents both the Buddha's teachings and the Buddha himself, who was prophesied to be a *chakravartin*, a "wheel-turner" or "revolutionary": either a great emperor or a great teacher. The wheel often has eight spokes to symbolize the Buddha's "Noble Eightfold Path", the spiritual and ethical means whereby humans may attain enlightenment (*bodhi*); eliminate *punya*; and hence reach *nirvana*—release from the cycle of rebirth.

The different Buddhist traditions have developed a rich and varied symbolism. All traditions depict the Buddha and other enlightened figures, and among the most universal images is the Buddha sitting in meditation, often at the moment of enlightenment, as in the nineteenth-century statue from the Temple of the Tooth in Kandy, Sri Lanka (opposite). The Mahayana traditions of Tibet and the Far East are noted for *mandalas* (left), cosmic diagrams used as aids to meditation and spiritual advancement.

The Buddha was not represented in human form until around the first century CE. Before then he was denoted by symbols such as the Dharma wheel or his footprints (opposite). He may also be represented by just his eyes, looking down in compassion on the world.

USHNISHA
A princely topknot developed into the *ushnisha* or "wisdom bump", denoting the Buddha's superior wisdom and knowledge.

EYES The Buddha's lowered, half open gaze denotes the "passive awareness" of the meditative state. They also express his universal compassion, looking down on suffering humanity.

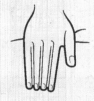

HAND GESTURE The Buddha reaches to touch the ground in the gesture called *bhumisparsha mudra*, calling the earth to witness to his enlightenment.

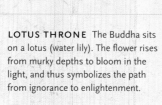

LOTUS THRONE The Buddha sits on a lotus (water lily). The flower rises from murky depths to bloom in the light, and thus symbolizes the path from ignorance to enlightenment.

TILAKA The spot (*tilaka*) in the center of the Buddha's brow marks the "third eye" or *ajna chakra*, the seat of spiritual insight and of "second sight".

ELEPHANTS
The Buddha's mother dreamed of a white elephant, which was taken to mean that her child would be a great ruler or teacher. Elephants also denote the Buddha's great strength of mind.

ROYAL PARASOLS
To Buddhists these shields from the heat of the sun denote protection from suffering, as well as being symbols of respect and honor.

THE AUSPICIOUS EMBLEMS

Buddhist art, especially in the Mahayana traditions, often uses a set of symbols known as the EIGHT AUSPICIOUS EMBLEMS (*ashta-mangala*). The ROYAL PARASOL stands for the Buddha, who was born a prince, and his heroic pursuit of enlightenment; it also alludes to the Four Noble Truths and Noble Eightfold Path, his core teachings—as does the DHARMA WHEEL (see main text). TWO FISHES originally denoted the sacred rivers Ganges and Yamuna, but came to symbolize good fortune. In Buddhism they also symbolize humanity in the "sea of *samsara*", the cycle of rebirth. *samsara* is also represented by the ENDLESS KNOT. The VASE denotes abundance, while the LOTUS (water lily) stands for purity and the path to enlightenment. The CONCH shell symbolizes the call of the Dharma. The VICTORY BANNER stands on Mount Meru and represents supreme spiritual attainment.

BUDDHAPADA
The Buddha is often represented by the *Buddhapada*, his footprints bearing symbols (above). Here they include most of the Auspicious Emblems (see box: an unbroken chain of circles replaces the endless knot); triangle and trident (the "Three Jewels" of Buddha, Dharma and Sangha, the monastic community); sword (wisdom); the sacred syllable *Om*; moon (*nirvana*), sun (enlightenment), hexagram (the universe) and swastika.

PATTERNS, SHAPES
& QUALITIES

THE SIMPLEST GRAPHICS OFTEN REPRESENT HUMANKIND'S GRANDEST CONCEPTS, FROM THE NOTION OF PURE BEING AS A POINT OF INFINITELY COMPRESSED ENERGY TO THAT OF ETERNITY AS A CIRCLE.

colors

Colors have always been used symbolically in human cultures, from prehistoric burial rituals, where red ocher denoted a hope for life in an afterworld, to rich Christian church vestments and vivid modern corporate logos.

WHITE

As the totality of light, in the West white symbolizes purity and the primal light of creation. White is also the color of the moon and femininity. Brides wear white as a token of virginity, angels wear it for spiritual purity. At Christian baptism white symbolizes innocence, and at Christmas and Easter it denotes the joyous birth and resurrection of Christ. However, white is also the color of ghosts and of the dead. In China, white is the color of autumn, linked with advancing age, and when someone dies a white cloth is traditionally hung over the doorway of their house.

BLACK

As the absence of light, black symbolizes negative forces, corruption, sin and nothingness—yet also the primordial darkness, replete with potential. In the West it symbolizes mourning, loss, danger (a black cat is a familiar of malign witches and represents bad luck) and black magic. In Christianity it is the color of Good Friday and Christ's crucifixion, while in ancient Egypt it was the symbol of resurrection and rebirth, of Osiris as lord of the underworld and of the fertile black soil of Egypt. Anubis, who conducted the dead to judgment, was also associated with black, as was Bast, the lunar goddess usually portrayed as a cat. In Hinduism it is the color of Kali and Shiva, the embodiments of Time, destroyer of all. In Chinese cosmology, black is linked with the north and winter, symbolized by the celestial Black Tortoise constellation, and with the element of water. Black can also denote honor—in Chinese theater, black-faced figures may be coarse but honest.

MANDALA

Some forms of *mandala* position believers within a sacred space, carefully balancing harmonious patterns with significant colors, usually white (east), red (west), green (north) and yellow (south).

GRAY

A marking of gray ashes on the brow denotes a Shaivite, a Hindu devotee of Shiva, the lord of destruction, and as the hue of ashes it is associated in Christian tradition with mourning ("ashes to ashes, dust to dust") and penitence ("sackcloth and ashes"). As the color of gray hair it is linked with wisdom and experience.

BROWN

The color of earth and soil, the substance from which, in many cultures, humankind was created. It is also the hue of excrement, detritus and degradation. In Christian monasticism simple coarse brown robes signify the individual's "death to the world", humility and a rejection of material pursuits.

ORANGE

Combining yellow (right) and red—the color of blood and fire, which has always denoted war and action, extroversion, passion and anger—orange is both fire and the sun. It is a widespread symbol of love, welcome and happiness, and as saffron it represents higher wisdom and the Buddhist spiritual path.

YELLOW

Yellow is the color of gold and the sun. Although in China yellow is highly auspicious, elsewhere, like green, it is ambivalent. A yellow ribbon is associated with those awaiting the return of a loved one and it has long been the official color of the US Cavalry, despite also symbolizing cowardice, treachery and disease.

THE COLOR OF GOOD FORTUNE

The first of the five colors of chinese cosmology (**RED**, **WHITE**, **BLUE**, **YELLOW**, **BLACK**), red (**CHI**) is the color of summer, the south and the element of fire. Red is the luckiest of all colors, and also symbolizes the sun, heaven, light, gold and prosperity; it most embodies the dynamism of **YANG**, and is traditionally held to possess the power to ward off demons, hence the walls of palaces and temples are painted this color. Red is linked with longevity; red cinnabar (mercury sulfide) was used by Daoist alchemists seeking the elixir of eternal life.

Red is unsurprisingly prominent at chinese New Year, but as the color of auspiciousness and celebration it features at many other chinese festivals and weddings. The Qing emperors (1644—1912) rejected the traditional red robes of their Ming predecessors, and wore mainly blue (also **QING**). But red was retained for the essential imperial sacrifices at the Altar of the Sun in Beijing. In Europe, the **RED FLAG** was an old banner of defiance and warning, which was adopted by socialist revolutionaries. The chinese communists furthered their own ends by exploiting the color's traditional auspicious associations.

RAINBOW SPECTRUM

In many cultures the spectrum is a celestial symbol, owing to its manifestation as the rainbow, widely seen as a bridge between Earth and heavenly paradise. Central Asian shamans wore rainbow colors to aid their spirit-flights and the iridescent rainbow goddess Iris bore messages from the Greek gods to the Earth. In South Asia, the rainbow is the bow of Indra, while in Tantric Buddhism the rainbow is the penultimate meditational state before the advent of enlightenment, symbolized by the clarity of pure light.

PINK

"Pink for girls and blue for boys" goes the saying, but more traditionally it was the other way around, pink (as a shade of red) being linked with fiery masculinity and pale blue, the color of the Virgin Mary, being more suited to girls. In the modern world it is associated with gay freedom and pride.

VIOLET

The tiny violet flower denotes meekness and both childlike innocence (the Christ child) and sexual innocence (the Virgin Mary), in paintings of the Adoration of the Magi. As a penitential color it may also be worn by Mary Magdalene.

EARTH COLORS

Native North American art often draws upon natural colors that symbolize a sense of profound connection to the environment in which they live. Pueblo artists of the Southwest, for example depict geometric and animal motifs such as serpents in black, white and a rich array of natural browns, reds and creams. Natural hues are also used in sacred Navajo sandpaintings, made from colored sands and earths. Such colors are also traditional for rugs. In the Northeast, around the Great Lakes, flattened porcupine quills dyed with plant pigments are used to adorn moccasins.

GREEN

The hue of abundant nature, green is universally linked with new life and growth, but it is also the color of death and decay. In the West the "Green Man" is a personification of nature, both powerful and wild, a reminder that it can be cruel as well as benevolent. Green can also symbolize naiveté, as well as envy and jealousy.

PURPLE

Purple unites blue and red and symbolizes achievement and inspiration as well as spirituality and inner transformation. In antiquity, purple dyes were expensive, thus used only for royalty. As the ecclesiastical color of Lent and Advent it is associated with the life and death of Christ the King.

CELESTIAL BLUE

The most tranquil of hues, **BLUE** is the color of the **SEA**, the great deep, and therefore of the womb-like waters of life and the creative feminine; it is also the color of the **SKY**, the heavens and of celestial mysteries, the element of **AIR** and the spirit. Blue is associated with a wide range of positive traits, including fidelity, chastity, constancy, truth, intellect, prudence, piety, peace, contemplation and serenity.

The **VIRGIN MARY** as Queen of **HEAVEN** wears blue, which can symbolize love, eternity and faith, and in Buddhism spiritual knowledge and the unclouded mind of enlightenment. In Hinduism blue is the color of **KRISHNA** and of **INDRA** as ruler of the weather. On the negative side, blue can symbolize depression, sadness and longing—melancholy feelings expressed in folk songs that developed into the music known as "the blues." In Chinese, **QING** covers a wide range of hues, including green, the deep gray of a thundercloud, and all shades of blue. The Qing dynasty, China's last emperors, adopted navy blue or indigo as their imperial uniform. Throughout China's dynasties, blue was the ritual color worn by the emperor for the annual ceremonies at the Altar of Heaven (dark blue) and the Altar of the Moon (light blue).

numbers

From the time that the Babylonians had begun to record their calculations in cuneiform (left), the thinkers of the ancient world believed that the laws of creation and the cosmos were revealed in numbers. The great Greek mathematician Pythagoras (ca. 580–ca. 500BCE) saw in the numbers 1, 2, 3 and 4 the arising of form, from point to line to surface to solid; while the dynamism of odd and even numbers reflected a dualistic universe of opposing forces. Yet these forces were mutually dependent: just as odd numbers could not exist without even numbers, good could not exist without evil, light without dark, birth without death, and so on.

The sequence 1, 2, 3 widely symbolizes the process of creation, from unity to duality to multiplicity. The Maya and Aztecs gave numbers as names to their gods, who ruled the cosmos with mathematical exactness. Many cultures assigned profound meaning to individual numbers and their multiples. Seven is widely seen in the Western tradition as the most auspicious of all numbers. In the East, multiples of eight are auspicious, and "eight times eighty millions" refers to an infinite or uncountable number.

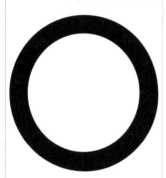

ZERO

Neither odd nor even, the absence of quality or quantity, zero symbolizes infinity, completion, totality, nothingness, the source from which the finite world arises and to which it returns. Coming to the West from India via the Arab world, zero was originally written as a dot, the fulcrum on which all calculation was balanced. In Zen Buddhism, the empty circle denotes the annihilation of the self, the attainment of *nirvana* and release from the round of birth, death and rebirth.

ONE

One, represented by a single stroke in numerals as diverse as Arabic, Latin and Chinese, is the first cause, divinity, the creator, God the Father. It is the undifferentiated oneness of primordial chaos, containing within itself the potential of all existence. In Confucian thought it is the perfect entity, and for the Greeks, before the invention of zero, it was the starting point of all calculation, the beginning. Psychologically it is the individual, the self or ego.

TWO

The number of partnership and balance, and cosmic dualities such as Father Sky and Mother Earth, spirit and matter, day and night, fire and water, right and left; but two is also tension and opposition, good and evil. Two symbolizes the moment of creation: in ancient Egypt, primordial chaos was the time "before there were two things". In China it is the interacting forces of *yin* and *yang*, opposing but complementary, each containing the seed of the other.

THREE

Widely held to be the number of perfect completeness, as reflected in the numerous sacred and divine trinities. In addition to the Christian triune deity of Father, Son and Holy Spirit, there are the Hindu Trimurti of Brahma, Vishnu and Shiva (creator, preserver, destroyer); the ancient Egyptian Osiris, Isis and Horus; Daoism's Three Pure Ones; and Buddhism's Three Jewels—Buddha, Dharma (teachings) and Sangha (disciples).

THE POWER OF THREE

The number three pervades all aspects of the celtic world. Goddesses took on threefold form (maiden, matron, crone), and stone figures of three little hooded men (**CUCULLATI**) brought good fortune. In legends, questions are posed three times, and artefacts bearing three sculpted heads signify the unity of all existence, the past, present and future embraced in the here and now. According to Julius Caesar, bards and druids never committed their wisdom to paper like the Greeks and Romans did. They memorized everything, a process that took twenty years for a druid. To aid the memory, wisdom was distilled into triads of three elements, for example: "The three founts of knowledge—thought, intuition, learning"; and "Three times for a fool's laughter—at what is good; at what is bad; and at what he cannot understand". When celtic peoples adopted christianity, the concept of the trinity was readily comprehensible. Triplet emblems used to this day are the **SHAMROCK** (right), the symbol of ireland and gaelic culture, and the **TRISKELE**, the three-legged badge of the isle of man. Threefold repetition is a common trope of folklore and legend, such as the Three Little Pigs, the Three Billy Goats Gruff, and the frequent granting of three wishes or three guesses.

FOUR

The number of the Earth, symbolized in China as a square to denote the four directions. There are four seasons, Four Elements in Western tradition (earth, air, fire, water), and four ages of man (infancy, youth, maturity, age). Four is equality, balance, good sense and trust; and in Christianity there are four cardinal virtues, and four evangelists and their gospels. Buddhism has its Four Noble Truths. As a feminine symbol, four is intuition, peace, shelter and protection.

FIVE

Five symbolizes the human body (head and limbs), and the magical pentagram (see page 129). It is also the hand or foot, and hence represents action, creativity, communication and movement. Five signifies the Torah, set out in the Five Books of Moses (Genesis to Deuteronomy). In China there are Five Elements (see box, page 120). The Five Pillars of Islam are professing the faith; prayer; almsgiving; annual fasting; and the pilgrimage to Mecca.

SIX

A number of mathematical perfection (6 = 1+2+3 or 1x2x3), of the double trinity (3+3), and of the days of active creation in the Bible. Six is thus linked with divine creative power, also found in the magical Seal of Solomon, which is the six-pointed star formed from two triangles. A cube has six faces, thus six is perfect symmetry. Conversely, six is one less than the perfect number seven, and it can represent imperfection and sin (see box, page 121).

SEVEN

Symbolizing the union of heaven (three) and Earth (four), seven is the perfect number in Classical and Judeo–Christian tradition. In ancient Greece seven was sacred to Apollo, and there were seven wonders of the world. The week has seven days. In Jewish tradition time is divided into "jubilees" of seven times seven years. Seven times seven days elapse between Passover and Shavuot (equivalent to Pentecost, which means "fiftieth [day]"). There are seven heavens, seven Christian virtues, seven deadly sins. Psychic gifts are traditionally attributed to seventh children, especially the seventh son of a seventh son.

THE WORLD OF FIVES

Most of the world identified four cardinal directions (north, south, east and west), but by ca. 250BCE the chinese had added a fifth—the **CENTER**. Naturally, in chinese cosmology, the center of the world was china itself, *zhongguo*—the middle kingdom or, less poetically, the central states, since the term was originally purely geographical, denoting the various kingdoms in the middle of the North china plain, the heartland of the chinese empire. For confucius, this denoted the limits of civilization. Five mountains represented these five cardinal and geomantic points, which are often depicted in chinese art (right).

The system of fives expanded to pervade chinese cosmology in the form of the **FIVE ELEMENTS** or "phases" (*wu xing*): **WOOD, FIRE, EARTH, METAL** and **WATER**, not so much literal substances as forms of energy. corresponding to these elements there are five emotions (anger, joy, desire, sorrow, fear); five Tastes (sour, bitter, sweet, acrid, salty); five weathers (wind, heat, thunder, cold, rain) and so on.

EIGHT

Formed in Arabic numerals by two zeros, eight symbolizes completion, infinity, a path without end or beginning, perfection. In Christianity, 888 is the number of Jesus, symbolizing his perfection and completeness (see box, facing page). The christening font is eight-sided, as were early baptisteries, and the shrine of the Holy Sepulcher in Jerusalem. It is a highly significant number in the East, too. There are eight auspicious Buddhist emblems, and the Buddhist Wheel of Life has eight spokes, and the eight-petaled lotus symbolizes enlightenment, attained by adhering to the Eightfold Path. Yogic physiology recognizes eight chakras.

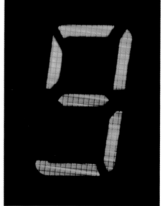

NINE

A trinity of trinities, three times three, nine is a potent number. The nine-layered Chinese pagoda symbolizes the ascent to heaven. Nine is also indestructibility and mystery, enhanced by the fact that all multiples of nine up to ninety (ten times nine) add up to nine (18 = 1+8 = 9, 27 = 2+7 = 9, and so on).

TEN

Formed by one and zero, ten is totality, the union of first cause (one) with infinity (zero). It is the number of human digits (ten fingers), and thus a basic number of completeness and of measurement. There are Ten Commandments in the Bible. The Romans denoted ten with a simple cross (X), like a saltire.

THE NUMBER OF THE BEAST

The ancient Romans, Greeks and Jews used letters for numbers, from which arose the system of GEMATRIA, or numerology, in which any name could be assigned a numerical value. Thus the six Greek letters for JESUS (ΙΕΣΟΥΣ) have the numerical values 10, 8, 200, 70, 400 and 200. This totals 888, a number that "reveals" the completeness and perfection of Christ, who exceeds the perfect number seven threefold.

The most famous example of gematria comes in the BOOK OF REVELATION, whose author describes "the BEAST", the great enemy of Christ, with a numerological conundrum: "Let anyone with understanding calculate the number of the beast, for it is the number of a person. Its number is six hundred and sixty-six". (Revelation 13.18.) The answer is EMPEROR NERO (above), a persecutor of Christians, whom many at the time (ca. 90CE) feared would return from the dead (he died in

68CE). The Hebrew for "Emperor Nero" was written QSR NRWN, derived from the Greek "Kaisar Neron" (Καισαρ Νερων). In Hebrew (which does not mark all vowels) the letters QSR NRWN have the numerical values 100, 60, 200, 50, 200, 6 and 50. Added together these make 666, aptly falling short of the perfect seven threefold just as Christ surpasses it.

ELEVEN

Composed of two masculine numbers that add up to the first female number (1+1 = 2), eleven is the union of male and female. For St. Augustine it suggested sin, falling between the perfect ten and the cosmic twelve. Some called it the Devil's dozen, but in Africa the number eleven is linked with fecundity.

TWELVE

Twelve yields the Trinity (1+2 = 3), and as three times four (Trinity in union with the elements) represents God's kingdom. It is associated with the heavens through twelve Zodiac animals, months, stations of the sun and hours of the day and night. The celestial resonance is also seen in the twelve-day festival of Christmas.

THIRTEEN & FOURTEEN

Considered unlucky in the West (it is identified with Judas), as a "baker's dozen" thirteen denotes generosity, "one for good measure". The moon waxes from new to full in fourteen days and from full to new in another fourteen. The moon's "imperfection" before the fourteenth may account for thirteen being inauspicious.

THE NUMBER 5040 & THE MEGALITHIC YARD

The product of 1 x 2 x 3 x 4 x 5 x 6 x 7 is 5,040, a so-called canonical number, which is also divisible by every number from one to ten. Plato gave it as the number of citizens in his ideal fictional city Magnesia, and divided by a hundred it is the mean diameter of the Stonehenge lintel ring (50.4ft). Prehistoric stone monuments, Egyptian and South American pyramids, the Temple in Jerusalem, Gothic cathedrals and many more constructions were all laid out in accordance with this and other geometrical and numerical principles, such as the Golden Number (see page 126). From his examination of hundreds of stone circles and other sites in Britain and France, Professor Alexander Thom (1894–1985) proposed that megalithic builders had also used a basic ancient unit of measurement which he named "the megalithic yard" (2ft 8.64 inches, or 0.8297m). This hypothetical unit is probably based on astronomical observation, since many of the stone circles Thom analyzed displayed alignments with heavenly events, such as solstices and equinoxes. Behind such monuments perhaps lay a belief that these sacred sites were able to focus and gather unseen energies, making them places where human consciousness sought access to hidden mysteries. This drew upon the observations of ancient Greek thinkers such as Pythagoras, who argued that music, arithmetic and geometry symbolized most accurately the true essence of creation. Pythagoras realized that the length of the strings of musical instruments were found to be intimately related to number ratios. Furthermore, music had a special power to alter human consciousness. The intervals and ratios between musical notes, the ratios in geometry and the astronomical periods all conform to mathematical rules. Plato concluded that both human life and the natural world are essentially the creations of number.

THE TAROT

Tarot is the name given to a deck of cards that became popular in the Middle Ages and may have originated in the Near East. There are seventy-eight cards, of which fifty-six are essentially the same as modern playing cards, with the addition of an extra court card, a knight. There are four suits called cups, pentacles (or coins), wands and swords (below), which correspond respectively to the modern suits hearts, diamonds, clubs and spades—"spade" is in fact from the Italian or Spanish *spada*, meaning sword.

In addition to the deck of numbered and court cards there is a set of twenty-two special "trump" cards (from Italian *trionfo*, victory or triumph). These depict a range of symbolic figures and objects, which are numbered from one (the Magician) to twenty-one (the World). There is also the Fool, a special card that is usually unnumbered but may be given the number zero or twenty-two.

The two groups of cards came to be known as the Minor Arcana (the fifty-six

that became the basis of the modern deck of playing cards) and the Major Arcana (the trump cards). "Arcana" means "hidden things", or symbols, and the terms reflect the fascination with which the trump cards in particular were held. The Major Arcana were much employed in divination and fortune telling, and their symbolism became extensive and open to a huge range of esoteric interpretations. The cards were understood as representing a spiritual quest, the life journey of the innocent Fool (right). The Major Arcana were also linked with Kabbalah and the twenty-two letters of the Hebrew alphabet, and with occult traditions of ceremonial magic such as the Order of the Golden Dawn.

Some of the many interpretations of the Major Arcana are given opposite. These eighteenth-century French cards follow a pattern known as the Tarot of Marseille, which dates back to ca. 1500 and was the basis for many later decks.

THE FOOL The only unnumbered card of the Major Arcana is the Fool. In Tarot games, this card was the trump-all, equivalent to the Joker in the modern pack. Esoterically, the figure of the Fool has been interpreted as Everyman, the holy innocent who embarks on the journey symbolized by the twenty-one other cards of the Major Arcana. He is shown here with a traveler's or pilgrim's staff, and spurred on by a cat representing spiritual motivation.

13

13. XIII. DEATH The number thirteen is traditionally linked with misfortune and in Tarot it is the number of Death, the Grim Reaper. Yet death is not evil but a necessary part of life's journey, and acknowledging without fear its presence and inevitability is a step to maturity. Coming just after the expiation of the Hanged Man, Death signifies a final severing of ties with the old self and the embarkation on the higher stages of growth.

FROM LEFT TO RIGHT:

1 I. *The Magician* (also called the Juggler or Minstrel): creativity and powers of (self-)transformation; **2** II. *The Popess* (High Priestess): morality and feminine insight; **3** III. *The Empress*: security, fertility, growth, feminine power; **4** IV. *The Emperor*: action, leadership, temporal power, masculinity; **5** V. *The Pope* (High Priest): spiritual enlightenment, vigor of the soul, masculine wisdom.

6 VI. *The Lover*: passion and love, union, marriage; **7** VII. *The Chariot*: self-mastery, success, the spiritual path of life and secular career; **8** VIII. *Justice*: discernment, balance, devotion to truth, maturity; **9** IX (VIIII). *The Hermit*: contemplation of truth, moral living, self-sufficiency, independence; **10** X. *The Wheel of Fortune*: dynamic movement, self-transformation, the acceptance of change for better or worse, worldly wisdom.

11 XI. *Strength*: the triumph of spiritual strength over physical; **12** XII. *The Hanged Man*: self-sacrifice, expiation of sin, selfless devotion; **13** XIII. *Death*: *See opposite page*; **14** XIV (XIIII). *Temperance*: equanimity, overcoming of egotism, base impulses and appetites; **15** XV. *The Devil*: deep self-examination, the trials of the spiritual seeker; **16** XVI. *The Tower* (or *House of God*): the final destruction of obstacles to self-realization.

17 XVII. *The Star*: the beginnings of spiritual transcendence; **18** XVIII. *The Moon*: divine feminine energy, inner mystic power; **19** XIX (XVIII). *The Sun*: divine masculine energy, supreme wisdom, joyous union with the divine; **20** XX. *Judgment*: the successful transformation, also in Christian terms, the ultimate reward of the virtuous: resurrection to eternal life; **21** XXI. *The World*: completion, wholeness, self-fulfillment, liberation, freedom, the transformed self.

BATELEUR · LA·PAPESS · L'IMPERATRICE · L'EMPEREUR · LE·PAPE
LAMOVREVX · LE·CHARIOT · LA·JUSTICE · L'HERMITE · LA·ROVE·DE·FORTVNE
LA·FORCE · LE·PENDU · TEMPERANCE · LE·DIABLE · LA·MAISON·DIEV
LE·TOILLE · LA·LUNE · LE·SOLEIL · LE·IUGEMENT · LE·MONDE

labyrinths

The intriguing labyrinth occurs worldwide and has been found on petroglyphs dating back several thousand years. A labyrinth may be unicursal, with one unmistakable, if convoluted, route to the center; or multicursal, like a puzzle maze, deliberately intended to "amaze" (literally confound and confuse) those who enter. Some distinguish labyrinths (unicursal) from mazes (multicursal), though the legendary Labyrinth of Crete was probably multicursal (see box, opposite). Labyrinths on the floors of churches and cathedrals are unicursal, walked by devotees on a symbolic pilgrimage or spiritual journey. Other variations are the meander, a maze pattern without an exit or entrance, and the endless knot, where paths cross over and under one another.

Some have seen entering the labyrinth as a symbolic return to the womb, followed by a spiritual rebirth when the traveler returned from the center to the outside world; or as a symbolic death and resurrection. For Christians the winding path of the labyrinth also represented the manner in which in life we deviate from the straight and narrow yet ultimately may still find our way, by means of faith, to forgiveness and eternal life. In the East, it may represent the journey through the fog of unknowing. Psychologists have interpreted the labyrinth as pathways of the brain, a representation of mental and physical obstacles to be overcome.

Labyrinths were also fashioned into protective amulets, and in medieval times they were depicted on houses to deter evil spirits.

MAZE OF LIFE
(*above*) The maze represents our meandering journey through life, with its frequent blind alleys, obstacles, wrong turnings, difficult choices and reversals. In its modern guise (above) it serves merely as a challenge game in which the first person to reach the center is the winner.

TROY TOWNS
(*left*) Welsh and Cornish shepherds once made unicursal labyrinths in the turf, with a narrow twisting pathway that eventually led to the center. They called these Caer Droia, which means "Troy Town" or "Town of Turnings". These labyrinths may have served for symbolic journeys of penance.

THE HEART OF DARKNESS

The myth of the Labyrinth of Knossos in Crete is a compelling tale that symbolizes the consequences of human transgression. King **MINOS** refused to sacrifice a fine **BULL** to the sea god **POSEIDON**, who angrily made Minos's queen, **PASIPHAE**, fall in love with it. At her command the royal craftsman, **DAEDALUS**, built a hollow **HEIFER** in which Pasiphae had intercourse with the bull. She subsequently bore a savage bull-man hybrid: the **MINOTAUR**, or Minos-Bull. Furious and horrified, Minos ordered Daedalus to build a warren of tunnels from which the Minotaur could never escape. This was the **LABYRINTH**—not in fact a single-pathed labyrinth, but a maze.

Minos conquered Athens and ordered its citizens to send seven boys and seven girls every year to feed the monster. One year, the children were accompanied by the hero **THESEUS**, who was determined to slay it. **ARIADNE**, Minos's daughter, fell in love with Theseus and gave him a ball of **TWINE**, which he unraveled as he went through the dark Labyrinth to the Minotaur's lair. He slew the beast (left) and led the children out by following the clue (thread) of twine. Theseus fled Crete with Ariadne—only to abandon her on an island. An innocent victim of her parents' sins, Ariadne was found by the god **DIONYSOS**, who married her and placed her crown among the stars.

In psychological terms, the Labyrinth has been interpreted as a symbol of our deepest anxieties and fears, and of suppressed illicit desires, reflected in the bestial conception. The Minotaur is a symbol of our primitive, animal nature.

CHARTRES LABYRINTH

Christians in northern and western medieval Europe would find at Chartres cathedral a unicursal labyrinth on the floor of the nave. The center symbolizes Jerusalem, and hence by walking the path to the center, the devotee was able to make a symbolic pilgrimage to the Holy City.

GONZAGA MAZE

One badge, or *impresa*, of the powerful medieval Italian Gonzaga dynasty was a simple unicursal maze sometimes depicted as an island with a mountain in the center, representing the Palazzo del Te in Mantua, which was erected on marshland. The dynasty's motto "*Forse che si, forse che no*"— "Perhaps yes, perhaps no"—aptly sums up the uncertainties of power as well as the manifold and difficult choices life presents when beset with daily decisions.

GLASTONBURY TOR

Twisting around the hill known as Glastonbury Tor in Somerset, England, are the apparent remains of an ancient labyrinth. Spiraling round the hill seven times, it may be an ancient ritual pathway that led to a sacred site on the summit of the hill, now marked by the remains of a medieval church dedicated to St. Michael— the archangel whose churches often replaced earlier pre-Christian sanctuaries (see page 87).

ENDLESS KNOT

The endless knot is a form of maze in which a line can always be followed back to its starting point. With no single starting or end point, it symbolizes infinity and the complexity and interconnectedness of life. In Christian Celtic manuscripts it also reflects the eternal truths of the gospels.

SKY LABYRINTH

Precolumbian labyrinth designs are found as far south as Peru. Depicted on a rock from Western Riverside county, California, the Soboba Hemet design (above) is technically a meander, without beginning or end. It takes swastika form, a widespread solar emblem, and perhaps represents the Sky Father, like some designs of the Hopi of Arizona. In some parts of the world labyrinths were incorporated into tombs, both to protect the dead from the living and to prevent the dead from returning from the underworld.

sacred geometry

Since the time of the ancient Egyptians and the great Greek mathematicians Pythagoras (sixth century BCE) and Euclid (third century BCE) there has been an enduring belief that the world is created on mathematical principles, and that geometry is one of the most powerful manifestations of this. A prime example is the so-called Golden Number, or Golden Ratio, known as *phi* (ϕ), 1.618 (more exactly 1.6180339887...). If a line ($a+b$) is divided into two unequal segments so that the ratio of the shorter segment (b) to the longer segment (a) is the same as the ratio of a to ($a+b$), that ratio is ϕ (1:1.618, or 0.618:1).

Considered aesthetically attractive, the ratio has fascinated mathematicians and artists since ancient times. Many Renaissance artists, including Leonardo da Vinci, used it in their work, and it was believed to be the geometric principle employed by God, the Divine Architect of the universe. Human constructions incorporating this ratio (left) symbolized the divine principle, and not only provided a harmonious environment for those who inhabited them but, it has been claimed, raised their spiritual consciousness. The great pyramids of Egypt, the Parthenon in Athens, Notre Dame cathedral in Paris, a Stradivarius violin, all include proportions based on the Golden Number. It is also found widely in nature—from the human body to the veins in a leaf.

SPIRAL
The spiral or whorl occurs in nature in many forms, such as seashells, whirlwinds and whirlpools, and in the unfurling of ferns and other plants as they pulse with new life. Its specific symbolism varies, but broadly speaking it is a symbol of great dynamism, denoting the unfolding force of creation.

CIRCLE
A representation of totality, infinity, wholeness and perfection. In many traditions, a circle is an emblem of the sun or the full moon. In the form of a ring, a circle denotes unity and unbroken harmony and the bond of community, friendship and marriage. In China, a circle or sphere symbolizes the infinite heavens.

OVAL
When metamorphosed into an ovoid shape the sphere symbolizes the cosmic egg (see page 162) and the power of limitless creative potential —the President of the United States exercises power from the Oval Office. In occult and shamanic lore the aura that surrounds the human body is oval shaped.

SQUARE
The square represents stasis and stability. In Indian and Chinese tradition, the square symbolizes the earthly realm, bounded by the four directions. At Beijing's Temple of Heaven (above), the circular ceiling, symbolizing the heavens, is supported on a square base of four pillars, symbolizing Earth.

MEDICINE WHEELS

scattered across the plains of North America are stone circles known as "medicine wheels", such as the Big Horn wheel in Wyoming, which is nearly 30m (100ft) in diameter with twenty-eight "spokes" and five small cairns around the rim and one protruding outside it. The spokes converge on a central cairn, the "hub" of the wheel. The purpose of the wheels is unknown. Many are on high ground, so may have solar or celestial symbolism—for example, the hub and protruding cairn of the Big Horn wheel align with the midsummer sunrise. Some wheel designs resemble patterns traced in Native American dances. Perhaps in general the medicine wheels represent sacred cyclical principles and focal points of "medicine" or spirit power.

DOUBLE SPIRAL

The interwoven double spiral represents powerful complementary and opposing forces, and as such encapsulates the dynamic energy of life and all creation. Variations on the double spiral are seen in the interwined snakes of the caduceus (see page 81), the swirling of yin and yang in the form of the taiji, the kundalini energy (see page 100) of Ayurvedic physiology, and in the double helix of DNA—the building block of life itself.

GOLDEN RECTANGLE

This figure is a rectangle in which the ratio of the short sides to the long sides is 1 to phi (φ), the Golden Number (see main text). It is found most famously in the designs of the Parthenon, the temple of Athene at Athens, and was used (perhaps more consciously) by the architect Le Corbusier.Like the square it represents security, balance, stasis and stability as opposed to fluctuation and uncertainty.

WHEEL OF FORTUNE

In European tradition, the Wheel of Fortune represents the unending and relentless round of good fortune and bad fortune, prosperity and indigence, and the permanence of change —all within the fixed framework of God's creation.

CUBE

As one of the five Platonic solids, a cube is an example of aesthetic beauty and symmetry, occurring naturally in crystal formations. The three-dimensional form of the square, the cube represents the Earth in all its solidity and permanence. In the Clementine Homilies, the apostle Peter declares that God took the form of a cube, the foundation stone at the center of the cosmos, giving rise to the dimensions of height, width and breadth. Its perfect regularity make it an emblem of truth, and as such it is a footstool for the personified figures of Faith and History. Islam's holiest site is the Kaaba (right) at Mecca, an ancient cubic structure said to have been founded by Abraham (Ibrahim). It is the point toward which Muslims pray daily, and which they circumambulate at the climax of the Haj, the great pilgrimage to Mecca.

THE EGYPTIAN PYRAMID

Egypt's pyramid tombs developed from a hillock that represented the primordial mound of creation on which the sun god came into existence, perhaps relating to an early belief that the deceased rose to the heavens to be numbered among the stars. By the time of the first pharaonic dynasties, the mound had become a rectangle with sloping sides, or **MASTABA** (Arabic for "bench"). The step pyramid of Djoser (ca. 2650BCE) at Sakkara essentially consists of six **MASTABAS** of decreasing size, one on top of the other. Experiments in building a true pyramid resulted in the bent pyramid of King Snofru at Dahshur (the gradient changes part-way up, probably because the original steepness was unstable). Nearby, Snofru then built the red pyramid, the first true example. Snofru's son Khufu or Cheops (ca. 2585—2560BCE) built the biggest pyramid of all, at Giza. Whether by accident or design, its proportions are close to the golden number (see page 126).

Every Egyptian pyramid was originally topped with a pyramidion, a miniature pyramid often inscribed and gilded to catch the sun's dawn rays, a daily imitation of the birth of the sun on the primal mound. Later obelisks, with their pyramidal points, were a variation on the same solar-primal mound symbolism.

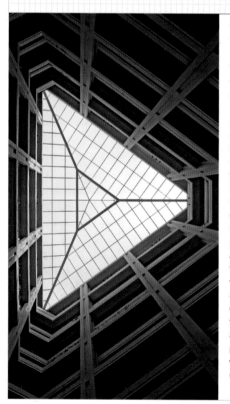

TRIANGLE

The triangle has a wide range of symbolism. The equilateral triangle with three identical angles symbolizes the Holy Trinity, the triune perfection and equality of Father, Son and Holy Spirit; in Hinduism it symbolizes the Trimurti, the divine triad of Brahma, Vishnu and Shiva, who preside over cosmic cycles as respectively creator, preserver and destroyer. An upward-pointing triangle is associated with the sun and fire, and male energy; the downward pointing triangle, from its association with the pubic triangle, is linked with female energy, rain and the moon.

HEXAGRAM

The hexagram, or six-pointed star, is perhaps best known in the form of the Star of David (Magen David), which has been used as a distinctly Jewish symbol since the Middle Ages and appears today on the national flag of the state of Israel. As the Seal of Solomon, the star is found in the Western magical traditions and Kabbalah as a symbol with powerful positive force. Consisting of two superimposed triangles, one pointing up and the other down, it symbolizes the concept of the microcosm as expressed in the Hermetic Axiom: "As above, so below."

ENNEAGRAM

The nine-pointed star (enneagram) is claimed in some Sufi traditions to represent the presence of God. In the Baha'i faith the star has auspicious numerological significance. The founder of Baha'i took the name Bahaullah, literally Glory (*baha*) of God (Allah). The numerical values of the Arabic letters for *baha* add up to nine. An irregular form of enneagram is used to represent personality types in the New Age system known as the Enneagram of Personality.

CONE

Combining the circle of infinity and perfection with the celestial symbolism of the triangle, the upward pointing cone symbolizes spiritual ascent, and the downward-pointing cone its opposite.

CYLINDER

The cylinder combines the circle and rectangle. Upright, a cylindrical shape may have phallic symbolism, as seen in the form of the impregnable round towers of myth and legend. A horizontal cylinder is like a tunnel and more feminine in symbolism.

HEPTAGRAM

The seven-pointed star shares the positive symbolism of the number seven (see page 119). In Christian tradition the heptagram represents the seven days of Creation and was used as an amulet against evil. On the badge of the Cherokee Nation it reflects the importance of seven in Native American lore, especially the profound responsibility to those who will come after, down to the seventh generation. As the Commonwealth Star, the heptagram represents the seven Australian federal states on the flag of Australia.

OCTOGRAM

In Islam the eight-pointed star has several forms. With the points around the edge of a circle it is referred to as al-Shamsa, the sun. In a complex combination of squares, circles, octagons and triangles, it symbolizes the mathematical perfection of God's creation.

SPHERE

The sphere or orb symbolizes infinity and the totality of divine creation. It represents the world, and also the vault of heavens. In Chinese art a sphere clutched by a dragon or a Dog of Fo represents the Pearl of Wisdom.

HEXAGON

In Christian tradition the hexagon represents death, perhaps because it is related to the number six, short of the perfect seven, the number of life (see also pages 119–121).

PENTAGRAM

The five-pointed star is the most common geometric star. It is a symbol of regeneration and renewal, whether it represents the biblical Star of Bethlehem or Venus, the Morning Star that heralds the new dawn. In Western magic, the pentagram symbolizes the four elements surmounted by the spirit and it is used in magical rituals to banish negative influences.

OCTAGON

With its eight sides, the number of Christ (who exceeds the perfect seven), an octagon symbolizes eternal life and resurrection. An octagonal rotunda was erected over the tomb of Christ (also called the Cave of Salvation) in what is now the Church of the Holy Sepulchre, Jerusalem. As a symbol of rebirth in Christ, the octagon is a traditional shape for the baptismal font, and for baptisteries. In sacred architecture an octagonal structure often supports a dome, forming a transition from square to circle (left, the Dome of the Treasury at the Great Mosque of Damascus).

ISLAM

Islam means "submission" or "surrender" to God, and Muslims ("those who submit") commit to a wholehearted obedience to the will of God, or Allah (a contraction of al-Illah, "*the* God" or "the One God"). Islam is also "being at peace" (*salam*) with God, since following the divine will brings about and underpins order in the universe.

God's will is expressed above all in the Quran ("Recitation"), revered as the literal word of God, directly revealed to Muhammad ibn Abdallah (ca. 570–632CE), the founder of Islam. Muslims acknowledge many prophets before him (including Abraham, Moses, and Jesus), but he is known as "the Prophet" and "the Seal of the Prophets" because the Quran is believed to be God's final word to humankind, and the symbol on Earth of God's power, mystery, mercy and compassion. Muslims prefer to be ritually pure when handling the holy book, which physically embodies God's presence and blessing (*baraka*).

The Quran is the basis of Muslim life and practice, which includes duties of prayer, compassion to the poor, ritual fasting and pilgrimage to Mecca (left), Islam's most sacred site. This illustration is predominantly in green, Islam's holy color. The Prophet's tribe had a green banner, and green is associated with paradise where the faithful are believed to wear green silk.

Islam has a rich tradition of illuminated manuscripts, although the Quran was never illustrated (for fear of idolatry). However, theologians became hostile to representational art on the grounds that to create an image of a living being challenged the divine creativity that Allah alone possesses. Thus, Islamic decoration consists mainly of exquisite calligraphy (passages from the Quran), and a rich repertoire of geometric and floral forms, as in the ornate interior of this mosque (right). The former symbolizes the presence of God on Earth, the latter his infinite perfection and complexity.

FIVE-POINTED STAR There are Five Divine Presences, and Islamic practice rests on the Five Pillars, or sacred duties, including prayer five times daily.

HEXAGONS Three is the number of heaven; doubled as six in the hexagon or six-sided shape it represents the "Circle of Heaven".

LEAVES & FLOWERS The stylized floral motifs seen in some of the hexagonal shapes and within the glazed "starburst" patterns represent the luxurious vegetation of paradise.

SHAHADA
The first of the Five Pillars, Islam's core duties, is the *Shahada* or confession of faith, often found as a calligraphic motif—as on the Saudi flag (above). Green is the color of spirituality.

BISMILLAH
"In the name of God, the Compassionate, the Merciful" is an invocation known as the *Bismillah*. It begins and ends every Islamic religious act and is often spoken in daily life. As a symbolic motif it represents divine mercy.

EIGHT-POINTED STAR
Eight is a celestial number in Islam. There are eight regions of paradise and eight angels support the throne of Allah on Judgment Day.

SIXTEEN-POINTED STAR Islamic star patterns are based on a circle, denoting infinity and eternity. The central circle symbolizes the one God and Mecca.

The star unfolds in seven layers, the perfect number: God has seven attributes. It ends in sixteen points: celestial eight doubled. The rich blues denote God's heavenly abode.

the cross

The simple geometric motif obtained by combining a vertical and a horizontal stroke is an ancient and universal symbol with hundreds of different forms, though arguably it is now most familiar as the chief emblem of Christianity, where it symbolizes Christ's saving sacrifice. It represents the meeting of heaven and Earth, of the union of opposites, and—since its arms can extend to infinity—of the cosmos and of eternal life, an *axis mundi* around which creation revolves. Its four points also symbolize the four elements and the four cardinal directions. It also denotes the Tree of Life, with its roots in heaven and its branches in the earth. It is linked with gods of the skies and the elements: Spanish Roman Catholic missionaries were surprised to find the cross as an emblem of the Mesoamerican wind and rain gods, Tlaloc and Chac, and T-cross amulets represented the hammer of the god Thor in pre-Christian Scandinavia and later.

The ancient cross known as the swastika, *fylfot* or hooked cross, unfortunately yet inevitably brings to mind Nazism, which adopted a tilted swastika as its cult emblem. However, it is in fact an older dynamic symbol of the sun, peace and the cycles of life, widely found as an auspicious emblem in Hinduism and Buddhism. Solar symbolism is the essence of the distinctive Celtic cross, which predates Christianity (see page 27).

DOUBLE CROSS

(*right*) The short upper crossbar of the patriarchal cross (borne before the chief archbishops of the medieval Church) symbolizes the placard bearing the inscription "The King of the Jews". Emblem of Anjou and Lorraine, the cross was once the badge of Joan of Arc, hence its adoption by the Free French forces during World War II.

BYZANTINE CROSS

(*left*) Widely used in the Orthodox churches, this cross also has three crossbars, but the third is at foot level, like a footplate. In early forms (left) it is level, but later it is slanted—said to represent the fate of the two robbers on either side of Christ. One mocked him, while the other was told that he would join Christ in paradise.

LATIN CROSS

This is the most widely used form of the cross and symbolizes the actual cross on which, according to St. Augustine, Christ died. Countless Christian churches are built with the nave, transepts and chancel forming the plan of a Latin cross (*crux ordinaria*).

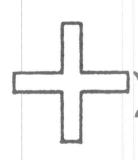

INVERTED CROSS

An upside-down Latin cross is the particular emblem of St. Peter, the "Prince of the Apostles", who according to the apocryphal Acts of Peter asked to be crucified head downward as a deliberate act of humility toward Christ, a scene depicted by Michelangelo and many other artists.

THE CROSS OF CHRIST

The **CROSS** was a rare symbol in the early church, both because christianity was illegal and because crucifixion was a shameful punishment for brigands and rebels. The cross was even used as a means for pagans to taunt christians. The **LABARUM** or **CHI-RHO** was more widely used, as well as the **CRUX DISSIMULATA** (disguised cross) in the form of an **ANCHOR, AXE** or **TRIDENT**. But after crucifixion was abolished and the faith itself became fully legal in 312, the cross was widely displayed, and as the faith spread it absorbed the auspicious symbolism of other cross forms among converted peoples. It is most widely found as the simple **LATIN CROSS**, but there are a wide range of other forms (this cross at Ravenna, right, is a decorative form with forked ends), many of which carry unique symbolism. The most common types are the **LATIN, GREEK, SALTIRE, DOUBLE,** and **TAU CROSSES**. It is also the symbol of numerous saints, not only those who, like peter and Andrew, were also crucified.

GREEK CROSS

The Greek cross (*crux immissa quadrata*) has four arms of equal length. In Christianity it is associated with St. George and, more broadly, with the centripetal energy of Christ, God descending to spread new life across the world. Many pre-Christian examples exist, including one from Knossos, ca. 1600 BCE.

MALTESE CROSS

This existed in Assyria and was reoriginated in the crusades with the military order of the Hospital of St. John of Jerusalem (also known as the Knights Hospitaller, and the Knights of St. John), who were later based in Malta. Each arm is splayed and ends in two points, giving eight directions.

TAU CROSS

Lacking the upright beyond the crossbar, this cross is named for its resemblance to the Greek letter tau (τ), or a capital T. It is also thought by some to be the likely form of the original cross. It was a pre-Christian symbol in Egypt, where it came to be associated with St. Anthony. It was also the cross of Mithraism.

PAPAL CROSS

The cross with three crossbars is a variant of the patriarchal double cross unique to the pope and known as the *ferula*. It is said, like the papal tiara, or triple crown, to symbolize the Trinity but this is not certain. Just as likely it refers to some threefold aspect of papal office: bishop of Rome, patriarch of the West and successor to Peter.

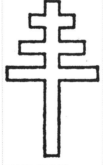

TEMPLAR CROSS

A Greek cross with splayed extremities to each of the arms was worn by the order of the Knights Templar, and was later the form of the Iron Cross, the military decoration for valor.

ANKH

When surmounted by a loop or circle, the cross becomes the Egyptian hieroglyph for *ankh*, "life". Grasped in the hand of a deity it represents the symbolic key to the mysteries of life and death.

SALTIRE

The saltire symbolizes martyrdom, in particular that of St. Andrew, who according to legend was crucified on a diagonal cross.

FORKED CROSS

The cross in the shape of a Y is linked with the Tree of Life. It symbolizes Christ, on the Cross, opening his arms of mercy.

LABARUM

The labarum is also called the *chi-rho*, since it combines the Greek letters chi (χ) and rho (ρ), the first two letters of Christ in Greek. It was a common emblem of Christ before the cross became widespread.

ROSY CROSS

A rose superimposed on a Latin cross is a symbol of the Virgin Mary, the "Rose without Thorns". It became the emblem of the order of the Rosy Cross, or Rosicrucians (see pages 48–49).

SYMBOLS FROM EVERYDAY LIFE

THE PARAPHERNALIA OF EVERYDAY LIVING—VARYING IN SCALE FROM AN EAR OF CORN TO THE DOME OF A VAST CHURCH—OFFERS A VAST STOCK OF SYMBOLS WHOSE MEANINGS MAY DERIVE FROM PRACTICAL OR CEREMONIAL USAGE, SOME ASSOCIATION IN MYTHOLOGY, OR THE IMPLICATIONS OF SHAPE OR FORM.

TOOLS & IMPLEMENTS

Domestic tools and implements represent our instinct for sustenance and survival. They may be used for creation or destruction and hence may possess a cosmic symbolism relating to cycles of life and the interplay of heaven and Earth.

WHEEL
In many cultures the wheel alludes to annual or seasonal cycles, or birth, death and rebirth. For Buddhists the spoked "Wheel of Dharma" (above) represents the truths taught by the Buddha.

BELL
An ancient form of alert, bells are symbols of awareness, vigilance and attentiveness. With their clear, pure notes they represent spotlessness: Jewish brides wear bells to denote virginity.

SCALES
The act of weighing one portion against another has been a symbol, of judging relative values, since antiquity. The ancient Egyptian "Books of the Dead" depict the deceased's heart being weighed on scales against the feather of Truth to determine the soul's virtue and fitness for paradise. This may be the origin of the Christian idea that all souls will be weighed on Judgment Day. The Roman goddess Iustitia (Justice) represents the law in Western tradition; she holds a set of scales to symbolize fairness and impartiality.

PLOW
When human societies turned to settled agrarian living, the plow became a natural symbol of a fruitful, pacific lifestyle. Peace is symbolized by the turning of "swords into plowshares". The plow is also often seen in sexual terms as the male organ penetrating and fertilizing the female earth. In India, it is thus a traditional symbol of kingly strength.

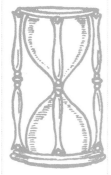

LIBERTY FOR ALL

ANCHOR

A traditional symbol of St. Nicholas of Bari, the patron saint of sailors, the anchor is a symbol of hope for all in troubled times. The anchor more broadly denotes the Christian virtue of hope, the "anchor of the soul" (Hebrews 6.19), which forms a trio of key virtues together with faith and charity (love). As a form of the cross, the anchor also represents salvation through Christ.

HOURGLASS

The Greek god Cronos, or Chronos, who symbolizes time and fate, holds an hourglass. Its two chambers signify the upper and lower worlds, life and death: the gradual emptying of the vessel is a common symbol of waning life, the "sands of time" running out. However, by turning the hourglass upside down, one is given the chance to begin anew, often with a change of heart.

TORCH

(*above*) A flaming torch denotes spiritual and intellectual enlightenment and truth. In ancient Greece, a chief priest at Eleusis was called Dadukos, or "Torchbearer", for his role in delivering messages from the gods. The torch as a modern Olympic emblem also derives from ancient Greece. As on the Statue of Liberty (above), it also denotes the light of liberty against the dark forces of tyranny.

LADDER

(*right*) The symbol of a ladder reaching from Earth to the heavens was common to many ancient cultures. In the Bible, the patriarch Jacob dreams of a ladder between heaven and the Earth with angels descending and ascending, signifying communication between God and humankind (Genesis 28.11–22). Celestial ladders also symbolize the ideas of aspiration and striving to achieve.

THE SYMBOLIC SHIP

A SHIP sailing on the SEA symbolizes vulnerable humankind seeking its destiny amid the vastness of the cosmos. In some ancient civilizations the dead were launched in boats in the belief that their souls would find a resting place beyond the seas (Indonesian spirit boat, left). The Egyptian god ISIS was honored every spring by launching a ship that was believed to protect seafarers from dangerous weather. In pre-Christian northern Europe, chieftains might be buried in ships to carry them on the afterlife journey: the seventh-century ship burial of a pagan king at Sutton Hoo in England is a famous example.

The main body of a church is called a NAVE (Latin *navis*, "ship"), likening the worshipers within to seafaring travelers on a shared spiritual journey, protected by God from the storms of misfortune. The idea of a ship as a self-sufficient community lies behind many symbolic images. The camel is the "ship of the desert" because of its ability to travel long distances without taking sustenance.

SPADE

The spade symbolizes the male principle, the phallus thrusting into the female earth and initiating the process of fertilization. The Roman god Saturn is sometimes depicted with the spade, alluding to his origins as an ancient Italian god of agriculture. The "spade" of playing cards is in fact a sword (Italian *spada*, Spanish *espada*), as it remains in Tarot (see pages 122–123).

SCYTHE & SICKLE

A scythe is the attribute of Father Time (see page 93) and of the traditionally skeletal, hooded figure of Death, the Grim Reaper. The crescent moon-like shape of the sickle is linked with the feminine principle and hence with fertility and lunar goddesses such as Demeter and Artemis (Diana). In communist symbolism, the sickle represents agricultural workers.

HAMMER

A stone hammer was the weapon of Thor, the Norse thunder god, and a symbol of protection in pagan Scandinavia: Thor-hammer amulets were still popular well into Christian times. But hammers are also building tools and represent constructive progress. In communism, a hammer is the symbol of the industrial working class, generally used in combination with the agricultural sickle (see left).

CUP & BOWL

A cup, bowl or dish carries feminine associations as a receptive vessel of sustenance, and their rounded forms also links such containers to eternal cycles of time and creation. The goblet or chalice is the vessel of life-giving elixir, as in the Holy Grail of medieval Arthurian legend. A symbolic or ornamental cup is commonly the trophy won in sports tournaments. As such it is a symbol of fulfillment and victory, but it ultimately derives from the Classical myth of the cup of ambrosia, the elixir of eternal life, drunk by the gods of Mount Olympus.

ANVIL

The anvil is a symbol of feminine creativity and the forging of life, especially combined with the masculine hammer. Greeks and Romans ascribed volcanic rumblings and eruptions to the subterranean forges of the smith god Hephaistos (Vulcan).

CROOK

The shepherd's crook symbolizes firm but kindly authority: bishops carry a crook, or crozier, to denote their care of the flock of Christ (see page 150). The pharaoh's stylized crook and flail symbolized his lordship of Egypt: they are emblems of Osiris, god of the underworld and the fertile land.

FLAG

A flag can represent the identity, unity, independence and sovereignty of a group or people. National flags often bear culturally significant colors and emblems. Many European flags have a cross, symbolizing their traditional Christian culture, and flags of Islamic countries often bear a crescent and star. The red-white-blue tricolor of revolutionary France inspired the flags of many other nations, especially those founded through revolutionary or anticolonial movements. The battle standard is a means of identification but also a sign of might and defiance. A flag flown at half-mast is a sign of general mourning.

PLATE

A plate is an emblem of plenty and achievement, perhaps owing to a custom of displaying or presenting the first fruits of the harvest on a platter, celebrating the fruitfulness of the earth. A silver or gold plate is often the trophy presented to winners of modern sports, notably in horse racing.

YOKE

A traditional symbol of oppression: the enemies of ancient Rome were said to "pass under the yoke" to symbolize their enslavement. But as a useful agricultural implement the yoke also has a positive meaning of discipline and teamship, a striving together in harmony.

weapons

The dual use of weapons—for defense and attack—gives them an ambivalent edge in symbolism. In aiding the "good fight", the cause of right, weapons have become associated with certain virtues: honor, justice and truth. In mythology, some weapons possess magical qualities that grant those that wield them a supernatural strength, or even invincibility, in the face of peril. As symbols of authority, weapons often developed highly stylized forms for use in ceremony or ritual, such as the gold mace that represents royal authority in the British parliament.

In many accounts, exemplary weapons with magical qualities were made of precious metals to denote their great value. In *The Iliad*, Homer describes King Agamemnon's breastplate and shield as a special blend of gold and silver (an alloy known as electrum), enhancing their charisma. In Christianity, weapons became metaphors of spiritual might, and "fighting the good fight" on behalf of Christ, the Prince of Peace. The language of physical battle became the language of spiritual progress, as in Martin Luther's famous hymn, echoing Psalm 46: "A stronghold sure is God our Lord, A trusty shield and weapon."

A heap of arms and armor appear in Western art and sculpture as traditional trophies of victory. But just as arms symbolize war and aggression, broken weapons indicate the cessation of hostilities.

KNIFE OR DAGGER

(*left*) Easily concealed, knives or daggers often carry a sinister overtone of betrayal or underhand business: they are commonly weapons of assassination. They are also the usual implements for ritual sacrifice, as when Abraham attempted to offer up his son Isaac in Genesis 22, before an angel intervened. In Aztec rites, humans were sacrificed with a knife of flint or of obsidian (left), a type of volcanic glass that symbolized death.

AXE

A near-universal emblem of power, authority and judgment. A double-headed axe was possibly a lunar symbol of the ancient Minoan rulers of Crete, and axe symbolism is found in many other cultures, often linked with solar or storm gods: in this sense it is related to the symbolism of the hammer. In parts of Africa, axe blows may form a part of rites to invoke rain. In ancient Rome, a bundle of sticks and an axe bound up together was borne before state officials as a sign of their authority: known as the *fasces* ("bundle"), it gave its name to Mussolini's Fascist party, of which it was the symbol.

SHIELD

(*right*) In Greek mythology a shield bearing the head of the Gorgon Medusa was an attribute of Athene (Minerva), and the virgin hunter Artemis also bore a shield to symbolize her role as a defender of chastity. In medieval Europe, shields were decorated with distinctive designs as a means of identification in battle: this was the origin of heraldry (see pages 78–79).

TRIDENT

(*left*) The trident of Poseidon (Neptune), Classical god of the sea, was likely a stylized lightning bolt. It is also held by Britannia, "ruler of the waves", the personification of Great Britain (left), and denotes either the British nations of England, Wales and Scotland, or the three kingdoms of England, Scotland and Ireland.

SWORDS OF POWER

The **SWORD** is the symbol *par excellence* of military and royal might, the weapon of warriors, knights (below) and kings. But like all weapons it can be used defensively, protecting the weak in the name of justice and honor, and by association it signifies valor and chivalry. It also symbolizes secular authority. The sword is the emblem of the profession of war as the **PEN** is of the ways of peace. In his 1839 play *Cardinal Richelieu*, Edward Bulwer-Lytton coined the memorable phrase, "The pen is mightier than the sword"—earlier still, Thomas Jefferson made a similar mention about Thomas Paine. A sword has the additional symbolism of powerful speech that cuts through lies: the **SWORD OF TRUTH**. The ambivalence of swords as both aggressive and defensive weapons is reflected in the image of the **DOUBLE-EDGED SWORD** to denote a situation with distinct benefits and drawbacks.

In medieval Europe, swords were the subject of many legends, such as the Arthurian **EXCALIBUR**, the sword endowed with powers of destiny for the one rightful sovereign who could draw it from the stone in which it was embedded. In form, the sword resembles the Christian **CROSS**, and hence crusader insignia often features a sword.

The blade's sharpness links the sword with discernment and enlightenment. In Hindu myth, **VISHNU**'s flaming sword is a symbol of pure knowledge, cutting through ignorance. The sword of **MANJUSHRI**, the Buddhist deity of wisdom, has similar properties and symbolism.

CLUB

The club is an archetypal symbol of brute force (right, held by a temple guardian in Thailand). One of the earliest armaments to be fashioned, it was the weapon of the hero Herakles (Hercules) in Classical mythology and of various Celtic heroes, such as the Dagdha, the patriarchal "Good God" of ancient Irish myth. One end of the Dagdha's massive club would strike a person dead, while a touch from the club's other end would bring the dead back to life.

LANCE OR SPEAR

A lance is wielded on horseback while a spear or javelin is thrown on foot. A lance denotes male chivalry and horsemanship. St. George (left) slew a dragon even though his lance snapped: a broken lance is one of his emblems. The Roman soldier who pierced Christ's side on the cross is often depicted as a cavalry officer with a lance. He is traditionally named Longinus, from the Greek for spear. A spear is also an attribute of the Greek goddesses Athene and Artemis.

BOW & ARROW

Among the oldest weapons known to humankind, the **BOW** and **ARROW** are ancient emblems of the hunter and warrior. The bow and arrows of the classical solar god **APOLLO** symbolize the **SUN'S** transformative powers: the bow stands for the sun's energy, with the arrows as its rays, vital and fertilizing as they penetrate the **EARTH**. In China, the bow is the symbol of the great divine archer **YI**. When ten suns appeared in the **SKY**, threatening to destroy the earth, Yi shot nine of them. A bow hung over a doorway signified the birth of a son.

The **RAINBOW** has sometimes been interpreted as a divine bow, as when God sets his bow in the sky to mark the end of the flood and his covenant with Noah (Genesis 9.13). Similarly, in Hindu myth, **SHIVA'S** bow represents divine force, and a bow is the attribute of **RAMA** (left, on Hanuman's shoulders). But the bow and arrow are not exclusively male symbols. In classical myth, the goddess **ARTEMIS** (**DIANA**) is the fierce huntress of the gods, whose arrows slew the seven daughters of the boastful queen **NIOBE** and in one account the hunter **ORION**. Apollo tricked Artemis into shooting Orion lest she fall in love with the hunter, and the idea of erotic tension between archer and victim is also seen in **CUPID'S** arrows of love, symbolizing the pleasure and pain of erotic attachment. The archer's balance of lethal power and bodily control is perfectly depicted in the zodiacal sign **SAGITTARIUS**, the Archer, a **CENTAUR** with drawstring extended and arrow poised.

Arrows in Christian art can signify martyrdom and immortality. **ST. SEBASTIAN** in particular is often depicted pierced with arrows, an ordeal he miraculously survived. **BROKEN ARROWS** and other neutralized weaponry can denote peace.

MACE

(*left*) Similar to a scepter, the ceremonial mace (gripped here by an imperial eagle) is far removed from the military bludgeon from which it is derived, with a flanged head designed to break through armor. A crowned mace is the symbol of royal authority in the British and other Commonwealth parliaments.

ARMOR

(*right*) Whether in medieval Europe or among the Samurai of Japan, a suit of armor both protected the warrior and marked him out as a person of high status, since few could afford one. The "knight in shining armor" is a classic Western ideal of chivalry, as demonstrated in the legend of St. George slaying the dragon to save the maiden: he is often represented as a medieval knight (see illustration, page 86). Armor remained a symbol of nobility and military prowess long after the development of firearms changed the nature of warfare.

WHIP OR SCOURGE

In many societies a whip was used symbolically to expel evil: in the gospels, Jesus is said to have driven out the extortionate moneychangers from the Temple in Jerusalem with a "whip of cords" (John 2.15). A knotted whip, or scourge, was particularly gruesome as it was designed to rip the flesh of beaten victims. Christ was flogged with a scourge before the Crucifixion and hence it is one of the Instruments of the Passion. In fact it was a popular weapon of punishment in the Roman empire and came to be a symbol of brutal oppression. A scourge is also a metaphor for vehement and scathing opposition. As the implement of self-flagellation, it is a symbol of penitence and an attribute of Mary Magdalene and other saints.

HINDUISM

HEADGEAR
This tenth-century statue depicts Vishnu (right) and Shiva (left) in their combined form of Harihara. Half of his headgear is Vishnu's regal crown, the other the elaborately piled-up matted locks of Shiva.

TRIDENT The weapon of Shiva is the trident (*trishula*), denoting creation, preservation and destruction, or other sacred trinities.

NANDIN Among the figures on the right of Harihara is his mount, the bull Nandin. Other figures include Shiva's son, the elephant-headed god Ganesha (see box).

Hinduism has no single founder, teacher or scripture, but most Hindus accept that the soul is reincarnated after death and that *karma*—one's actions in this life—will affect the nature of lives to come. *Moksha*, or liberation from the infinite cycle of rebirth, comes by attaining supreme wisdom through right living and devotional practice, which can include offerings to deities and yogic meditation. Any practice that enhances life—such as medicine, dancing and building—can be an act of devotion.

The illustration above shows the marriage of Vishnu and his consort Lakshmi, attended by other deities. The many Hindu deities are understood as manifestations of one Supreme Being, often called Brahman (not to be confused with the god Brahma). This being takes many forms in order to be accessible to humans. Some deities are familiar to all Hindus (see box, right)—for example, Vishnu and Shiva (see main image). Others, such as Brahma and Varuna, are less prominent now than in earlier times. There are also countless local divinities.

Conical towers at Hindu temples symbolize Mount Meru, the celestial home of the gods. Important Hindu sacraments and rites of passage, such as weddings, are held in the presence of a sacred fire (*agni*), which represents the cosmos as a validating witness; and it is through being consumed in fire that the body is symbolically returned to the cosmos at death.

AUMKAR
The *aumkar* represents the sacred syllable *Om* that is uttered at the start and end of Hindu prayers. The syllable is understood as having three sounds (*a-u-m*). For many it was the first sound in the cosmos, and is the embodiment of true knowledge.

YANTRA
Devotees of the esoteric spiritual path known as Tantra use *yantra*s as focal points for meditation in the pursuit of liberation (*moksha*). Like Buddhist *mandala*s (see page 115), *yantra*s are symbolic diagrams of the cosmos.

WHEEL
Vishnu's bladed discus-like wheel (*chakra*) cuts through ignorance. It has a stem like a lotus, another of Vishnu's attributes.

CONCH Vishnu's conch trumpet symbolizes the sound of creation. Such trumpets have been used in sacred rites since ancient times.

KALKIN The figures on Harihara's left include Kalkin, Vishnu's tenth and future avatar (see box), a warrior on a white horse who will establish a new era.

GODS & SYMBOLS

The most prominent Hindu deities are **VISHNU**, **SHIVA** and the **GODDESS (DEVI)**, who has many manifestations, such as **SHAKTI**, **DURGA** and **KALI**. Vishnu has ten **AVATARS**, forms in which he battled evil in the world, the most popular being **KRISHNA**, a youth frequently shown with blue skin (like Vishnu) and playing a **FLUTE**, and **RAMA** (hero of the *Ramayana* epic). Shiva and his consort **PARVATI** (a form of the Goddess) are represented by the **LINGA** and **YONI**. The marriage of Vishnu and **LAKSHMI** (see illustration, far left), symbolizes the ideal union of husband and wife.

Other popular deities include the monkey god **HANUMAN**, and **GANESHA** (below), who overcomes obstacles and is worshiped before any task or journey. He is part **ELEPHANT** (to crush large obstacles) and rides a **MOUSE** (which gnaws through small ones).

Many deities are multiarmed to denote their omnipotence, each hand bearing a weapon or other symbolic attribute. Most deities also have associated animals.

clothes

At all times, and in all cultures, clothing and other accoutrements of personal dress have been strikingly visible expressions either of individuality, independence and free will; or of conformity, dependence and the ceding of individual autonomy to that of a group. Dress may convey national or cultural allegiance, or religious faith. Trades and professions may call for special clothes suited to the work, and these in turn become symbols of certain qualities, like the Freemason's apron or the artisan's skullcap worn by the Egyptian god Ptah to denote his role as a creator. In Christian art, several holy figures may be recognizable from their dress: St. John the Baptist usually wears a rough tunic of animal hides from his time spent in the wilderness, while St. Jerome, translator of the Bible into Latin, is sometimes portrayed in the (anachronistic) scarlet robes of a cardinal. For Adam and Eve, the wearing of clothes to cover their nakedness symbolized the loss of innocence.

Membership of certain professions or groups, such as the army, navy, police, church, law, judiciary or hospital medicine, often requires the wearing of uniform, literally a "single form" of dress, to convey one's level of skill, rank, or position in the group, especially if it is a strictly hierarchical organization such as the church or military. Church robes may involve a range of symbolic colors to reflect the church season, rite or festival. Uniform also implies the acceptance of a group ethical code, often explicitly avowed by the taking of an oath.

Prison inmates have to wear uniforms to convey their submission to authority and loss of individual freedom. Formal occasions such as weddings and funerals often demand a semiuniform—such as morning suits or mourning dress—by which guests express respect for whoever is the focus of the occasion (the bridal pair or the deceased in these cases). Even when uniform is not compulsory, as in most business, an implicit "dress code" may express the wearer's authority and, by implication, probity (see also pages 150–153).

HEADWEAR

As a marker of office or status, such as a bishop's miter, or a Native American chief's headdress (right), a form of headwear can represent the wearer's authority. Special headgear—such as the Jewish yarmulka, or skullcap, or the Sikh turban—can denote one's faith. Baring the head is a common sign of respect; but in Judaism it is customary to cover one's head in the presence of God. (See also **CROWN**, page 151.)

ERMINE

A broad collar or trim of white ermine (stoat) fur, spotted with black ermine tails, was expensive since it required the winter pelts of several stoats. Hence, it was a marker of royal or noble status (above).

VEIL

The **VEIL** is a widespread symbol of modesty and also denotes respect for, and deference to, social superiors and the divine. When **MOSES** returned from Mount Sinai, he had to wear a veil to protect his followers from the bright reflection of God on his face. Many women wear the **MIQTAB** (veil) in Muslim society as a sign of modesty, and at Christian weddings it is customary for the bride to be veiled, marking her pure state until she is married. The veil is an attribute of the personified figure of **CHASTITY**. It can also carry a sense of deception. In the Bible, **JACOB** mistakes veiled **LEAH** for **RACHEL**, and as a consequence has to work another twelve years for his father-in-law **ISAAC**.

A famous holy relic in the Vatican claims to be a linen veil with which a woman named **BERENICE** (right, **VERONICA** in Latin) mopped the face of **CHRIST** as he carried his **CROSS** to Calvary. His features are said to have been miraculously imprinted on the veil, which is known in Latin as the *vera icon*, or "True Image", an anagram of Veronica.

SHOE OR BOOT
Slaves walked barefoot in antiquity, so shoes represented freedom. In England it was once customary to throw a shoe after a bride and groom to wish them luck on their journey through life. Two shoes express a similar wish in China, since *xie* means "shoe", "harmony" and "together". Boots can have more aggressive overtones. As a child, the deranged Emperor Gaius was nicknamed "Little Boots" (Caligula).

GLOVE
Gloves were a sign of status: if worn by members of the clergy they indicated "clean hands" that were unsullied by corruption. Yet "glove money" is a bribe, originating from the old custom of a client slipping to his lawyer a pair of gloves to represent him. In the expression "hand in glove", the idea of one thing fitting snugly into another implies a cozy relationship, perhaps even illicit collusion.

TOGA
The great symbol of Roman citizenship was the toga, a formal garment consisting of a long, broad piece of woolen cloth that was elaborately wound round the body. Senators and emperors wore togas edged with purple, an expensive dye, as a sign of status. The equivalent dress for respectable women was the *stola*, a long pleated dress. A woman in a toga was assumed to be a prostitute.

CLOAK OR MANTLE
Elisha took up Elijah's mantle to denote his succession as prophet of God (2 Kings 2.13): hence, "taking up the mantle" means taking over responsibility. The cloak (Latin *cappella*) of St. Martin was a famous relic kept in a special shrine at Tours, France. The relic's name was transferred to the shrine itself and later to any similar structure: hence the word "chapel". A cloak also has overtones of (malign) concealment.

DRAGON ROBES
The emperor of China wore a yellow silk robe richly embroidered with dragons and other imperial symbols. The emperor alone had the right to wear the five-clawed imperial dragon (*long*). Lesser notables wore robes decorated with four- or three-clawed dragons.

GAUNTLET
In medieval chivalry, to be without gauntlets symbolized that one was unarmed and unhostile. Throwing down the gauntlet was a challenge to a knight or noble on equal social terms; taking it up expressed acceptance of the challenge.

GIRDLE OR BELT
The girdle carries a double meaning of submission, or chastity, and empowerment. In Classical myth, Aphrodite (Venus), had a magic girdle that made her irresistible; and the "Girdle of Isis" represented vitality and purity in ancient Egypt. The Virgin's Girdle is a celebrated Christian relic. Warriors "girded up their loins", donning a belt to carry weapons.

SANDAL
Sandals symbolize fleetness, and winged sandals are an attribute of the messenger god Hermes (Mercury) and also the hero Perseus: he used them to slay the sea monster Ceto.

TUNIC
A tunic fits closely to the torso, so by analogy the body in Christian tradition is called the "soul's tunic". In Greek myth, Herakles' death was caused when his tunic was doused in a poison lethal to the touch (see page 179).

food & drink

In the ancient world it was natural to associate nature's bounty with divine blessing. A good harvest showed divine favor, a poor one retribution for disobedience or disloyalty. Grace is spoken in many faiths at table to give thanks to God for providing food. Festivals celebrate turning points in the farming year; most Jewish religious festivals, for example, owe their origins to the agricultural cycle. The idea that divine bodies can be appeased by feeding resulted in sacrificial meals, the burnt offering of Jewish tradition (see page 166), ambrosia for Greek gods, and, more generally, banquets in honor of the gods. Other celebrated feasts include the Wedding at Cana, in which wine symbolizes the spirit of heaven, as opposed to the water of earthly life; and the miraculous Feeding of the Five Thousand, in which the bread and fish are the symbols of everlasting life.

BREAD

As a basic source of nourishment, bread is a symbol of life. In a spiritual metaphor, Christ is described as the "bread of life" (John 6.35), food for the soul. Yeast, as a component in the baking process, is a symbolic factor: unleavened bread in Jewish thought represents purity and sacrifice; leavened, or risen, bread suggests spiritual transformation. In some cultures breaking bread signifies death.

FISH

Significant meals involving fish can be traced back to the mystery religions when believers partook of a sacramental meal of fish, bread and wine (later reflected in the Eucharist). Fish were worshiped by the ancients for their fecundity and in their honor a fish dish was taken on a Friday, a practice embraced by Christianity when abstaining from meat-eating on Fridays, the day that Christ died.

WHEAT & BARLEY

A more basic foodstuff of life than bread, the staple crop wheat is symbolized as immortal sustenance. In the Greek Eleusinian Mysteries, Demeter, goddess of fertility, is worshiped by initiates contemplating a single grain of wheat in the belief that a good harvest will be produced by doing so. The miracle of spring regrowth from the previous year's seeds contributed to wheat becoming a symbol of resurrection in the New Testament.

RICE

As the staple grain of the East, rice mirrors the life-giving qualities of corn and wheat in the West. Chinese mythology says rice grew naturally until communication between heaven and Earth broke down; then peasants had to labor in the paddies to produce a harvest.

GRAIN OF THE GODS

As the staple crop of many American civilizations, corn acquired the symbolism of benevolence and prosperity. The emergence each spring of abundant ears of corn, which died and regrew the following year, imbued the crop with a sense of divine origin, an essential that belonged to the gods.

In Egypt the dying and rising of corn were figured in the god Osiris who oversaw funerary proceedings and judged the fortune of the dead. In Mesoamerica the Maya and Aztecs both worshiped grain gods who were responsible for the fertilizing process and therefore crop yield. The stalks and ears of maize were venerated as icons of fertility deities in the homes of Aztec peasants, and sometimes worn as charms by warriors.

The native peoples of the American southwest classify corn as one of the "three sisters", together with beans and squash. Corn is a symbol of fruitfulness, and corn pollen is often carried by an individual in their medicine bag to enhance fertility and to make offerings to the spirits.

MANNA

While the Israelites wandered in the wilderness of Sinai, on the brink of starvation, manna miraculously came down from heaven for them to eat. Moses said it was bread of heaven: "like coriander seed, white; and the taste of it was like wafers made of honey" (Exodus 16.31). The term has been adopted universally as the symbol of a surprise substance.

MOON CAKES

Moon cakes are eaten by the Chinese to celebrate the mid-autumn festival. Round pastries are made of lotus seed paste and duck-egg yolks to provide sustenance for family and friends while watching the moon.

GOURD

One of Daoism's Eight Immortals has a gourd as an emblem. Its association with longevity is symbolized in smoke rising from a gourd, representing the liberation of the spirit from the body.

MUSHROOM

The mushroom is also associated with immortality in the Daoist tradition. The Queen Mother of the West is often depicted with one (see page 51). The hallucinogenic quality of some have imbued them with a sense of mystery and revitalization.

PASSOVER

The Seder meal is eaten by Jews at the festival of Passover to commemorate the Exodus from Egypt (when the angel of death "passed over", sparing the Israelites). Constituents of the meal represent elements of the escape: the blood of the sacrificed (paschal) lamb means salvation (in Christianity, Christ is represented as the Lamb of God who shed his blood at Passover); unleavened loaves are a reminder of the hurried flight, there having been no time to add yeast; eggs represent the promise of a new beginning; and bitter herbs symbolize the suffering in Egypt.

TOMATO

Native to the Americas, the tomato plant was believed by the Pueblo people of New Mexico to possess supernatural qualities—those who saw tomato seeds being eaten were said to be blessed with the power of divination. This belief turned to mischief in the eastern part of the country, where the tomato became associated with witchcraft. On transferring to revolutionary Europe, and in particular France, the redness of this fruit symbolized bloodshed and it became popular with republicans as a side dish.

THE LAST SUPPER

The final meal celebrated by Christ and his disciples before his crucifixion broadly symbolizes the replacement of the old values of Judaism with the new teachings of Christ. Consumed when the Passover meal was celebrated, the wine (representing blood) and bread (representing body) of Christ were taken in the belief that the disciples, and subsequently all followers of the faith, would thus partake of the new spirit of eternal life. That this was a sacrificial meal lies behind the meaning, and hence Christians celebrate it as the Eucharist, "giving thanks" to God for sacrificing his son. The earliest church ritual included a fish, symbol of the eternal Christ, in their commemoration. Renaissance painters customarily depicted the Last Supper as a sacramental rite, with Christ pouring wine into a chalice and consecrating the loaf in priestly fashion, and often with John the Evangelist resting on Jesus (as in this fresco, below, from 1460).

HONEY

The sweet, golden character of honey, a source of inspiration for artists, poets and prophets, made it seem to be of divine origin, able to produce eloquent words of wisdom.

PUMPKIN

Pumpkins represent recklessness and empty-headedness. Hence at Halloween, a time of spiritual chaos, pumpkins are paraded as hollowed-out skulls with mad expressions.

WATERMELON

(*right*) Thought to have originated in Africa, watermelons were being cultivated in East Asia by the eleventh century and by the late sixteenth or early seventeenth they had reached England. In Southeast Asia watermelon is a symbol of fertility on account of its many seeds. Depictions of watermelon are common in Mexican Day of the Dead art.

WINE

Because grapes could be pressed and their juice turned into a mysterious potent liquid, wine adopted a symbolism for benign transformation. It signified the power of nature, fertility and resurrection from death. As wine frees inhibitions, it is also associated with revealing the truth, especially from liars. In his *Natural History*, Pliny the Elder claimed "in vino veritas"—"in wine [there is the] truth". In Islam, wine represents the promise of paradise.

SOMA

For Hindus soma is an intoxicant that symbolizes the gods' vigor. It fills the imbiber with divine power. Soma is identified with the moon, its vitality restored each month by the sun. Soma's strength is represented in Hindu art by an eagle or bull.

CAULDRON OF THE OTHERWORLD

The idea of cauldrons producing magic potions is widespread in mythology. In Celtic lore, cauldrons provided inexhaustible cornucopia and had the power of revitalizing wounded warriors. The Irish god Dagda went one step further and restored life in a never-emptying cauldron. Witches' brews were mixed in cauldrons to produce magic spells.

MEAD

In Celtic lore, mead was the immortal nectar of the gods. It was also drunk at the main Celtic festival of Samain because the gods' representatives on Earth, the priests, joined in the festival. Owing to the fact that mead is fermented honey, its sweetness was associated in some cultures with truth.

ELIXIR OF LIFE

(*left*) Medieval alchemists believed that a magical powder or fluid, known as "the elixir of life", could bestow the gift of immortality on the person who drank it. The Chinese ingested certain substances we now know to be toxic, such as quicksilver, or mercury, and sulfur, in the belief that these would promote longevity. "Elixir of life" was also a term for the "philosopher's stone", the means by which base metals could be transmuted into gold. In fact the alchemical process became a metaphor for a spiritual journey to enlightenment. In Tibetan Buddhist art (left) in particular, deities, saints and teachers may be depicted with a vase that contains the elixir of immortality.

BACCHANALIA

In ancient Greece and Rome, orgiastic, drunken feasts were held in honor of the god of wine—Dionysus (Greece) and Bacchus (Rome). Bacchanalian revels involved the ritual drinking of sacred wine, which symbolized the ecstatic union of the celebrant and the deity. The mystic cult promised an afterlife of perpetual revelry to initiates.

symbols of office

Performers of particular skills or trades are often singled out by their special clothes or other practical tools of their work. In Europe, this was once much more marked than it is now: for example, English physicians were recognizable by their silver-topped staffs, while scholars wore a black cap and gown at all times in public.

However, members of elite groups—rulers, nobles, warriors, priests, healers, poets, agents of justice, members of guilds, and other office-holders—have often been denoted by distinctive and purely symbolic robes, badges, and other accoutrements to indicate not simply their special functions but also their status within the social hierarchy. In the modern world, such symbolic trappings and paraphernalia may be confined to special ceremonies and festivals, like the special "vestments" worn by clerics of the Roman Catholic, Orthodox, Anglican and other Christian traditions. However, priests may wear a special "dog collar" with normal clothes, and the pope wears a white robe as head of the Roman Catholic Church: the color is associated with divine righteousness (Mark 9).

Private societies such as the Freemasons and other special groups may have their own particular language of symbols, denoting group identity and separation from the outside world.

SCEPTER

The scepter, similar to the mace of battle, is a symbol of supreme authority. In ancient Greece, the holder of the scepter had sole right to pronounce judgment. In many civilizations the scepter denoted ruthless punishment and bore such emblems as the eagle or gods of thunder and destruction. Christian monarchs bear golden scepters, often topped by a cross of Christ and borne at the coronation in the right hand (the hand that wields power).

ORB

The orb, literally "world" (Latin *orbis*), is a golden sphere topped by a cross: it symbolizes Christ's rulership over the universe, and by extension his sanction to the earthly monarch who governs in his name. In Britain it denotes the monarch as "Defender of the Faith", a titled bestowed by the pope on Henry VIII (ironically, since he later rejected papal authority) and borne by monarchs ever since. The orb is held in the left hand (the hand of peace) at coronations.

CROZIER

(*right*) The crozier is an elaboration of the shepherd's crook and symbolizes a bishop's pastoral role as overseer—the literal meaning of "bishop" (Greek *episkopos*)—of the faithful flock, in direct succession to the apostles of Christ, who is the Good Shepherd. It also symbolizes the bishop's disciplinary role as leader of a see (episcopal region), preventing errant sheep from straying from the fold of orthodoxy. The semicircular hook has also been held to represent the downpouring of God's blessings on his flock through the pastoral care of the bishop.

CROWN

The supreme emblem of royal authority is the **CROWN**. In the classical world, crowns or diadems signified celestial power granted by the gods. Unlike later European crowns, those of Greece and Rome were often quite simple—for example, of **OAK** leaves (sacred to **ZEUS/JUPITER**) or **LAUREL** leaves (sacred to **APOLLO**). The Roman emperor wore a crown of **ROSES** denoting victory, which was considered to be a blessing of the **SUN GOD**; it was parodied in Christ's **CROWN OF THORNS**, placed on his head when he was sarcastically hailed as "King of the Jews".

The "typical" crown shape, a metal band with dentelated upper edge, derives from early European stylized versions of Roman laurel crowns. By the high Middle Ages, crowns had become distinctly grandiose, made of precious metals and gems to symbolize the wearer's status and bearing a **CROSS** to signify the universal dominion of Christ, in whose name the monarch ruled. In modern kingdoms, a representation of the crown is often an official emblem of the state. In Europe, British monarchs are now alone in having a formal sacred rite of coronation.

Emperors of China wore elaborate headdresses decorated with golden imperial dragons (**LONG**) and **PEARLS** denoting wisdom. The empress wore a similarly elaborate headdress portraying her symbol, the fabulous Chinese **PHOENIX** or **FENG**.

AMPULLA & ANOINTING SPOON

The ampulla is the flask containing holy oil, or chrism, used to anoint sovereigns in a ceremony with biblical origins in the anointing of the Israelite kings (1 Samuel 10.1). The act symbolically affirms the blessing of God and the Church on the new ruler.

SOLOMON'S THRONE

As the seat of kings, the throne is a symbol of quasi-divine authority. One of the most elaborate thrones was that of King Solomon (1 Kings 10.18–20), which became the inspiration of subsequent thrones in the Judeo–Christian world, symbolizing the ruler's power and wisdom. A basic frame of ivory, to represent incorruptibility, was overlaid in solar gold, meaning divine wisdom. Two lions, signifying power, denoted Israel and Judah, the two provinces of Solomon's kingdom. At the top of six steps leading up to the throne were a further twelve lions—to signify the tribes of Israel.

RING & BRACELET

Its form as an unending circle gives the ring the symbolism of eternity, continuity or an unbreakable vow. It is thus worn to indicate a sacred office—for example, a monarch might put on a ring at a coronation to denote his or her "marriage" to the land and people. A nun wears a ring similarly to represent her sacred "marriage" to Christ. The Pope wears a "Fisherman's Ring" as Christ's apostolic overseer of the faithful, the *pisciculi*, or "little fish". The bracelet or arm-ring similarly signifies eternity: the Egyptian pharaoh, for example, wore one that bore a scarab to indicate life after death.

ROD

The rod, or wand, of office derives from the simple stick or staff, the most basic of weapons but also the traveler's support. As an ancient symbol of divine and magical power, it can represent the potency of the phallus or the accusatory pointed finger. In England, various royal and parliamentary officers are known by the wand they bear on ceremonial occasions. At the annual State Opening of Parliament, "Black Rod" knocks on the door of the House of Commons to request that Members of Parliament come before the Queen. His request is initially refused, symbolizing the rejection of autocracy.

MILITARY RANK INSIGNIA

The Roman army was the first western military to develop a hierarchy of officers, with STRIPES on their tunics to denote rank. Modern military ranks developed in the eighteenth century when soldiers and officers began to wear badges to indicate status. In armies, non-commissioned officers (lance corporal or private first class; corporal; sergeant) are denoted respectively by one, two and three CHEVRONS on the sleeve (left). Commissioned officers (from second lieutenant upwards) generally wear rank symbols on the epaulette, or shoulder strip, with various combinations of BARS, STARS, "PIPS" and (in monarchies) CROWNS. The highest officers often wear additional insignia and the most senior generals (also called marshals or field marshals) receive a ceremonial BATON.

Navies worldwide have a similar system to armies, except that in most cases all ranks wear sleeve insignia. For officers this generally consists of gold BANDS, the topmost band often with an ANCHOR LOOP or one or more stars symbolizing navigation skills. Air forces and marines may follow either system.

PRESIDENTIAL SEAL

Created by President Rutherford B. Hayes in 1880 as the personal emblem of the President of the United States, the presidential seal adorns the ceiling and carpet of the Oval Office, the president's personal flag, all White House documents, presidential transportation and even china used for official dinners. The seal itself is a version of the Great Seal of the United States, whose main element is a heraldic bald eagle with an olive branch of peace in one talon and arrows of war or defiance in the other, ringed by fifty stars representing the states.

PAPAL TIARA

Popes were crowned with the conical triple tiara from the Middle Ages until 1963, and while no longer part of papal regalia it remains on the arms of the Holy See and Vatican City. It is surmounted by a cross and bears three crowns, variously interpreted as symbolizing the threefold domains of the pope as bishop of Rome, as spiritual leader of the Church, and as temporal ruler of the States of the Church (now confined to the Vatican City). It is also held to represent the Trinity and the three prime Christian virtues of faith, hope and love.

GARTER

Orders of chivalry in various countries have their own distinctive emblems. In Britain, the highest order is the Garter, reputedly instituted ca. 1348 by King Edward III. According to one account of the order's creation, a lady's garter slipped down at a royal ball, causing ribald laughter among the men and greatly embarrassing the lady. The king at once picked up the garter and silenced the mockery by declaring chivalrously in French: "Honi soit qui mal y pense"—"Shame on him who thinks ill of it." The phrase is the motto of the order.

MANDARIN SQUARES

Officials in imperial China wore embroidered badges on their robes to indicate rank. Known as "mandarin squares" (buzi), the squares were first introduced by the Ming emperor Hongwu in 1391 and were worn until the end of the monarchy in 1912. Different offices were symbolized by various auspicious creatures: thus the highest ranking civil officials wore a crane (above), a highly favorable creature representing wisdom, longevity and venerability. The most senior military officials wore the qilin, a horned beast that denoted protection.

CAP

Caps may be awarded as marks of rank, honor or achievement. Sports players chosen for national teams may be awarded a cap bearing the team colors or emblem, and being "capped" is considered a high honor. More formal caps are worn as emblems of high office. The scarlet biretta of a cardinal is called a cap, as is the mortarboard worn by academics on formal occasions. A "Cap of Maintenance" is borne before British sovereigns at their coronation as a sign of authority.

DUNCE'S CAP

A pointed, conical cap, once believed to enhance the power of thought, was associated with the medieval theologian Duns Scotus. In the Reformation his name became a byword for outmoded ideas, and so the "Duns" or "Dunce" cap was a symbol of stupidity and regressive thought.

MITER

The episcopal miter is pointed with an open cleft at the top and may be richly embroidered, often with a cross. It is preeminently the formal headgear of abbots and bishops, including archbishops and cardinals. In art, St. Bernard may be identified by three miters on the ground, alluding to the legend that he refused a bishopric three times.

PHARAOH'S CROWNS

The pharaoh wore two distinctive crowns in his role as "Lord of the Two Lands" of Upper and Lower Egypt. The *hedjet*, or white crown, of Upper Egypt and the *deshret*, or red crown, of Lower Egypt (above) were worn individually and also combined as a single crown, the *pschent*, to represent the whole kingdom. For certain rituals he wore a plumed crown, the *atef*, associated with the god Osiris, or the blue and gold *khepresh*, or "war crown". Often, he is also depicted wearing the *nemes*, a headcloth of blue and gold stripes. All these crowns bore the uraeus, the golden image of a rearing cobra-goddess, said to protect the pharaoh by spitting venom into the face of his enemies.

CAP OF LIBERTY

(*right*) The Phrygian cap was first worn by freedmen of ancient Phrygia in Asia Minor. Dyed red to suggest sacrificial endeavor, this felt cap was worn in the French Revolution to symbolize the struggle for liberty and the downfall of monarchical tyranny. It is an attribute of "Marianne", the female personification of the French Republic.

musical instruments

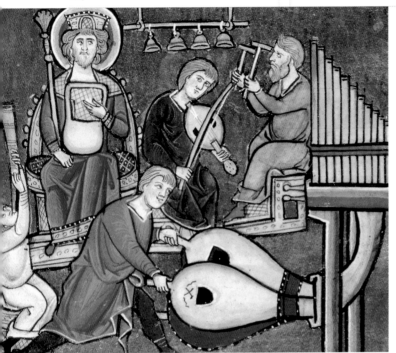

The materials, shapes and sounds of musical instruments have provided a rich source of symbolism since simple animal-bone flutes were first used thousands of years ago. Depictions of revelry on Egyptian sarcophaguses imply that their music was believed to contain sexual energy and played a ritual role in the passage to the afterlife. Chinese musical instruments are classified by the eight materials of their design (wood, stone, hide and so on); many are held to imitate the sounds of nature and are therefore associated with those elements. In early Christian and medieval art, instruments symbolized key events and human attributes: thus, angels announce the Last Judgment with trumpets, and serenade the blessed in heaven with harps and lutes, while St. Paul famously likened a Christian without love to a mere "resounding gong or clanging cymbal" (1 Corinthians 13.1), suggesting hollow insincerity. To thinkers of the Renaissance, the contours of stringed instruments suggested body shapes, as reflected in terms such as ribs, neck and waist.

The association of musical instruments with eternal values was important in the East. Tibetan Buddhists use a handbell to signify the clarity of supreme insight into the emptiness of all things.

TAMBOURINE
An instrument of percussive joyousness, the tambourine is an instrument used in celebration and rituals associated with happiness. In the Bible, triumphal processions, typically after a victorious battle, are led by women playing tambourines, and tambourines appear in Egyptian depictions of feasts and afterlife rituals.

SISTRUM
The sistrum, a kind of rattle, was associated with Hathor, the maternal Egyptian goddess of love, music and dancing, and it was played in rituals to generate a happy mood. When Hathor's cult was subsumed into that of Isis, the instrument became an attribute of that goddess, too. In ancient Israel it was played to accompany dances.

BAGPIPE
Bagpipes are folk instruments in several parts of Europe and beyond. In the margins of medieval manuscripts depictions of grotesque peasants playing bagpipes symbolized rural society's coarseness when compared with the life of the cloister, town or palace. In modern times bagpipes may be symbols of national self-determination, most notably among the Scots.

FLUTE
The fife or piccolo, types of small flute, often accompany the drums of war, their high pitch designed to be audible above the clamor of battle. The Hindu god Krishna is by tradition a master of the flute, which he is depicted playing (above) as he cavorts with dairymaids, or *gopis*, including his beloved Radha. In Mozart's opera *The Magic Flute*, the playing of the instrument has Masonic ritual symbolism.

HARP & LYRE

The lyre and its relative the harp are among the oldest of all instruments—a sumerian relief of ca. 2500BCE depicts a lyre—and numerous legends attest to their power. According to Greek mythology, the lyre was invented by Hermes (Mercury), who stretched strings over the empty shell of a turtle. However, Mercury was forced to give up the instrument to Apollo as punishment for stealing his cattle, and in classical culture the lyre-bearing Apollo (right) is the god of music and artistic inspiration. He was the leader of the nine Muses, from whom the word "music" derives. The lyre was designed to accompany song, and its greatest exponent in classical myth was Orpheus, whose playing beguiled Hades into releasing Orpheus' wife Eurydice from the underworld. Christ was sometimes depicted as Orpheus with his lyre, surrounded by creatures (Christ's followers) enraptured by his song (the gospel message).

PAN PIPES

The pan pipes (or syrinx) were played by shepherds in Greek mythology. Named after the mischievous Greco-Roman nature god Pan, the instrument was associated with vice and guile. Pan taught Daphnis, the originator of bucolic poetry, to woo the nymph Chloe with pan pipes. Also in a pastoral setting, the Renaissance paintings of the Adoration of the Shepherds show them playing pipe to the infant Christ. A similar instrument is popular in the folk music of Andean South America.

TRUMPET

The traditional role of the trumpet was to herald or proclaim the presence of royalty and sound the start of battle, notably through a cavalry charge. In a religious context it was associated with divine aid, victory and salvation. In the Old Testament, trumpet calls announced the presence of God. Thus in the Israelite conquest of Canaan, trumpets signaled divine approval of the fall of Jericho (Joshua 6). The sound of the divine or angelic trumpet is said to herald the Last Judgment. Renaissance painters used a trumpet as an attribute of Fame (right).

CYMBALS

A common instrument of triumph, a pair of brass or bronze cymbals were used in ancient Jewish ceremonies to accompany the Psalmist in songs of praise. However, in the Christian church, cymbals were associated with hell and were prohibited. Small finger-cymbals (*tingsha*) feature in Tibetan Buddhist rites.

ORGAN

Dubbed the "Queen of Instruments", the organ is widely used in churches, its sound a fitting symbol of divine majesty. The composer J.S. Bach (1685–1750) filled his many organ works with sacred symbolism. One example, "St. Anne", has three fugues denoting the elements of the Trinity.

VIOLIN

The resemblance of its curved body to the female form has meant the violin has been traditionally regarded as a "feminine" instrument.

MUSES

In Greek mythology the Muses were divine nymphs, followers of Apollo and the source of creative inspiration. In art they may be identified by their instruments, though these can vary: Euterpe, music and lyric poetry, double flute or trumpet; Thalia, comedy and pastoral poetry, violin; Melpomene, tragedy, horn; Terpsichore, song and dance, lyre, harp or violin; Erato, lyric and love poetry, tambourine, lyre or triangle; Calliope, epic poetry, trumpet; Polyhymnia, heroic hymns, portable organ or lute.

DRUM

An ancient instrument, the drum is widely used in sacred rituals. For Native Americans, the drum symbolizes the cosmos, the round arch of the heavens and the inseparable unity of past, present and future; its beating represents the human pulse and the eternal rhythms of nature. The drum beats time for warriors who are heading into battle, or it marks the slow solemn rhythms of a funeral procession. In Western art Satan often beats a drum.

SHOFAR

The *shofar*, or ram's horn, was used to rally the Israelites for war or religious ceremony. Thus, it was blown when "Israel transported the ark of the covenant" (1 Chronicles 15.28). It is used in synagogues to announce festivals.

buildings

Buildings have furnished a rich and profound vein of symbolism, ranging from the medieval idea of God as "cosmic architect" to modern-day "firewalls" and "glass ceilings". Few types of edifice are more symbol-rich than those made for worship of the divine. Holy buildings in the various traditions of the world are often deliberately designed to evoke cosmic power. The Egyptians built pyramids and obelisks to reflect the sun god's perfect light, and East Asian Buddhists designed pagodas (left) with diminishing tiers to signify spiritual ascent. The ancient Hebrew tabernacle was the precursor of the Jewish Temple and synagogue, and also the Christian church, and represented the dwelling place of God on Earth. Like other sanctuaries, the tabernacle followed precise geometric dimensions that reflected spiritual progression from the outer world through veiled chambers to the inner sanctum, or "Holy of Holies".

Buildings and the act of construction are central symbols of Freemasonry. One of its main emblems is the pyramid, flat-topped to signify that humankind's work of spiritual ascent is unfinished (see pages 158–159). In psychology, houses and rooms symbolize states of mind that may be revealed in dreams. According to Carl Jung, a house in a dream often symbolizes the self, and any uncomfortable feelings experienced in it, such as the reluctance to enter certain rooms, suggests repressed emotion in one's waking life.

BRIDGE

The bridge is a common symbol of passing from one state of being to another. Journeys of initiation into Chinese secret societies were made by crossing a series of bridges. The difficulty of entering into the blissful afterlife is symbolized in Islam by the Bridge of Paradise, which is only as wide as a hair. The pope is the "Pontifex Maximus", a title originally borne by Roman rulers that means "Greatest Bridge-Builder", symbolizing the emperor's role as high priest and chief intermediary between the gods and humankind.

DOOR

Both literally and symbolically a door may denote the threshold between the outer world and a holy inner place. Christ is described as "the door" (John 10.9) to salvation. A door was also an alchemical symbol of transition.

WINDOW

Windows signify receptivity to enlightenment and wisdom. A round window can represent the eye and consciousness, especially at the top of a tower, analogous to the head of a person.

DOME

A universal symbol for the vault of heaven. Mosques have domes because the Prophet Muhammad described a heavenly vision of a mother-of-pearl dome on four pillars. The first Buddhist *stupas*, memorial shrines for relics of the Buddha and other elders, took the form of a round dome on a square base, symbolizing Earth and heavens (dome).

PILLAR

As essential supportive structures, pillars or columns stand for stability and strength, and by extension for the upholding of the established order, hence referring to a person as a "pillar of society". Egyptian obelisks (right) glorified the sun god Ra and the pharaoh, the "son of Ra". Monuments such as the victory columns of Roman emperors bear an obvious (phallic) symbolism of male prowess. The "Pillars of Hercules" was the Classical name given to the Strait of Gibraltar at the mouth of the Mediterranean Sea.

STAIRS

In leading to a higher or lower plane, stairs or steps stand for the ascent of the soul to knowledge of the divine, or descent to the depths of the unconscious and realm of the occult. The spiral staircase can represent a person's dependence on an abiding principle such as God or love, symbolized by the central post. (See also **LADDER**, page 136.)

TOWER

The tower is a common symbol of the folly of human aspirations, most famously in the biblical account of the Tower of Babel in the Book of Genesis. The tower, built in a bid to reach heaven itself, was doomed to failure. Towers are also symbols of watchfulness, especially in a religious sense of guarding against impending doom or judgment. In psychoanalytical symbolism, the tower represents the erect phallus: the motif of the hero saving a maiden from a tower is seen as a metaphor for sexual maturity.

THE HOUSE OF GOD

secular Roman **BASILICAS**—large rectangular public halls—were the model of many early churches. The main hall became the **NAVE**, from Latin *navis*, "ship", symbolizing the church as a vessel of safe souls; and the place at the far end of the hall, where Roman judges once sat, became the **SANCTUARY** (chancel and apse). Here stand the **ALTAR** symbolizing God's presence and, in a cathedral, the bishop's **THRONE** (*cathedra*). The basic ground plan often forms the shape of a **CROSS**, with two areas called **TRANSEPTS** projecting from the nave. A **DOME** over the crossing symbolizes the vault of **HEAVEN**. The main nave was literally "oriented", with the altar in the orient, or **EAST**, the rising **SUN**, symbolizing resurrection. Church furnishings may be rich in symbolism: thus, the lectern often bears an **EAGLE**, emblem of St. John and his gospel.

DIVINE MOUNTAIN

The conical towers of some Hindu temples represent the homes of the gods, cosmic mountains such as Mount Kailash, or Meru, which is Shiva's residence and the navel of the world.

KIVA

Circular or oval in shape, *kiva*s are partly subterranean ritual chambers of the Hopi and Pueblo peoples. A *kiva* usually has a central recess to symbolize the point at which the first humans emerged from the underworld.

MIHRAB

Perhaps the most important feature of a mosque is the *mihrab*, or prayer niche, which indicates the *qibla*, or direction of Mecca, toward which all Muslims must direct their prayers.

KUMBUM

The fifteenth-century Kumbum temple at Gyantse monastery, Tibet, is a three-dimensional form of *mandala*, a Buddhist sacred cosmic diagram. It takes the form of a stepped pyramid topped by a round drum and conical spire, symbolizing the journey from Earth to the spiritual world and ultimate enlightenment. Denotes any vision of radical social renewal.

NEW JERUSALEM

The New Testament prophesies a celestial city descending to Earth as the "New Jerusalem", a perfect society over which Christ will rule (Revelation 21). By extension, it denotes any vision of radical social renewal.

FREEMASONRY

Known to its members as the Craft, Freemasonry is an all-male fraternal society with branches, or "lodges", worldwide. Its activities—setting aside popular conspiracy theories—center on belief in a Deity, the support of its members, probity in professional and private life, and charitable works. Its deep roots lie in the medieval guilds of stonemasons who created the most important buildings of the age: the great cathedrals. The professional masons saw themselves as undertaking, quite literally, the work of God, and as the successors of Hiram of Tyre and others who built and furnished King Solomon's Temple in Jerusalem, as described in 1 Kings 6–8.

The more recent origins of Freemasonry lie in Britain in the years around 1600. Its precise relationship to existing stonemasons' guilds is unclear, and in any case it was soon open to men from other professions. In Freemasonry, rather like alchemy, the true labor is not physical but spiritual: to turn the rough stone of the soul into a cut and dressed ashlar, to build in oneself a perfect Temple of the spirit, just as the masons

of antiquity built the Temple of the Lord. Building the Temple is the central metaphor of Freemasonry. Tools of the stonemason's trade, such as the square and compasses, are important symbols (above and opposite). Freemasons rise through three Degrees from Entered Apprentice to Master. Initiation into each Degree takes place in symbolic rituals, details of which are kept secret both from outsiders and members of lower Degrees.

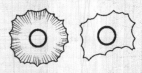

SUN & MOON Like the checkerboard pavement, sun and moon represent cosmic dualities: dark and light, positive and negative. Lunar and solar cycles are also important in Freemasonry.

INFINITY KNOT A symbol of eternity and of the eternal Creator, and also of the bonds binding the Brotherhood of Masons.

GAVEL & CHISEL The gavel, or hammer, and chisel are the basic tools for turning the raw stone of the soul into the perfect dressed block that can form part of the New Temple.

MASONRY & THE FOUNDING FATHERS

The first lodge in America was founded in 1733. George Washington was a Mason, as was Benjamin Franklin, and much speculation has surrounded the extent to which Freemasonry influenced the founding of the United States. Some symbols adopted by the new republic were highly familiar to Masons. Perhaps it is best to conclude that certain Masonic symbols of the striving of a common Brotherhood before God were readily adaptable to the aspirations of the Founding Fathers. Among the most striking is found on the reverse of the **GREAT SEAL OF THE UNITED STATES** (right, on a dollar bill). It shows the **UNFINISHED PYRAMID**, above which shines the all-seeing **EYE OF PROVIDENCE** (see opposite page). In Freemasonry the pyramid (left) denotes striving toward building the perfected self and the creation of the **NEW JERUSALEM**, a new ideal society. Hence the motto on the Great Seal: *Novus ordo seclorum*, "A new order of the ages".

BIB The turned-down bib of this nineteenth-century French leather apron indicates that its wearer was a Master Mason.

BEE HIVE Like the apron itself, the hive and swarm of bees are emblems of the Masonic ideals of work and industriousness.

ALL-SEEING EYE The Eye of Providence, or Eye of God, radiates from a triangle symbolizing the Holy Trinity and divine knowledge and enlightenment.

SWORD & RULE The sword represents truth and the mason's rule fair measure. Other tools depicted include the triangle and level.

THE TEMPLE A key Masonic idea is building the New Temple, both the ideal self and center of the New Jerusalem or perfect society of justice and harmony.

SQUARE & COMPASSES These denote a correctly lived life, using discrimination and judgment. Masons meet "on the square", which implies acting honorably.

TWO COLUMNS Two bronze pillars, named Jachin and Boaz, flanked the porch of Solomon's Temple. They are said to denote the male and female principles.

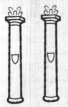

SEVEN STEPS A mystic number of spiritual ascent. The upper steps denote the Degrees of Entered Apprentice, Fellow Mason and Master Mason.

MYTHS

AN ATTEMPT TO COMPREHEND THE UNIVERSE AND THE HUMAN CONDITION, MYTHS TACKLE THEMES INCLUDING THE ORIGIN OF THE COSMOS; BIRTH AND DEATH; AND JEALOUSY AND BETRAYAL. OFTEN VERY ANCIENT, THESE POWERFUL PRODUCTS OF THE HUMAN IMAGINATION REMAIN A RICH SOURCE OF SYMBOLISM.

CREATION

The puzzle of how the universe came into being is central to most creation myths. A primeval watery mass or a dark void, holding the potential of all existence, are common themes, while elemental forces are often personified as cosmic giants.

DUALITY
In many creation myths time begins when One becomes Two, a process of order emerging from chaos. This accounts for primal dualities: male/female, light/dark, sky/Earth. Thus, in Maori myth the first being divides into the male sky (Rangi) and female Earth (Papa) (above).

COSMIC CYCLES
Primal energy, as an uncontrollable force, is both creative and destructive. An extension of this is the cyclical nature of the universe. Worlds are perpetually brought into being, ended and recreated. Tibetan Buddhists depict the endless cycle of becoming as the "Wheel of Life" (above).

COSMIC SERPENT
In many ancient cultures the serpent was believed to be androgynous and so is a common emblem of the self-creating deity. It is the primordial ocean out of which all becomes, and to which all returns. It is raw nature, the animating spirit that generates power in the earth. From the cosmic serpent comes all procreative life and fertility. The coiled serpent is a symbol of latent power. In Egypt, the serpent Apep symbolized primeval chaos. It lived in the underworld (see page 172), where it had to be destroyed every night so that order could return each day. (See also page 83.)

CHURNING THE OCEAN
Hindu myth describes how the gods and lesser gods uproot a sacred mountain, Mandara, wind the cosmic snake Vasuki around it, pull on each end of the snake to churn up the primordial sea. This produces the sun, moon, other features of the cosmos, and finally the elixir of immortality.

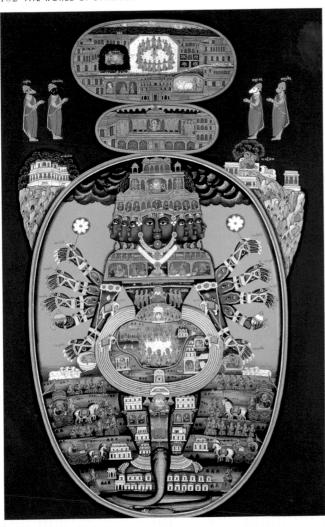

COSMIC EGG

Found as far apart as West Africa, Egypt, India, China and Oceania is the striking concept that creation began when a **COSMIC EGG** was produced out of a formless void. The egg contains all creation, which begins when the egg breaks open. Some cultures claimed that the egg was fertilized by a **SERPENT**, others that a giant **BIRD** laid the egg in the primeval **OCEAN**. Both versions occur in the myths of the Egyptian god **AMUN**. In one account, the snake form of the god was the first being in the primeval waters, where it fertilized the cosmic egg; in another, Amun took the form of a **GOOSE** to lay the egg from which all life was born. For the Dogon of Mali, a vibration set up by the creator god **AMMA** cracks the egg to release the divinities order and chaos. In Chinese myth, the egg contains **PAN GU** (see above right).

GENESIS

In the Bible, creation is not the result of divine conflict but an ordered process over the course of six days. On the first day God divides light from darkness; on the second, he divides the waters above and below the firmament (heaven). The rest of creation follows over the next four days, crowned by the creation of humankind. The account draws upon ancient Middle Eastern mythological traditions and, rather than offering a literal scientific explanation of how the universe began, aims primarily to glorify God's greatness and majesty.

PAN GU

In Chinese mythology, the divine ancestor of all things was Pan Gu, a cosmic giant who grew for 18,000 years inside a cosmic egg before bursting out and splitting the egg in two parts: light (*yang*), representing the heavens, and darkness (*yin*), representing Earth. After another 18,000 years Pan Gu lay down and died, and parts of his body mutated into features of the heavens and the landscape: Pan Gu's eyes became the sun and moon, his hair and beard the stars, his breath the wind and cloud, and his voice thunder.

NUN

In Egyptian mythology the world was created, according to some accounts, when a mound of land arose from Nun, the watery abyss, at the beginning of time. The mound, which was symbolized in pyramidal form, provided a perch on which the Benu bird, a manifestation of the sun god, could alight, symbolizing the dawn of the world. The Benu is often depicted as a grey heron (above).

DRAGON OF THE WATERS

The depiction of a primordial power-struggle in the early Babylonian creation epic was highly influential in the ancient Middle East. In it, the primordial waters of wisdom and the blind forces of chaos are personified in the form of the female dragon Tiamat. Marduk, as champion of the gods, slays Tiamat by cutting her body in two, one part forming the sky, the other the Earth.

DREAMTIME

Australian Aboriginal myth tells of a primordial period known as the DREAMTIME, during which ancestral heroes in human and animal form traveled across Australia creating the features of the landscape and the laws by which people lived. However, Dreamtime also represents a state of being that can be accessed in the present through ritual. Participants in rites believe that they temporarily become their ancestors, and can draw upon their power by recalling the primordial events and by striking sacred sites linked with the ancestors, such as ULURU (see page 108). Death and mortality is commonly explained as the consequence of human wrongdoing. Their ancestors had the chance of immortality, but even they failed to lead perfect lives.

THE GREAT SERPENT

(*above*) The concept of the serpent as a prime force in creation is important in African mythology. The Fon people of Benin describe the creative power of the bisexual deity Mawu-Lisa as flowing in the form of a great snake, Da Ayido Hwedo. This power, also in the rainbow and all water, is coiled around the Earth, holding it together.

YMIR

(*right*) Norse mythology symbolizes the primeval forces of creation as a giant, Ymir. As in the similar Chinese and Indian accounts of Pan Gu and Purusha, the violence of creation is represented in the giant's dismemberment: in this case the giant's body represents the Earth, his skull the sky and his blood the sea.

BATTLES OF THE GIANTS

Cosmic battles involving primordial giants are sometimes interpreted as symbols of the struggle for social evolution against the disruptive forces of anarchy. Greek myth recounts that the Olympian gods led by Zeus fought both the giants and the Titans for dominance.

OMETECUHTLI

For the Aztecs, Ometecuhtli was the self-created, dual-gendered primordial cosmic being. From this being all the other gods were produced.

PURUSHA

In Hindu tradition the sacrificed body of Purusha, a primordial giant, is the source of the cosmos and all gods and creatures. For Hindus it is vital for the maintenance of the universe to continue making ritual sacrifices as a reenactment of the giant's cosmic sacrifice.

EARTH DIVER

Native American myths recount how the first land was brought up from the bottom of the primordial ocean by a creature that lived in the waters. In the Cheyenne account, the deity Maheo ("All Spirit") made the great waters and all the birds and water creatures. But the birds grew tired and took turns to dive for land. Finally, Coot brought up a little soil that grew in Maheo's hand. Soon only Grandmother Turtle had the stamina to carry the soil on her back, where it grew and grew to make the dry land. (See also page 83.)

SEAS OF HEAVEN & EARTH

In the Islamic creation account, the original one primordial ocean separates into the higher and lower waters: the fresh, sweet sea of heaven, and the salty, bitter waters of Earth.

the flood

Cataclysmic floods that wipe out humanity are common to the mythology of many peoples. Often the deluge is divine punishment for humanity's misdeeds. The event is generally an act of renewal: whatever its cause, the flood signifies not so much an ending as a new beginning: the establishment of a reformed and wiser human society, and a restored covenant with heaven.

The best-known flood story is the biblical account of Noah, a virtuous man who alone is forewarned by God and survives by building a ship, or ark, in which he and his family keep pairs of every animal species that will be used to repopulate the Earth. This theme of one man's, or one couple's, survival of a cosmic deluge has roots in ancient Mesopotamian myth (see box opposite) and also finds echoes in other cultures. The Greeks told of the gods flooding the world in a catastrophe that only Deucalion and his wife Pyrrha survived. In Hindu myth, the first man, Manu, likewise survives a flood by building a ship. Often the one chosen to survive is semidivine or, like Noah, of great virtue.

NOAH'S ARK

(*right*) This Islamic painting depicts the prophet Nuh (Noah) in his ark as described in the Quran. In Genesis 6, however, the ark is a rectangular vessel, which recalls the cubic ark of Utnapishtim in the Epic of Gilgamesh (see box opposite). As the vessel of divine protection it is more symbolic of the cosmos than of a real ship.

MANU

In Hindu myth, Manu, the first man, rescues a small golden fish that grows to enormous size, then he releases it into the sea. Later the fish, Matsya, warns Manu of a deluge, and tells him to build a boat and stock it with the seed of all things. When the flood comes, the boat is pulled to safety by Matsya, which turns out to be the first avatar of the god Vishnu (left), who appears whenever the world is in danger.

DEUCALION & PYRRHA

In Greek myth, the Titan Prometheus warns his son Deucalion of a flood. He and his wife Pyrrha build a boat and survive. After the flood the oracle at Delphi tells them to throw behind them the bones of Gaia, the Earth. The "bones" are rocks: those that Deucalion throws become men, those thrown by Pyrrha, women: this recreation of humans by humans symbolizes the autonomy of humankind.

ATLANTIS

The Greek philosopher Plato wrote that the continent of Atlantis was a flourishing island kingdom beyond the Pillars of Hercules (Strait of Gibraltar) that was suddenly destroyed by the sea in a single day and night. For Plato the tale of Atlantis was a metaphor for the transience and uncertainty of the world in which we live. The mythical place, which may have roots in the destruction of the volcanic Mediterranean island of Thera, became a symbol of a lost utopia, or of the ideal benevolent society, as in *The New Atlantis* by Francis Bacon (1627).

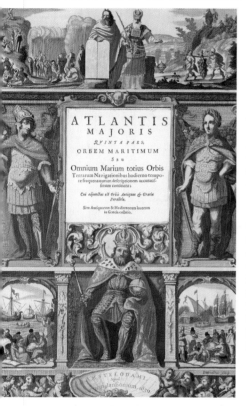

THE BABYLONIAN FLOOD

The flood myths of ancient Mesopotamia predate the biblical account of NOAH and probably reflect the unpredictable deluges of the Euphrates and Tigris rivers. These versions are strikingly similar to the Bible in their broad outline, the main difference being that the one biblical GOD becomes the several gods of Mesopotamia. In each, heaven is angry with humanity and seeks to destroy it, but ultimately offers it a second chance on account of one man's virtue and piety. The Sumerian story of ZIUSUDRA is the oldest, but it is very fragmentary. Utnapishtim's tale is in the EPIC OF GILGAMESH, one of the oldest works of literature (ca. 2000BCE).

The fullest story is that of ATRAHASIS. Humans are created to serve heaven, but the gods cannot bear their noise, so ENLIL sends several calamities to destroy them, ending in a flood. The wise god ENKI (below, far right) forewarns the pious king Atrahasis, who builds a boat in which he, his family and various animals survive. The other gods cannot manage without human labor and after seven days the flood recedes and Atrahasis, like Noah, makes a sacrifice to heaven. Enlil agrees not to destroy humanity, only to limit its numbers. To reward his piety, Atrahasis is made immortal and placed among the gods.

FIVE SUNS

(*left*) Aztec cosmology told of Five Suns representing five successive world eras. Confrontations between the gods led to cosmic struggles that led to the destruction of each era and the establishment of the next. The current era, the Fifth Sun, arose after the end of the Fourth Sun when a great flood transformed the people into fish.

GOURD CHILDREN

According to the Maio and Yao peoples of south China, the thunder god caused a flood that destroyed humanity except for two children, who hid inside a gourd. They later repopulated the Earth. The myth draws upon the fertility symbolism of the gourd, which derives from its abundance of seeds.

FINTAN THE WISE

Irish myth adapts the biblical flood story in a distinctly Celtic manner, introducing the element of magical transformation. It is said that before the coming of the Gaels, there were five waves of earlier settlers in Ireland. The first were led by Cessair, daughter of Bith, son of Noah, who arrived forty days before the Flood. The cataclysm wiped out all Cessair's folk save for Fintan Mac Biochra, who survived by transforming into a creature. He lived for 5,500 years as a salmon, an eagle and a hawk, and after returning to human form he was able to give an account of all the events of the time of the Flood to the people who came after.

sacrifice

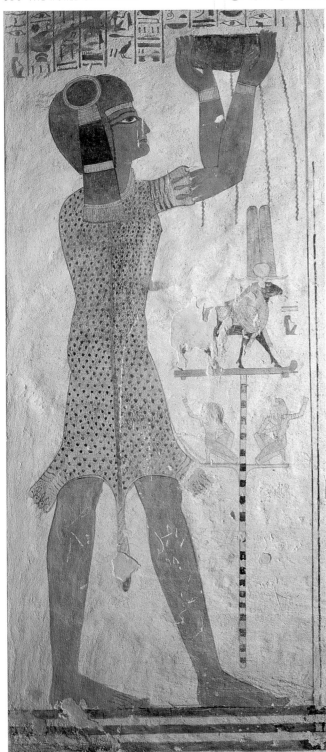

The idea of offering up something of supreme value to the divine as a symbol of obedience, repentance or love features in many myths. Generally, the higher the value of the sacrifice, the greater the divine favor in return, and one common theme is that of sacrificing an only son or daughter. In Christian tradition this is supremely exemplified in the idea of Jesus as the sacrificial Lamb of God (see box). To offer something as a gift to the gods or to God is to render it holy—"making holy" is the literal meaning of "sacrifice"—and separate it from the profane world. In biblical Judaism the sacrifice made by Noah after the Flood was a burnt offering (literally "burnt whole"—in Greek *holos kaustos*), which rose to God in the form of its pleasing aroma. (The term Holocaust was transferred to the mass murder of the Jews by the Nazis, seen as the cataclysmic sacrifice of an entire people.)

The need felt by ancient societies to elaborate a ritual system of sacrifice indicates the ambiguity with which humanity perceives its place in the universe, in its propensity both to distance itself from, and to seek a closer approach to, the divine. At the same time as embodying a sacred "otherness", the sacrificial act unites the sacrificed and sacrificer in a cosmic oneness.

SCAPEGOAT

(*below*) In several ancient traditions a substitute sacrifice for a king was offered in order to appease the gods. In Hebrew tradition, the sins of the community are confessed and symbolically transferred to a "scapegoat", a goat that was allowed to escape into the desert to die. This custom became ritualized as a Jewish ceremony held to mark Yom Kippur, the Day of Atonement.

ABRAHAM & ISAAC

In Genesis 22, God commands the patriarch Abraham, in order to test his faith, to sacrifice his only son Isaac. At the last moment, an angel appears and shows Abraham a ram caught in a thorn bush, which he sacrifices instead. For Muslims, the Dome of the Rock in Jerusalem marks the place of the event (above). The episode symbolizes selfless devotion to God; for Christians it prefigures the Crucifixion, the sacrifice of Jesus, who then returns to life.

AZTEC SACRIFICE

The Aztecs believed that the continuity of the world could only be guaranteed with a regular and plentiful sacrifice of human victims to the sun god, who was seen to bathe in "blood" every night at sunset. Elaborate ceremonies were staged in which the victims were bathed and finally killed at the top of the sun god's temple with a sharp flint knife, with which the priest (above, right) would cut out the still beating heart. The body was then dismembered.

SATI

In the historic Hindu custom, now outlawed in India, known as *sati*, or suttee, widows would be burned on the funeral pyres of their late husbands, sometimes by force. The act symbolized the devotion of the goddess Sati, who immolated herself after her father humiliated her husband Shiva. The idea that the widow should be sacrificed to serve her husband in the afterlife was also known, though not regularly enacted, in Egypt, Greece and Scythia.

IPHIGENIA

Ambition so ruthless that it overrides even the love of a father for his child is the potent message behind the myth of Agamemnon's sacrifice of Iphigeneia. In a blood bargain with the gods, the leader of the Greek force against the Trojans took the most beautiful of his daughters to the sacrificial stone in return for a favorable wind for his battle fleet. In one version, Iphigeneia was saved by Artemis, goddess of the hunt, and became her priestess.

CHRIST THE LAMB

In the New Testament, the death of **CHRIST** is regarded as a sacrifice for sin. He is described as the **LAMB OF GOD** that takes away the sins of the world (John 1.29), following the Jewish idea of sacrificing the paschal lamb at **PASSOVER**. Christ's **BLOOD** is said to have cleansed humankind of the sinfulness instituted by the disobedience of **ADAM**. The blood is represented by the **WINE** of the **EUCHARIST**, or **LORD'S SUPPER**, the prime rite of the Christian church. By drinking the communion wine, Christians believe they are partaking of the redemption and future resurrection to eternal life brought by Christ, the "true **VINE**". Hence in Christian art **GRAPES** symbolize eternal life and resurrection. In medieval Europe, the **PELICAN** was mistakenly said to feed its young with blood drawn from its own breast (above); the bird became another symbol of Christ's sacrifice.

HORSE SACRIFICE

The ancient high kings of Ireland began their reigns with a ritual bath in a broth made from the flesh of a sacrificed horse. The act symbolically imbued the king with the strength, speed and virility of the horse.

MITHRA

Mithra was the Persian god of war, justice and the sun. In the Roman empire he became the focus of Mithraism, a mystery cult centered on the sacrifice of a bull as an act of renewing creation and bestowing immortality—hence the cult's appeal to Roman soldiers, who might face death in combat. Followers of Carl Jung interpreted the slaying of the bull as symbolizing the victory of man's spiritual nature over his bestial side.

MOUNT TAI

Five sacred mountains are revered in China, corresponding to the cardinal directions plus the mystic center. The most sacred is Mount Tai, on which emperors performed sacrifices to heaven. The mountain is linked with sunrise, birth and renewal.

ODIN THE DIVINER

The ruler of the Norse gods, Odin lived in Valhalla (see page 171) among fallen heroes. He sacrificed an eye to gain secret knowledge of runes, mystical symbols used in divination. Prisoners taken in battle were sacrificed to Odin, whose priests divined future success in battle.

CHRISTIANITY

There are many Christian denominations, but most share the belief that God is a triune ("three-in-one") deity, consisting of three "persons": Father, Son and Holy Spirit. God became incarnate in the form of Jesus of Nazareth, his son, who was conceived by a virgin, Mary, through the Holy Spirit. At once fully divine and fully human, for Christians Jesus was the Messiah, the savior and redeemer of humanity, and his appearance was the key event in human history. Jesus died on the cross (ca. 30CE) but Christians believe that he was physically resurrected from the dead, and that through him all the faithful will also be resurrected to eternal life at the end of time.

Over two millennia Christian artists and artisans have employed and generated a vast symbolic repertory. The central Christian symbol is the cross, which comes in many forms (see pages 132–133) and represents Christ himself, his redeeming sacrifice and his promise of resurrection to eternal life for all believers. However, the cross became widespread as a symbol only after the Roman empire abolished crucifixion early in the fourth century. Before then, many Christians were reluctant to associate Jesus with the bandits, rebels and criminals for whom the shameful penalty of crucifixion was usually reserved. Indeed, pagans sometimes used the cross to taunt Christians that their Lord was a common felon. As memories of the penalty faded, the use of the cross increased.

Among the earliest Christian symbols were the chi-rho monogram (see opposite) and the image of a fish, denoting Jesus as the "Fisher of Men" and his followers as *pisciculi* or little fish. Christ was also portrayed as the sacrificial Passover "Lamb of God", and as the "Good Shepherd" of his flock.

PELICAN A popular medieval symbol of Christ's divine, self-sacrificial love, often known as the pelican-in-her-piety—who dies so that her young may live. (See also page 167.)

CUP OF SACRIFICE The chalice is the wine cup of the Last Supper and of the Christian rite of Eucharist (holy communion), holding the "blood of Christ". Above it is the host, or eucharistic bread, "the body of Christ".

HALOES

In christian art a holy figure is commonly denoted by a circle of light known as a **HALO**, or **NIMBUS**, radiating from their head. christians probably adopted the halo from depictions of greco-roman rulers and gods. To begin with it was principally a symbol of power, and hence the halo was originally (from ca. 400CE) confined to depictions of the **TRINITY** (father, son, holy spirit) and **ANGELS**. As it evolved into a general symbol of holiness, its use was extended to **SAINTS**. christ, and sometimes **GOD THE FATHER** and holy spirit, may have a special halo that includes the **CROSS** (see christ, right). god may also have a triangular halo denoting the Trinity. The **AUREOLE** is a halo around the whole figure. It is especially linked with jesus (above) and the **VIRGIN MARY**, and is also commonly found in the stylized almond shape known as a **MANDORLA**.

GRAPEVINE

The grapevine became a common Christian symbol of spiritual and physical resurrection. Jesus says "I am the true vine" (John 15.1); he rose from the dead as "the first fruits of those who have died" (1 Cor. 15.20). Jesus (and then the Church) being the vine, the true believers are its branches. In the Eucharist, believers partake of wine, the "blood of Christ". A cluster of grapes may also represent the Promised Land.

KEYS OF PETER

Christian saints can often be recognized by their specific symbols. Peter carries the "keys of the kingdom of heaven" conferred on him by Christ (Matt. 16.19), marking him out as "prince of the apostles". Crossed keys are a symbol of the papacy, which claims Peter as the first pope. Uncrossed, "the office of the keys" represents the authority Christ gave to forgive the sins of those who repent.

HAND OF GOD
The hand emerging from heaven is a symbol of God the Father. Alpha and omega (AΩ), the first and last letters of the Greek alphabet, denote God as the beginning and end of all things (Revelation 22.13).

CROWN OF VICTORY
Symbolizing divine sovereignty and Christ's triumph over death, it is flanked by the nails and scourge of the Passion (his suffering that ended in death on the cross).

CHI-RHO
The letters X (chi=kh) and P (rho=r), begin the name Christ in Greek. The chi-rho monogram was a common symbol in early Christianity.

TITULUM
The letters INRI stand for *Iesus Nazarenus Rex Iudaeorum* (Jesus of Nazareth, King of the Jews). Placed above the cross, the *titulum*, or title, was intended to be sarcastic, but for Christians it was Truth.

death & the afterlife

Most cultures have represented in rich symbolic terms their beliefs surrounding death and what happens afterward. For many, the dead transfer to heaven, often a place above the vault of the sky or beyond the seas; or it may be a more ambiguous location, a present but invisible terrain where the dead live in a sort of parallel world, represented as an earthly ideal such as a beautiful garden with evocative scents, flowers and "birds of paradise". The Duat, for example, was a perfected Egypt, with a great river, symbolic of the Nile, and plentiful fields of crops on each bank. The idea of sacred enclosure is also represented by the notion of paradise as an enchanted island, an ultimate sanctuary: the Green Isle of Ireland, Apollo's Island of the Blessed, the Avalon of Arthurian legend and the Eastern Isles of the Chinese Immortals. Paradise is sometimes a haven for the elite; for example, Valhalla was reserved for the bravest Norse warriors, the Elysian Fields for Classical heroes (see below).

It is a widespread idea that humankind once existed ordinarily within such a pleasant and perfect world, only to err and be divinely punished with the experience of an imperfect life on Earth. Thus, ideas of an afterlife heaven in which to experience a blissful existence are compensation for the hardships of now. Psychologically there is recompense too, because the dead, unlike the living on Earth, get their just deserts. For the damned the destination is hell, often said to be an underworld fraught with terrors, such as demonic beasts and countless forms of suffering. For the morally virtuous, the heavenly paradise is characterized by harmonious music and light—a place where they can experience eternal contentment and perhaps reunion with their forebears.

GRIM REAPER

(*left*) The Grim Reaper personifies death as a hooded, skeletal figure bearing a scythe, with which he relentlessly harvests souls. He is sinister but not necessarily malign, since death is inevitable; nor is he seen as the cause of death. In art the Reaper is a *memento mori*, a reminder of mortality.

THANATOS

The Greek god of death was the son of Night and Darkness and the twin brother of Hypnos, Sleep. He is depicted as a winged youth (left), because death is always vigorous and active. Thanatos may wear a sword, a natural attribute for someone the eighth-century CE writer Hesiod described as "pitiless as bronze".

DAY OF THE DEAD

A Mexican festival linked to the Catholic All Saints' Day and All Souls' Day (November 1 and 2), the Day of the Dead honors deceased family and friends. Graves are adorned with marigolds, sugar-candy skulls, and the dead's favorite food and drink, in the belief that on this occasion departed souls return to visit the living. The ritual dates back to at least the Aztec period.

VALHALLA

In Norse mythology, Valhalla was Odin's feasting hall and the home of slain warriors in Asgard, the residence of the gods (left). The warriors destined for Valhalla were chosen on the battlefield by goddesses called Valkyries. Within walls made of shields and a roof of spears, the heroes fight each other daily while waiting for Ragnarok, the battle at the end of time (see page 181).

HADES

Hades, literally "the Unseen", was the name of the Greek god of the dead and also his realm. Cold, bleak, dark and haunted by demons, in psychoanalytical terms Hades is the epitome of mental repression. The realm was guarded by the three-headed dog Cerberus, and once a soul was inside there was no escape—though some figures such as Persephone and Orpheus did succeed in leaving. The ferrying of newly deceased souls across the River Styx to Hades symbolizes the passing of the soul from the body to its new state of being.

ELEUSINIAN MYSTERIES

(*left*) Secret rites were held at Eleusis in Greece in honor of Demeter, the goddess of crops and earthly fertility. Initiates took part in such activities as sea-bathing, processions and religious drama in order to attain a happy afterlife. Demeter was the sister of Zeus, the sky god, and Hades, the underworld god, symbolizing the interrelationship of the elements.

ELYSIAN FIELDS

(*right*) One of the realms of the Greek underworld, the Elysian Fields, or Elysium, was a refuge for fallen heroes such as Achilles, the Greek hero of the Trojan War, and Aeneas' father, the Trojan hero Anchises. Some living mortals were permitted to visit Elysium. In Virgil's *Aeneid*, Aeneas entered it and learned the workings of the universe from his father.

ET IN ARCADIA EGO

The nostalgic yearning for a blissful age, especially the carefree days of youth, came to be symbolized by the Latin phrase ET IN ARCADIA EGO, often translated "I too once lived in Arcadia", in which Arcadia (a historic region of Greece), represents a lost pastoral idyll. But in seventeenth-century Italy, when the term was coined, it had a more profound meaning. A more accurate translation is: "Even in Arcadia I (am to be found)". The word "I" means DEATH, and the phrase is therefore a MEMENTO MORI, a reminder that youth, beauty and happiness will not last forever. The phrase is the title of two famous paintings by Nicolas Poussin (1594—1665), who depicted simple shepherds deciphering the inscription on an ancient tomb (above).

TARTAROS

Tartaros was the deep abyss of the Greek underworld, a worse abode even than Hades. It was here that the souls of the most wicked, like Sisyphus (left), suffered eternal torment. Tartaros was depicted as a chamber with bronze walls and gate, and lay so deep that an anvil thrown from heaven would take nine days to reach it.

OSIRIS & HORUS

In Egyptian myth, the god Osiris (left) was the first ruler, but was slain and dismembered by his rival Seth, the god of disorder. At the instigation of Osiris's wife Isis, his body was reassembled and then embalmed by the god Anubis, making Osiris the first mummy. Isis magically revived Osiris for long enough to conceive Horus, who subsequently overthrew Seth. Osiris became the ruler of the underworld (see below), judge of the dead and lord of fertility. Every deceased pharaoh was identified with Osiris, while every living pharaoh personified his son Horus. The two gods' parallel reigns, one over the land of the living, the other over the dead, symbolized stability and the continuity of order.

PURE LANDS

(above) The largest Buddhist tradition in Japan is known as "Pure Land" and is so-called from a western paradise known as Sukhavati or the Pure Land, the realm of the Buddha Amitabha (Amida in Japanese). Originating in China, and found also in Vietnam, the tradition appealed to the poor, who had little time for the intensive meditation necessary to gain enlightenment. Its main belief is that it is possible to be reborn in the Pure Land simply by piously invoking Amida's name. Once they are in Amida's blissful paradise of peace and plenty, his followers will be able to awaken their "Buddha nature" and attain *nirvana*, release from the endless cycle of rebirth.

THE EGYPTIAN AFTERLIFE

The ancient Egyptians had various concepts of the afterlife, which were seen as complementary. Souls might ascend to become one of the eternal stars or join the SUN god RE in his BARQUE OF MILLIONS that traversed the SKY each day and the underworld at night. Or souls might descend directly to the UNDERWORLD to be judged before its ruler, the god OSIRIS. The deceased's HEART was weighed in SCALES against the feather of MA'AT (truth or righteousness). If the scales balanced, the soul was declared blessed and proceeded to DUAT, a paradise that resembled an ideal Egypt (below). But if the heart tipped the scales, it was heavy with sin and was devoured by the monster AMAMET, or AMUT, a personification of hell. This annihilation of the soul was the worst possible fate.

The blessed soul took the form of a BA, a human-headed bird that could flit between Duat and the world of the living. Duat—which was ambivalently located either in the underworld or in the night sky—was inhabited by many fabulous creatures, such as SHABTIS, mummy-figurines buried with the dead that were believed to come alive to act as servants. Malign creatures included the giant serpent APEP. Every night Apep tried to destroy the sun god as he passed in his barque through Duat, but it was always slain by the fierce god SETH, allowing cosmic order to prevail and the sun to rise anew.

INANNA IN THE UNDERWORLD

The Sumerian goddess of sex and fertility was Inanna (the Babylonian Ishtar), who personified the planet Venus. She features in a myth in which she descends to the underworld and is slain, but is then revived and returns to the Earth. Like the Greek myth of Persephone, who descends to Hades but is allowed to return to the Earth for part of the year, the story symbolizes the dying of the vegetation in winter and the revival of life in the spring. More generally it represents the hope of renewed existence in the afterlife.

JOLLY ROGER

"Roger" was slang for a thief, and the term "Jolly Roger" was given to various outlaw flags flown by pirates of the 1600s and 1700s. They were intended to alarm ships into submission without a fight: some flags were plain black, for death (the likely fate of those who resisted), and others the traditional red flag of defiance. The most famous Jolly Roger bore a white skull and crossbones on a black background, and became the "pirate flag" of popular tradition.

PENGLAI

(right) In Daoist myth, immortals inhabit a legendary island in the East China Sea named Penglai. The isle represents a state of bliss and the legendary mushrooms of immortality can be found there. The link between the east and eternal life in Chinese cosmology comes from its association with spring, the season of renewal and vigorous growth.

AGNI

Cremation is a key element in Hindu beliefs about the soul's release at death. When the body is burned it is believed that Agni, the god of fire, carries the soul to a blissful existence in the heavens, from where it will be reincarnated.

CELTIC OTHERWORLD

As the place of the blessed dead, the Celtic otherworld is a land of eternal feasting, joy and youth, like the Irish Tir na n'Og, or Land of Youth. In Arthurian legend, Avalon is the mystical paradise that receives the dying King Arthur. In his twelfth-century account of Arthur, Geoffrey of Monmouth calls Avalon the "Isle of Apples", and apple trees feature in Celtic myth as trees of the otherworld that bear fruit with magical sustaining properties.

SEVENTH HEAVEN

There is an elaborate description of paradise in Muslim tradition: eight gates open to it, and one hundred steps lead through a series of seven levels— the seven heavens. Each is inhabited by different figures in sacred history, but the seventh heaven, the highest, is reserved for God, the highest class of angels and Muhammad. The Kabbalists also followed a similar sevenfold heavenly system, which has roots in ancient Mediterranean cosmologies.

WHEEL OF LIFE

In Buddhist belief the Wheel of Life represents *samsara*, the eternal cycle of life, death and rebirth. It depicts the seven realms of existence into which one may be reborn, from the realm of animals to the realm of gods. The best realm is the human realm, which offers the chance of release from *samsara* through the practice of Dharma, the Buddha's body of teachings.

TOWERS OF SILENCE

(left) Zoroastrians, followers of the pre-Islamic religion of Iran, do not bury or cremate their dead, because they believe that the elements of earth, fire and water must be kept pure. Since ancient times, therefore, corpses have been exposed on top of circular stone structures to be devoured by birds.

ANCIENT EGYPT

The people of ancient Egypt communicated in a uniquely symbolic manner. The motifs that appeared on buildings, monuments and everyday objects were not merely decorative but conveyed the ideas and beliefs that underpinned society. For example, the role of the pharaoh (king) as protector of his people was expressed in the common depiction of the king with his arm raised, smiting the enemies of Egypt with a mace. This royal image is found from the earliest dynasties until the early centuries CE, when the Roman emperors who then ruled Egypt were portrayed as pharaohs along with the whole panoply of traditional symbolism.

The form of a building or object could also fulfil a symbolic function. The Great Pyramids of Giza represented the primordial mound from which life originated, as did the raised platform in the dark inner sanctuary of Egyptian temples, on which stood the cult image of the god or goddess.

Nowhere is the Egyptian predilection for symbolic communication better exhibited than in their written language. Hieroglyphs, literally "sacred carvings", were said to have been invented by the ibis-headed deity Thoth (left), the scribe of the gods. The mystique of hieroglyphs is partly owing to the fact that they fell out of use and ceased to be understood for around 1,500 years. Later visitors to Egypt were intrigued by these strange, often very beautiful and intricate symbols that adorned ruined temples and tombs. Many endowed them with mystical and even magical significance.

In fact, most hieroglyphs represent single sounds or groups of sounds, like our alphabet. Others are stylized images of what they represent: so the word "owl" is simply an image of an owl. The third type shows what a word means in context: thus "to answer" ends in a sign of a man with his hand to his mouth, to show that the word refers to "speaking".

EYE OF HORUS

The eye of the solar god Horus, with whom each living pharaoh was identified, was a common amulet. On this pectoral (chest ornament), the Eye is flanked by two uraei on the barque of the sun god.

SCARAB
The dung beetle represented the sun god at dawn, rising from the underworld replete with potential, like the dungball that held the beetle's egg.

URAEUS

The uraeus, or image of a rearing cobra, was associated with Wadjet, the patron snake goddess of Lower Egypt and protector of the pharaoh.

ANKH

The "handled cross" or "key of life" was a symbol of immortality. In Roman times the *ankh* symbol was retained by the Copts, the native Christians of Egypt, as a form of the Christian cross.

DJED
Shaped like a pillar and perhaps depicting a stylized spinal column, the *djed* represents stability. This was seen as a masculine and royal quality and was associated in particular with the god Osiris.

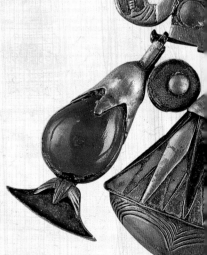

SUN & MOON The "two lights" of the sky were seen as the eyes of Horus. His left eye, the moon, had been injured by the god Seth, lord of chaos, and therefore shone less brightly.

PAPYRUS The papyrus stood for Lower Egypt, the marshy Nile delta where the reed grew in abundance. At the bottom of this pectoral it alternates with the lotus, or water lily, the heraldic plant of Upper Egypt.

THE EGYPTIAN PANTHEON

The sun-god RA and the solar deity HORUS were often depicted as a high-flying hawk or as a hawk-headed man. The father of HORUS was OSIRIS, lord of the underworld, the dead and fertile soil. His skin was GREEN or BLACK (the colors of death but also renewal, since new growth was green and the Egyptian soil was black). He was depicted as a pharaoh with the royal symbols of CROWN, CROOK and FLAIL. Another god associated with death and the afterlife was ANUBIS. He had black skin and the head of a jackal, an animal that haunted cemeteries.

The ancient fertility goddess HATHOR was often depicted as a COW or a woman with cow's EARS. Hathor's cult merged with that of ISIS, divine mother and protector of the pharaoh. Her name means "throne", and this is her symbol. Female HIPPOS are fierce protectors and the hippo-goddess TAWARET (above) was a favorite domestic deity.

NEKHBET

Just as the cobra-goddess Wadjet was the protector of Lower Egypt, the vulture-goddess Nekhbet was the patron of Upper Egypt. Like the hawk-winged scarab in the main image, Nekhbet clutches the hieroglyph for "eternity" in each talon.

the quest

Heroes in pursuit of an actual or symbolic goal have always fired the mythic imagination. Quests often follow the pattern of a great journey, involving a series of dangerous, even seemingly impossible challenges intended to test the hero's courage, strength, ingenuity and honor. Some heroes are blessed with divine protection and may be taught suitable skills in preparation for their trials, as when Chiron the wise centaur instructs Jason in hunting and warfare. But only the purest in heart will succeed in attaining their goal.

The goal may be spiritual enlightenment, or eternal life. In the latter case, the hero is usually disappointed, but may reach an acceptance of human mortality, as in the Sumerian epic of the hero Gilgamesh. In overcoming the obstacles placed before him, the hero finds release from mental burdens and a kind of fulfillment. Psychologically the quest can be seen as an allegory of the mystery of existence, in which the hero represents the individual, struggling— but perhaps also coming to terms—with the pitfalls of human life.

EPIC OF GILGAMESH
(*right*) This Sumerian story is one of the most ancient of quests, dating in part to ca. 3000BCE. Born two-thirds divine, Gilgamesh goes in quest of immortality, only to find that human efforts to live forever will always be futile.

PERSEUS
The classic hero of Greek myth, protected and armed by the deities Athene and Hermes. His curved sword, polished shield, winged sandals and helmet represent divine speed, strength and virtue. Using his shield as a mirror, Perseus cuts off Medusa's head of snakes that represent evil and sin.

THE GOLDEN FLEECE
(*above*) The Greek hero Jason is given the near impossible task of retrieving the Golden Fleece of Colchis, itself is a solar emblem of aspiration. The flying ram from which the fleece was shorn is sacred to the god Zeus. For Jason to secure the seemingly unattainable he must overcome dark forces, represented by an ever-awake dragon that guards the fleece. The tree on which the fleece hangs symbolizes the Tree of Life, and the prospect of divine immortality.

THE HOLY GRAIL

The quest of the HOLY GRAIL by the knights of KING ARTHUR was among the most famous of medieval legends. It is essentially a search for immortality. The grail itself is usually said to be a chalice in which, at the crucifixion, JOSEPH OF ARIMATHEA caught drops of the BLOOD OF CHRIST, which gives eternal life. According to British legend, Joseph took the chalice to Britain, where it was lost. It is up to Arthur and his knights of the ROUND TABLE (right, paralleling christ's disciples) to find the precious object.

For the celts, the grail symbolized the HEART as the center of life, and in christianity the grail is also the SACRED HEART of christ. The loss of the grail symbolized the loss of paradise and innocence, and separation from christ. Thus the quest is a bid to find christ, the spiritual center of humankind, and spiritual renewal. The Arthurian knights are spiritual initiates, who must encounter on their way a number of challenges that bring them close to death.

only GALAHAD is granted a vision of the grail because of his spiritual and moral purity. On completing the quest, his soul ascends directly to heaven.

THE ODYSSEY

Homer's epic poem *The Odyssey* describes the ten-year return voyage of Odysseus (known to the Romans as Ulysses) following the Trojan War, which itself had lasted ten years. Described as a "man of many devices", this son of King Laertes of Ithaca, a Greek island, is presented as the personification of resourcefulness and fidelity. He is the archetypal returning hero who has to set things right after a prolonged absence from his home. After twenty years' away, Odysseus proves his worthiness by liberating his wife Penelope from the suitors who have been harassing her, and assumes his rightful crown. Penelope herself is the paragon of wifely fidelity, refusing the suitors' advances, convinced that her husband will one day return.

VOYAGE OF BRENDAN

A very popular tale in medieval Europe was the *Voyage of St. Brendan*. It tells how Brendan, a historical sixth-century Irish monk, sailed the Atlantic on a quest for the paradisial Isles of the Blessed. The monk and his friends had fantastic adventures, including landing on a great fish (above). Some believe that the tale reflects a genuine voyage that took the monk to North America.

XUANZANG

The Chinese monk Xuanzang (602–664CE) traveled to India on a sixteen-year pilgrimage to collect Buddhist scriptures. This famous real expedition was the basis of the 1582 novel *Journey to the West*, one of the most popular books in Chinese literature, in which Xuanzang and his two divine companions face eighty-one ordeals devised by the Buddha to test Xuanzang's sincerity.

AENEAS

The hero of the *Aeneid* by Virgil represents man in thrall to his destiny, in this case to become the ancestor of the Romans. Having fled burning Troy with his family, Aeneas wanders the Mediterranean. He falls in love with Queen Dido of Carthage, but his fate drives him to abandon her and sail for Italy.

PROMISED LAND

God's directive to the patriarch Abraham to seek a special land for his descendants, the Israelites, has always lain at the heart of the Jewish faith. The Promised Land "flowing with milk and honey" became symbolic of any ideal society or utopia.

THESEUS

Theseus was sent by his father, King Aegeus of Athens, on a mission to Crete to slay the Minotaur, the monstrous man with a bull's head. Psychoanalytically, the myth of destroying the monster at the heart of the Labyrinth expresses the overcoming of our deepest fears and suppressed emotions.

VISION QUESTS

In Native American tradition, shamans undergo "vision quests" to the sacred world. By entering trances they visit the sacred land of the dead to obtain from ancestors the power to heal, and also to cause sickness to enemies of the tribe.

THE LABORS OF HERAKLES

The quintessential hero of Classical antiquity was Herakles, known to the Romans as Hercules. His most famous exploits began after the goddess Hera drove him into a fit of madness, in which he slew his entire family. As a penance, Herakles had to work for twelve years for King Eurystheus of Tiryns, who set the hero a series of twelve labors, or challenges.

The usual sequence of the Labors, which reach their culmination in the west, the land of the setting sun, and finally at the gates of the underworld, has been seen as a metaphor for life's journey from birth to death. The Labors have also been viewed as the struggle to master vices and inner "monsters" of the psyche. Herakles has been identified as a "solar" hero, the Labors being interpreted astrologically as the sun's journey through the twelve signs of the Zodiac: the Nemean lion is associated with Leo, the Hydra and Stymphalian birds (as creatures of water) with Cancer, the Cerynean hind with Capricorn, and so on.

1. NEMEAN LION
(*right*) Offspring of the monsters Typhon and Echidna, the lion of Nemea had a hide impervious to weapons, so Herakles strangled it. His success in overcoming this creature, coupled with the lion's general association with the sun, symbolize victory over death, an idea represented by Herakles' donning of the lion's pelt.

2. LERNEAN HYDRA
Living in the swamps of Lerna, the Hydra was a many-headed water-serpent, a symbol of untameable nature. When Herakles cut off one head, two more grew in its place, symbolizing humankind's inability to conquer vices. In the end, Herakles' nephew helped him to overcome the beast by quickly cauterizing each neck before a new head could grow.

3. CERYNEAN HIND
Herakles had to capture a hind with golden horns and bronze hooves without harming it, since it was sacred to the goddess Artemis. Herakles slightly wounded the hind, but blamed King Eurystheus for the injury. In psychological terms the episode reveals that possessiveness leads to harm, despite one's best efforts.

4. ERYMANTHIAN BOAR
As his fourth labor Herakles was ordered to bring back to Eurystheus, alive, a monstrous boar that was devastating the region around Mount Erymanthus. He succeeded in capturing the beast in deep snow and returned with it. However, the king was so afraid that he hid inside an urn (left), highlighting his own cowardice.

5. AUGEAN STABLES

Herakles had just a day to clean years' worth of dung out of the cattle stables of King Augeas. Drawing on his initiative as well as his physical strength, he succeeded by diverting two rivers through the stables. This has been seen symbolically as adopting radical new perspectives to tackle long-held fears.

6. STYMPHALIAN BIRDS

The hero had to rid Lake Stymphalos of man-eating birds with iron claws, wings and beaks. He used a bronze rattle to scare them out of the trees and then shot them one by one. The lake has been held to symbolize a stagnant soul mired in vice, represented by the birds.

7. CRETAN BULL

Herakles was sent to Crete to capture a fire-breathing bull, said to have been the one that fathered the Minotaur (see page 64): he choked the bull and took it to Greece. The Herakles story perhaps has roots in some ancient Greek subjugation of Crete, where the bull was a totemic beast.

8. MARES OF DIOMEDES

The hero went to Thrace to capture a herd of ferocious man-eating mares owned by King Diomedes. Like Dr. Frankenstein and Dr. Moreau, the king was destroyed by the monsters he sought to control: Herakles tamed the mares by feeding Diomedes to them.

THE DEATH OF HERAKLES

using ARROWS tipped in the HYDRA'S venomous blood, Herakles slew a CENTAUR who tried to rape his second wife, DEIANEIRA. The dying centaur persuaded Deianeira to apply his own blood to Herakles' shirt as a love potion. But the centaur's blood was tainted with Hydra's venom, and when Herakles donned the shirt he died in agony. His semi-divinity was no proof against death. But Herakles' end was crowned in glory, for he was then taken up to OLYMPUS as a god, fully divine and immortal.

9. GIRDLE OF HIPPOLYTA

Eurystheus ordered Herakles to get for his daughter the beautiful girdle of Hippolyta, queen of the Amazons, a martial race of women of Asia Minor. Herakles defeated the Amazons, killed Hippolyta and returned with the girdle. This has been understood as an affirmation of Greek patriarchy over foreign matriarchy.

10. CATTLE OF GERYON

To get the red cattle of Geryon, a three-bodied cowherd, Herakles sailed beyond the known world to an island in the Ocean, the river encircling the Earth. He made a channel to the river by prising apart two mountains, creating the Pillars of Hercules (Strait of Gibraltar), and killed Geryon to get the cattle. Herakles' ship was the *Cup of Helios* (the sun god) and the story is full of solar symbolism.

11. APPLES OF THE HESPERIDES

Herakles ventured west again, sailing between the Pillars to recover golden apples growing on a tree tended by the Hesperides, nymphs of Mount Atlas. To obtain this fruit of immortality, Herakles first had to slay the dragon Ladon. On the journey Herakles encountered the Titan Atlas, who held up the world. Depictions of Herakles by the apple tree may be a source of the depiction of the tree of Eden as an apple tree.

12. DESCENT TO THE UNDERWORLD

Herakles had to bring back alive the three-headed dog Cerberus, which guarded the gates to the underworld. In dragging away the "hound of hell" by brute force, Herakles shows that it is possible to overcome the dread of death; but death itself cannot be destroyed.

the end of time

Ideas about the end of time vary from one culture to another, but for many the final cataclysm also symbolizes a cleansing and renewal, with a new world arising from the old, sometimes with only a few virtuous individuals or an elect as survivors. This was the case with the Norse myth of Ragnarok, and it is also to be found in the Christian vision of the New Jerusalem. In Mesoamerican and Hindu cosmology, the end of the world happens as part of an endless cycle of cosmic creation, destruction and re-creation.

Judeo-Christian and Islamic traditions speak of a final Day of Judgment in which the sinful are separated from the virtuous. Jewish expectations of a Messiah who will deliver them from persecution on earth and establish the rule of God lie at the roots of Christian beliefs in the Second Coming of Jesus to usher in the end of history. Both Jewish and Christian scriptures describe in graphic images the signs that will herald the end: earthquakes, fires and floods, will presage a final conflict between the forces of good and evil, like the battle of Armageddon in the Book of Revelation (see box).

DESCENT INTO HELL
(*left*) *The Gospel of Nicodemus* (ca. fourth century CE) recounts Jesus' descent to the underworld between his death and resurrection. Breaking down the gates of Hades, he freed many holy people who had lived before his time, such as Adam and Eve and the prophets. This foreshadowed the Last Judgment, when all the blessed dead would be resurrected.

MARY THE INTERCESSOR
In Roman Catholic belief, the Virgin Mary was taken, body and soul, up to heaven three days after her death. In heaven she acts as a merciful intercessor between believers and Christ. The cult of the Virgin Mary as intercessor for the faithful flourished especially in the Middle Ages, when many Christian minds were gripped by terror of the Last Judgment. One way to avoid damnation, it was believed, was to plead with the Virgin for protection through formulaic prayers such as the *Hail Mary* (*Ave Maria*). It was believed that Mary passed such prayers to Christ, who in turn passed them to God.

BRAHMAKALPA
(*right*) According to Hindu cosmology the entire lifetime of the Earth is but a single Brahmakalpa, one day and one night of Brahma, the first god in the ancient triad or Trimurti (Brahma, Vishnu and Shiva). Overseen by Vishnu, the Preserver, the world runs its normal course during Brahma's day, but under the eye of Shiva, the Destroyer, the world declines steadily during Brahma's night and comes to an end in a cataclysmic destruction by fire—whereupon Brahma, the Creator, restores the world anew at the dawn of a new *kalpa*. Some scholars have calculated that a *kalpa* lasts 8,640,000 years.

THE LAST JUDGMENT

The BIBLE includes various cataclysmic visions of the end of time, such as those of EZEKIEL and DANIEL. The BOOK OF REVELATION (also called the Revelation to John or The Apocalypse of John), is the only one in the NEW TESTAMENT. Probably written in the reign of the persecuting emperor DOMITIAN (81–96CE), it is full of striking symbolic images. JESUS, the LAMB, will open the SEVEN SEALS of world history. Disasters that will befall the earth are represented as FOUR HORSEMEN, and SEVEN ANGELS pour SEVEN GOLDEN BOWLS of plague on sinful humanity. A struggle will unfold between good, symbolized by a WOMAN AND CHILD, and the evil SEVEN-HEADED DRAGON, or SATAN. A great BEAST, identified by the NUMBER 666, represents the ANTICHRIST (see also page 121). The forces of good will give battle at ARMAGEDDON and the WHORE OF BABYLON, referring to ROME, will fall. The holy ones will reign for a MILLENNIUM before Satan returns briefly. Finally the dead will be judged from the BOOK OF LIFE at the LAST JUDGMENT, and a NEW HEAVEN and NEW EARTH will arise for the righteous, together with a NEW JERUSALEM.

PAHANA

Some Hopi saw the arrival of Europeans as the onset of the end times, with iron serpents (railroads) and a giant spider's web (telegraph lines) ensnaring the land. But amid widespread destruction the Pahana ("True White Man") would bring wisdom and conduct a Day of Purification on the eve of a new world.

RAGNAROK

Norse myth envisioned the final disaster as Ragnarok, the "Twilight of the Gods", when gods, humans and the old world would all be consumed in a massive cataclysm. A new idyllic world would then arise.

RAS TAFARI

For Rastafarians the end began in 1930 when Ras Tafari (Haile Selassie as God incarnate) became emperor of Ethiopia. On Judgment Day he and the lost children of Israel (the descendants of African slaves) will be reunited on Mount Zion in Africa.

SAOSHYANT

In Zoroastrian myth the final age will see the Earth flooded by molten metal that will purge the living and dead of sin. Through a savior, Saoshyant, all will be taken up to the realm of the supreme deity Ahura Mazdah.

SATAN

In the Book of Job, Satan ("Accuser") is one of God's court who afflicts Job to test his faith. But later Satan came to be seen not as God's agent but his enemy: the Devil, the source of all the world's evil, the tempter of humanity and the leader of the rebel angels who had been expelled from heaven. Satan heads a great host of demons, who in Christian belief are defeated by the heavenly host led by St. Michael.

THE MAYAN PROPHECY

The calendar of the Maya, who are renowned for the complexity of their calendar and accuracy of their astronomic calculations, predicted that the present age would come to an end on December 22, 2012. This belief, which has acquired some New Age followers, is based on the conjunction of the winter solstice meridian with the center of the Milky Way, an astronomical event said to signal a shift in the Earth's magnetic field. A "dark rift" in the Milky Way represents the Mayan road to the underworld and symbolizes the birth canal of the next world age.

AZTEC FIVE SUNS

The Aztecs believed that conflict between four deities, each representing a quarter of the universe, led to the catastrophic end of each of the Five Suns, or cosmic eras. Jaguars destroyed the first Sun, a hurricane the second, fire the third and flood the fourth. The fifth (present) Sun is destined to be destroyed by earthquakes.

further reading

Allan, T. *The Symbol Detective.* Duncan Baird Publishers: London, 2008.

Battistini, M. *Symbols and Allegories in Art.* Getty Publishing: Los Angeles, 2005.

Battistini, M. *Astrology, Magic, and Alchemy in Art.* Getty Publishing: Los Angeles, 2007.

Becker, U. *The Continuum Encyclopedia of Symbols.* Continuum: London, 2000.

Beer, R. *The Encyclopedia of Tibetan Symbols and Motifs.* Serindia Publications: London and Chicago, 2004.

Bently, P. (General editor.) *The Dictionary of World Myth.* Facts on File: New York, 1995.

Binder, P. *Magic Symbols of the World.* Hamlyn: London, 1972.

Black, J. and Green, A. *Gods, Demons and Symbols of Ancient Mesopotamia: An Illustrated Dictionary.* The British Museum Press: London, 1992.

Boardman, J., Griffin, J. and Murray, O. (Editors.) *The Oxford History of Greece and the Hellenistic World.* Oxford University Press: Oxford and New York, 2001.

Buckland, R. *Signs, Symbols & Omens: An Illustrated Guide to Magical & Spiritual Symbolism.* Llewellyn Worldwide: Woodbury, Minnesota, 2003.

Campbell, J. *The Hero with a Thousand Faces.* Princeton University Press: Princeton, New Jersey, 1949.

Campbell, J. *The Power of Myth.* Bantam Doubleday Dell Publishing Group: New York, 1989.

Carr–Gomm, S. *Dictionary of Symbols in Art.* Duncan Baird Publishers: London, 2000.

Carr–Gomm, S. *The Secret Language of Art: The Illustrated Decoder of Symbols and Figures in Western Painting.* Duncan Baird Publishers: London, 2008.

Carter, G. (Editor.) *The Illustrated Guide to Latin American Mythology.* Studio Editions: London, 1995.

Chamberlain, J. *Chinese Gods: An Introduction to Chinese Folk Religion.* Blacksmith Books: Hong Kong, 2009.

Chevalier, J. and Gheerbrant, A. (Trans. by J. Buchanan Brown.) *The Penguin Dictionary of Symbols.* Penguin Books: London, 1996.

Cirlot, J.E. (Trans. by J. Sage.) *A Dictionary of Symbols.* Routledge: London, 1971.

Cohen, D. *The Secret Language of the Mind.* Duncan Baird Publishers: London, 1996.

Cooper, J.C. *An Illustrated Encyclopaedia of Traditional Symbols.* Thames & Hudson: London, 1978.

Cornelius, G. and Devereux, P. *The Language of Stars & Planets: A Visual Key to Celestial Mysteries.* Duncan Baird Publishers: London, 2003, and Chronicle Books: San Francisco, 2003.

Drury, N. *The Dictionary of the Esoteric.* Watkins Publishing: London, 2004.

Drury, N. *The Watkins Dictionary of Magic.* Watkins Publishing: London, 2005.

Eberhard, W. *A Dictionary of Chinese Symbols.* Routledge: London, 1988

Eliade, M. *The Myth of the Eternal Return.* Princeton University Press: Princeton, New Jersey, 1992.

Eliade, M. *Essential Sacred Writings from Around the World.* HarperSan Francisco: San Francisco, 1992.

Eliade, M and Mairet, P. *Images and Symbols.* Princeton University Press: Princeton, New Jersey, 1991.

Fontana, D. *Dreamlife: Understanding and Using your Dreams.* Element Books: Shaftesbury, Dorset, 1990.

Fontana, D. *The Secret Language of Symbols: A Visual Key to Symbols and their Meanings.* Duncan Baird Publishers: London, 1993, and Chronicle Books, San Francisco, 1994.

Frankl, E. and Platkin Teutsch, B. *The Encyclopedia of Jewish Symbols.* Jason Aronson Inc. Publishers: Lanham, Maryland, 1996.

Fraser, J.G. *The Golden Bough: A Study in Magic and Religion.* Oxford University Press: Oxford and New York, 1994.

Fried, J. and Leach, M. (Editors.) *Funk and Wagnall's Standard Dictionary of Folklore, Mythology and Legend.* Thomas Y. Crowell: New York, 1972.

Gettings, F. *The Arkana Dictionary of Astrology.* Arkana: London and New York, 1990.

Green, M.J. *Dictionary of Celtic Myth and Legend.* Thames & Hudson: London and New York, 1997.

Hall, J. *Dictionary of Subjects and Symbols in Art.* Westview Press, Inc.: Boulder, Colorado, 2007.

Hart, G. *The Routledge Dictionary of Egyptian Gods and Goddesses.* Routledge: London and New York, 2005.

Holroyd, S. and Powell, N. *Mysteries of Magic.* Bloomsbury Publishing: London, 1991.

Hope, J. *The Language of the Spirit: A Visual Key to*

Enlightenment and Destiny. Duncan Baird Publishers: London, 2003, and Chronicle Books, San Francisco, 2003.

Huxley, F. *The Way of the Sacred*. Geofrey Cave: London, 1989.

Impelluso, L. *Nature and Its Symbols*. Getty Publishing: Los Angeles, 2005.

Innes, B. *The Tarot*. Arco Publishing: New York, 1978.

Jung C.G. *Analytical Psychology: Its Theory and Practice*. Routledge: London, 1986.

Jung, C.G. *The Archetypes and the Collective Unconscious*. Routledge: London, 1991.

Jung, C.G. *Man and His Symbols*. Laurel Press: New York, 1997.

Kokkinou, S. *Greek Mythology*. Intercarta: Athens, Greece, 1989.

Kurrels, J. *Astrology for the Age of Aquarius*. Anaya Publishers: London, 1990.

Liungman, C.G. *Symbols – Encyclopaedia of Western Signs and Ideograms*. HME Publishing: Lidingö, Sweden, 2004.

Merrifield, R. *The Archaeology of Ritual and Magic*. Batsford: London, 1987.

Morgan, P. *Buddhism*. Batsford: London, 1989.

Miller, M. and Taube, K. *An Illustrated Dictionary of the Gods and Symbols of Ancient Mexico and the Maya*. Thames & Hudson: London and New York, 1997.

O'Connor, M. and Airey, R. *Symbols, Signs & Visual Codes*. Southwater Publishing: London, 2007.

Opie, I. and Tatem, M. (Editors.) *A Dictionary of Superstitions*. Oxford University Press: Oxford and New York, 2005.

Owusu, H. *Symbols of Native America*. Sterling: New York, 1999.

Owusu, H. *African Symbols*. Sterling: New York, 2007.

Pickering, D. *Cassell Dictionary of Superstitions*. Weidenfeld Nicolson Illustrated, 1995.

Powell, T.G.E. *The Celts*. Thames & Hudson: London, 1983.

Rawson, P. *Tantra: The Indian Cult of Ecstasy*. W.W. Norton: London, 1984.

Saunders, N.J. *Animal Spirits*. Duncan Baird Publishers: London, 1995, and Little, Brown & Company Inc., Boston, 1995.

Scholem, G. On the *Kabbalah and its Symbolism*. Schocken Books: New York, 1969.

Spence, L. *Myths and Legends of the North American Indians*. Kessinger Publishing: Whitefish, Montana, 1997.

Thompson, C.J.S. *Lure and Romance of Alchemy*. Kessinger Publishing: Whitefish, Montana, 2003.

Tresidder, J. *1001 Symbols*, Duncan Baird Publishers: London, 2003, and Chronicle Books: San Francisco, 2003.

Tresidder, J. (General editor.) *The Complete Dictionary of Symbols in Myth, Art and Literature*. Duncan Baird Publishers: London, and Chronicle Books: San Francisco, 2004

Tresidder, M. *The Language of Love*. Duncan Baird Publishers: London, 2004, and Chronicle Books: San Francisco, 2004.

Van Over, R. *I Ching*. New American Library (US), 1971

Vitebsky, P. *The Shaman*. Duncan Baird Publishers: London, 2000, and Little, Brown & Company Inc.: Boston, 2000.

Waterstone, R. *India*. Duncan Baird Publishers: London, 2002, and Thorsons: New York, 2002.

Welch, P.B. *Chinese Art: A Guide to Motifs and Visual Imagery*. Tuttle Publishing: North Clarendon, Vermont, 2008.

Wilkinson, R.H. *Symbol & Magic in Egyptian Art*. Thames & Hudson: London, 1999.

Williams, C.A.S. *Chinese Symbolism and Art Motifs*. Tuttle Publishing: North Clarendon, Vermont, 1988.

Willis, R. (General editor.) *World Mythology*. Duncan Baird Publishers: London, 2006, and Oxford University Press: New York, 2006.

Zimmer, H. (Edited by Joseph Campbell.) *Myths and Symbols in Indian Art and Civilization*. Princeton University Press: Princeton, New Jersey, 1992.

Zimmerman, L.J and Molyneaux, B.L. *Native North America*. Duncan Baird Publishers: London, 2002, and Little, Brown & Company Inc.: Boston, 2002.

index

acknowledgments & picture credits

acknowledgments

The following artists produced the commissioned artwork in this book, listed below with page number and position:
t = top, c= center, b = bottom, l = left, r = right

Neil Gower: 33b, 175

Olaf Hajek: 2–3, 4–5, 6–7, 22–23, 24, 32, 92, 104, 114, 134, 160

Katarzyna Klein: 3br, 22cl, 23bc, 25, 27bc, 33cl, 33c, 33cr, 36br, 41c, 53tr, 93, 103, 115, 118br, 135, 161

Clare Melinksy: 27br, 34bc, 35, 40c, 45tr, 45bl, 46tr, 53tl, 53br, 55tl, 55tr, 55cl, 55cr, 70bc, 73tr, 94c, 117tl, 125c, 148bl

Gary Walton: 29bl, 29bc 51bl, 63tl, 71bl, 72cr, 73tl, 77cl, 77c, 77cr, 82tl, 82tc, 82tr, 83tr, 95bl, 105cl, 105c,105cr, 107tl, 125cr

Mark Watkinson: 30–31, 38–39, 48–49, 60–61, 68–69, 78–79, 90–91, 100, 112–113, 130–131, 142–143, 158–159, 168–169

picture credits

The publisher would like to thank the following people, museums and photographic libraries for permission to reproduce their material. Every care has been taken to trace copyright holders. However, if we have omitted anyone we apologize and will, if informed, make corrections to any future edition.

AA = Art Archive, London
ADO = Alfredo Dagli Ort
AKG = akg-images, London
BAL = Bridgeman Art Library, London
BL = The British Library, London
BM = © The Trustees of the British Museum
BN = Bibliothèque Nationale, Paris
BSP = Big Stock Photo
Dr = Dreamstime.com
EL = Erich Lessing
EM = Egyptian Museum, Cairo
GDO = Gianni Dagli Orti
iS = iStockphoto.com
ML = Musée du Louvre, Paris
NAM = National Anthropological Museum, Mexico City
PC = Private Collection
Sc = Photo Scala, Florence
Sh = Shutterstock.com
V&A = Victoria and Albert Museum/© V&A Images, London. All rights reserved
WFA = Werner Forman Archive, London

t = top, c= center, b = bottom, l = left, r = right

Page 8 Map of universe showing seven stages of the sun at the center of the world and signs of the Zodiac, from *The Fine Flower of Histories*, by Ottoman historiographer Seyyid Loqman Ashuri, 1583. (AA/Turkish and Islamic Art Museum, Istanbul/ADO); **9** Stone tablet of a Mayan calendar used in Guatemala and Mexico (iS/Leeuwtje); **10bl** Great Western Railway Company coat of arms (AA/Eileen Tweedy); **10tr** Communist star with sickle and hammer (Sh/Sinisa Botas); **11** An enameled altar cross. Mosan, ca.1160–1170; from France or Belgium, with five scenes from the Old Testament (BM); **12** Meenakshi Sundareswarar temple in Madurai, South India (Sh/Aleynikov Pavel); **13** *Taiji* (Sh/Khramtsova Tatyana); **14** Statue of the Buddha, China (Sh/kentoh); **15** *Ba* amulet from the tomb of Prince Hornakht, ca. ninth century BCE (WFA/EM); **16t** Bronze devil face, antique door (iS/xyno); **16b** Till Eulenspiegel, peasant–trickster of folktales, depicted on a 10 Pfennig Notgeld issued by the Brunswick State Bank, 1921. Designed by Günther Clausen (AKG); **17** Ergotimos and Cleitias (6th century BCE): detail of the fight between Lapiths and Centaurs on the François Vase (Sc – courtesy of the Ministero Beni e Att. Culturali/ Archaeological Museum, Florence); **18tl** Archway into the south ambulatory of Wells Cathedral, Somerset (Br Lawrence Lew, OP); **18b** The temple of Angkor Wat, Cambodia (Getty images/National Geographic/Martin Gray); **19** Tiled pattern on a mosque in Isfahan, Iran (Sh/javarman); **20** *The Tree of Knowledge of Good and Evil*, colored woodcut from *Geheime Figuren der Rosenkreue*, 1785–1788 (AKG/BN); **21** Illumination to the alchemical treatise *Splendor Solis*, probably Augsburg, late 16th century (AKG/Staatsbibliothek Preußischer Kulturbesitz, Berlin – Cod.germ.fol.42,); **25b** "Grand design" spiral galaxy known as Messier 81, or M81, a composite from NASA's Spitzer and Hubble space telescopes and NASA's *Galaxy Evolution Explorer*. M81 is about 12 million light-years away in the Ursa Major constellation (NASA/JPL-Caltech/ESA/Harvard-Smithsonian CfA); **26tl** Detail from the fence around Versailles Palace showing a bust of King Louis XIV (iS/Robert Kirk); **26br** Winged scarab beetle from a door of the temple of Edfu (iS/Pierrette Guertin); **27tl 1** Japanese flag (Sh/ARTEKI); **2** Uruguayan flag (Sh/Andrew Chin); **3** Argentinian flag (Sh/Adam Golabek); **4** Taiwan flag (Sh/c); **5** Antigua-and-Barbudan flag (Sh/Hintau Aliaksei); **6** Malawian flag (Sh/Kheng Guan Toh); **27tr** Helios on the sun wagon, painting on Greek vase, Canosa, 330 BCE (AKG/Staatlische Antikensammlungen & Glyptothek, Munich/EL); **27c** Hindu swastika on the exterior of a temple (Sh/Ami Parikh); **28–29c** Composite image showing the Moon at each stage of a lunar month (Science Photo Library/Eckhard Slawik); **28bl** Eskimo mask from the village of Andreofsky: the face represents the spirit of the moon, the board around the face symbolizes air, the hoops signify the levels of the cosmos, and the feathers represent stars. (WFA/Sheldon Jackson Museum, Sitka, Alaska); **28br** Crescent moon on top of a mosque dome (Dr/Dcubillas); **29tr** The Moon from Tarot cards by Antonio Cicognara 16th century (AA/Carrara Academy, Bergamo/ADO); **30tl** Blue zodiac clock with gold detail and decoration (iS/Baloncici); **30bl** Chinese zodiac symbols (Sh/fly); **31c** Planisphere or celestial map showing astrological symbols, from Atlas minor, *Sive Geographia compendiosa in qua orbis terrarun ostenditur*, 1784, published in Amsterdam by A. Zurne (AA/Bodleian Library, Oxford (2027a.49)); **34bl** Olive tree with a split trunk (Dr/Brandpoint); **34tr** Buddha statue entwined by tree roots (iS/Anthony Brown); **35tr** Oak in the forest at Mazury, Poland (Sh/Piotr Skubisz); **36cl** Chinese pine branch papercut (Sh/John Lock); **36bl** Illustration of a flowered almond tree (Sh/Ann Triling); **36tr** Yew trees bordering churchyard with Celtic cross, Dyfed, southwestern Wales (Photoshot/NHPA/David Woodfall); **37tl** Olive branch (Sh/Laurent Renault); **37cl** Painted landscape with three cypress trees on a sunny day by Ellen Beijers (Sh); **37r** California Redwood forest (iS/Kelly Cline); **38tl** Abraham (in medieval armour) presents the tenth part of his booty to the priest-king Melchizedek (Gen 14. 17–24). Detail from the Verdun Altar, by Nicholas of Verdun, 1181. Klosterneuburg (Austria), collegiate church. (AKG/EL); **38br** The union of Islam, Christianity and Judaism, by Rabbi Jacob Emden of Altona, Germany, eighteenth century (PC); **39c** *Tree of Life* by Mark Penney Maddocks, showing the ten spheres (AA/Eileen Tweedy); **40tl** Detail of exotic fruit, from *Still life with Peacock* by Luis Portu, 19th century, Mexico (AA/Queretaro Museum, Mexico/GDO); **41tl** Silver-gilt trinket box in the shape of a peach (Dr/Miao); **41tr** Cherries (iS/MHJ); **41bl** Relief with grapes and egg and dart designs on the Baal Temple, Palmyra, (Roman) Syria, 32CE. (AKG/Hedda Eid); **42tr** Lemon tree. Reproduction of vintage botanical book (Sh/Vladislav Gurfinkel); **42bl** Prayer with illuminated border, from Flemish manuscript *Book of Hours of Philippe de Conrault*, ca.1480 (AA/Bodleian Library, Oxford – Douce 223 fol 148v); **42br** Raised relief depicting "Welcome" pineapple (Sh/Mary Terribery); **43tl** Castanee-Chestnuts. Illustration to *Tacuinum sanitatis in medicina*, a Latin version of an Arabic health book. Italian, Verona or Lombardy, late 14th century (AKG/Austrian National Library, Vienna -Cod.ser.nov. 2644); **43cl** Plums (iS/Tania Oloy); **43bl** Chilies drying (Sh/vlas2000); **43tr** Bird on a walnut, section of a margin painting in the *Book of Hours of Antoine le Bon*, Duke of Lorraine, 1533 (AKG/BN– NA lat. 302, fol.53); **44tl** Detail of inlaid marble decor inside the Red Fort, Delhi, India (Dr/Rene Drouyer); **44bl** St. Catherine of Siena holding a lily, detail of an embroidered banner in the convent of the Dominican sisters in Stone, Staffordshire. Work of the Leek School of Embroidery, founded in 1879. (Br Lawrence Lew, OP); **44br** Late Victorian tile with Japanese chrysanthemum design (Sh/Christopher Elwell); **45tl** Rosy heart, detail of a gravestone in Munich (iS/xyno); **45tcr** Violet (iS/Roman Dekan); **46tl** Statue of a *boddhisattva* with lotus buds, Tokyo, Japan (iS/

Nikontiger); **46tc** Traditional Chinese peony papercut design (Sh/John Lock); **46c** Ivy, detail of a carving on a gravestone (Sh/Steve Lovegrove); **46br** Border of mistletoe and ladybird in the *Book of Hours of the Virgin*, Flemish, 1500 (AA/BL); **47tl** Leaf from *Master Shen Fengchi's Orchid Manual: Vol. IV*, 1882 (ink on paper) by Zhenlin Shen (fl.1882) (BAL/FuZhai Archive); **47cl** Poppy wreath on a war memorial (iS/William Murphy); **47cr** Chinese wood carving of birds and flowers, including marigiolds (Sh/ Apollofoto); **48tl** Cross with roses on an old gravestone, Munich (iS/xyno); **48–49c** *Mons Philosophorum*, colored wood engraving after a 1604 original, from *Geheime Figuren der Rosenkreuzer aus dem 16ten und 17ten Jahrhundert*, published by J.D.A.Eckhardt, Altona, 1785 (AKG); **49b** *Theosophische Werke*, by Jacob Boehm, Amsterdam, 1682: Light and darkness. All Things originated from the fire/root as a twofold birth in light good and darkness/ill (PC); **50bl** Taj Mahal, Agra, India (Dr/Nrg123); **50r** Floral tiles, Topkapi Palace, Istabul, Turkey (Sh/Certe); **51tl** Detail of Flora from *La Primavera* (Spring), by Sandro Botticelli, ca.1477–1478 (AKG/Rabatti – Dominige); **51cl** Garden of Gethsemane stained glass, Victorian (Sh/Keith McIntyre); **51tr** *Madonna of the Rose Bush* by Martin Schongauer, Dominican church, Colmar, France, 1473 (AA/GDO); **52tl** The Tree of the Knowledge of Good and Evil, detail of the reliefs on the façade of Notre Dame, Paris (Dr/Nikos Koravos); **52cr** View of Burghley House, seat of the Marquis of Exeter, landscaped by Capability Brown. Engraved and published by Robert Havell, 1819 (BAL/The Stapleton Collection/PC); **52br** General view of the Chateau and the Pavilions at Marly by Pierre-Denis Martin. Oil on canvas, 1722 (BAL/Giraudon/ Château de Versailles); **53tl** King Solomon and the animals, ca.1595, Indian miniature, 16th century (BAL/The Trustees of the Chester Beatty Library, Dublin – In. 04,f.74r); **53bl** Zen rock garden in Ryoanji temple, Kyoto, Japan (Sh/ Stanislav Komogorov); **54tl** Cosmological diagram, from the *Book of Byrthferth*, ca.1090 (BAL/St. John's College Library, Oxford – St.Johns 17 f.7v); **54bc** Chac, Maya god of rain (BSP/Shiver); **54c** *Ejiri in Suruga Province (Sunshû Ejiri)*, a color woodblock print by Katsushika Hokusai, 1830–1833 (BM); **54br** Noah with the ark in his arms, detail of a Victorian stained glass window in St Michael & All Angels, Fringford, Oxfordshire (Sh/Sybille Yates); **55br** Haida ceremonial robe (detail) appliquéd with a figure of a two-headed eagle (WFA/Canadian Museum of Civilization); **56tr** Tutankhamun's burial mask (Dr/Prehor); **56bl** Ancient Andean gold mask (Sh/Carlos E Santa Maria); **57cl** Achillion Palace, Corfu (Sh/Netfalls); **57bl** Icon of the Holy mother and Christ child (Sh/Agata Dorobek); **57tr** Statue of Mercury (Dr/Sergey Rusakov); **57br** German Iron Cross, military medal awarded for bravery (BSP/Brendan Montgomery); **58tl** Jade Lion Statue, Chinese (Sh/Vivian Fung); **58tr** The Emerald Buddha statue in Wat Phra That Doi Suthep, Bangkok, Thailand (Sh/Valery Shanin); **58b** Mosaic double-headed serpent, probably worn ceremonially as a pectoral. *Coatl* (serpent) is associated with several gods such as Quetzalcoatl (Feathered Serpent), Xiuhcoatl (Fire Serpent), Mixcoatl (Cloud Serpent) or Coatlicue (She of the

Serpent Skirt), mother of the god Huitzilopochtli. Aztec/ Mixtec, from Mexico 15th–16th century (BM); **59tl** Cut diamond (iS/Max Delson); **59tr** Semi-precious stones, including agate and amethyst (iS/Raigorodski Pavel); **60tl** Alchemist with the philosopher's stone, illustration from a 16th century manuscript alchemical roll of the writings of George Ripley, 15th-century English alchemist (AA/ Bodleian Library, Oxford – Ashmole Rolls 52); **60–61c** Senior and Adept under the tree of love, illustration from the alchemical manuscript *Splendor Solis* probably produced in Augsburg, 1582 (AKG/BL – Ms. Harley 3469, fol.17); **61br** Lion devouring the sun from D. Stolcius von Stolcenberg, *Viridarium Chymicum*, Frankfurt 1624 (PC); **62tl** Groom holding a saddled horse, gouache miniature, Pakistan, ca.1840 (V&A); **62bl** Fox on armorial bearings (PC); **62bc** Coyote head on a replica of a pre-1903 Tlingit totem pole at Sitka National Historical Park, Alaska (iS/ Nancy Nehring); **62br** Capitoline wolf, Etruscan with Roman twins added. (Sh/javarman/Capitoline Museum Rome); **63tc** Roman mosaic of a tiger hunting a white bull (Sh/Bill Perry/Capitoline Museum Rome); **63br** Crowned lion's head on the façade of the Pitti Palace, Florence (iS/ PeskyMonkey); **64t** Hanuman, Hindu deity, from a temple in Tirupati in South India. (iS/Daniel Laflor); **64b** Detail of the Ishtar Gate from Babylon, 6th–7th century BCE (Sh/ Martina I Meyer/ Pergamon Museum, Berlin); **65tl** Carving on a Buddhist temple wall, Beijing (Dr/Szefei); **65tc** *The Dying Stag*, engraving published by R. H. Stoddard, ca.1883 (iS/Constance McGuire); **65b** Agricultural scene with detailed depictions of the grain harvest in the Tomb of Menna, Thebes (Gabana Studios Germany/Manna, Egypt); **66l** Colorful mural of an elephant carrying people in a *howdah* across a green landscape, India (Sh/Jeremy Richards); **66r** Boar eating the fruit from a shrub found in a Greek temple in ancient Corinth (iS/Brianna May/ Archaeological Museum, Corinth); **67tl** Jesus as the Good Shepherd, Victorian stained glass (iS/Pattie Calfy); **67tr** *Cave Canem* – "Beware of the dog", mosaic, Roman (AA/ Archaeological Museum, Naples/ADO); **67cl** Vintage US postage stamp with a bison (iS/Ray Roper); **67c** Rabbit hieroglyph, Karnak (Gabana Studios Germany/Manna, Egypt); **67br** Egyptian statue of a cat carved from Aswan granite (BSP/myskatevi); **68cl** Blue *hamsa*, good luck charm on Hebrew bible BSP/samc); **68br** Jewish star on the wall of a synagogue (iS/Arie J Jager); **69c** *Temple Instruments*, illustration on the title page of the Perpignan Bible, 1299 (AKG/BN – Cod. Hebr.7, fol.12v); **70tl** Floor mosaic with different species of saltwater fish, an allegory of all the races of the Christian people, in Aquileia Cathedral, Friuli-Venezia Giulia, Italy, 4th century (AKG/De Agostini Picture Library); **71c** Large inlaid carving representing a bonito fish, or, when inverted, a shark. The annual bonito hunt was a major ritual event for the village. Carrying such a carving in the canoe was intended to lure the bonito while repelling predatory sharks. Solomon Islands (WFA/ BM); **71bc** Dolphin fresco at the Minoan palace of Knossos, Crete, ca.1500BCE (BSP/Paul Cowan); **72tl** Koi carp, symbol of fortune, Chinese painting (BSP/WittyVlad); **72bl** Copy of 13th-century illumination in the *Alexander Romance*,

facsimile engraving published 1878, showing Alexander the Great lowered in a glass barrel to observe the life of the ocean (iS/Steven Wynn); **73tr** Raphael with Tobit and his fish, detail of a stained glass window depicting the archangels, in St Sulpice, Fougères, Brittany (iS/Stan Tiberiu Loredan); **74tl** Ornate archway in City Palace, Jaipur, Rajasthan, decorated with peacocks (Sh/ JeremyRichards); **74bc** Relief of Horus in the Chapel of Anubis, Djeser-djeseru, Hatshepsut's funerary temple, Luxor (Gabana Studios Germany/Manna, Egypt); **75t** Eagle totem pole, Stanley Park, Vancouver (iS/RonTech2000); **75cr** Dove mosaic in the Orthodox church at Bethany, Jordan, site of Jesus' baptism by John the Baptist (Sh/ Darrell J Rohl); **76tl** Raven totem pole in Alaska (Sh/ Michael Klenetsky); **76tr** *Leda and the swan*, copy of a lost original by Leonardo da Vinci (AA/Galleria Borghese, Rome/ADO); **76bl** Oriental fabric with crane design (Sh/ trendywest); **77tr** Phoenix, relief on the Klong Son temple in Koh-Chang island, Thailand (Sh/aaleksander); **78tl** Vintage French postage stamp (Sh/Halima Ahkdar); **78– 79c** Coat of arms of Christopher Columbus, Genoese explorer, from the manuscript *Book of Privileges*, 1492 conceded to Christopher Columbus, by Catholic monarchs of Spain, Ferdinand and Isabella (AA/Museo Navale, Pegli/GDO); **79tr** Imperial Russian double-headed eagle with St. George, orb and scepter (iS/Nikolay Alexandrov); **80tr** Snake on a gravestone (iS/pixonaut); **80bl** Hungarian commemorative silver medal from 1914 depicting Herakles destroying the Hydra (iS/Daniel Baumgartner); **81t** Overview of Serpent Mound, Ohio (Corbis/Richard A Cooke); **81cl** Eygptian mummy casket (BSP/Scott); **81c** Statue of Shiva, Grand Bassin temple, Mauritius (iS/ Laurent); **81cr** Coatlicue, She of the Skirt of Snakes, goddess of the earth, life and death, Aztec, Mexico (DBP/ NAM); **81br** Caduceus symbol on a building, Munich (iS/ xyno); **82tr** Medusa head bas-relief detail on the Casa de Pilatos, Seville (iS/Roberto A Sanchez); **82bl** Adam and Eve with the serpent stained glass window (iS/Manuela Krause); **82br** Crocodile god Sobek, Kom Ombo temple, Egypt (BSP/pajche); **83bl** Dragon on the side of the Rathaus (City Hall) in Munich (iS/Stan Rippel); **84tl** Gold bracelet from the tomb of Amenemope mounted with a lapis lazuli scarab bearing aloft the gold solar disc (WFA/EM); **84bl** Butterflies adorning the door of an antique Chinese cupboard (Sh/qingqing); **84br** Death's head hawk moth (Getty images/Dorling Kindersley/Frank Greenaway); **85bl** Beehive and bees, 15th-century French manuscript on herbalism (AA/Biblioteca Estense, Modena/GDO); **85c** Gold necklace of fly pendants traditionally awarded for valor in battle, from the tomb of Queen Ahhotep I (1590– 1530BCE) at Dra Abu el-Naga, Thebes (AA/EM/ADO); **86tl** *Saint George and the Dragon* by Paolo Uccello, ca.1470 (Sc/ The National Gallery, London); **87tr** Ancient Chinese dragon design (Sh/sunxuejun); **87bl** Red lacquer Chinese vase with depiction of a dragon (BSP/Juha Sompinmäki); **87cr** Colorful dragon sculpture (Sh/Photobank); **87br** *Dragon and Tigers* by Hashimoto Sadahide, 19th-century woodblock print, Japan (V&A); **88tr** Pair of griffins, gilded wood (iS/Rafael Laguillo); **88clt** From *Book of Lady*

Meshsekeb, papyrus, Egyptian, 11th–10th century BCE (AA/Egyptian Museum, Turin/GDO); **88clb** Sphinx, Giza (Sh/sculpies); **88br** Chimera, statue of a winged lion with a fish tail, Amsterdam (Dr/Marianne Lachance); **89tc** Unicorn at Linlithgow Palace, Scotland (iS/Alejandro Sanz Torrente); **89tr** An *amorino* or Cupid astride the centaur Nessus. Overcome by lust, Nessus abducted Deianeira, the wife of Herakles but was killed by a poisoned arrow from the hero's bow. Engraving by C. Randon of a 10th-century statue, 19th century (iS/HultonArchive); **89b** Andromeda rescued from the monster by Perseus riding Pegasus, Parisian, c.a1410–1411 (BAL/BL – Harl 4431 f. 98v); **90bl** *Dings* with a pagoda at a Daoist temple, Xi'an, China (Sh/Nataliya Hora); **91c** Daoist priest's robe with central *yin-yang* symbol surrounded by the eight trigrams, Chinese, 19th century (V&A); **93bc** *The Dream of the Cavalier*, by Antonio P. y Salgado Pereda, oil on canvas ca.1650 (AKG/Academia de San Fernando); **94l** *Adam and Eve*, painting on the exterior of Haus Clagüna, Ardez, Engadina, Switzerland (Dr/Claudio Giovanni Colombo); **94br** Corn Mother by Joe Cajero, Jr. (Corbis/AINACO); **95tr** A panel from the *Codex Fejérváry-Mayer* (pre-1521) shows how Tezcatlipoca tempted the Earth Monster to the surface of the great waters by using his foot as bait. In swallowing his foot she lost her lower jaw. Hideously crippled she was unable to sink and thus the Earth was created from her body. (WFA/Liverpool Museum, Liverpool); **95bc** Blanket based on a creation myth sandpainting design: two supernatural "holy people" flank the sacred maize plant, which was their gift to mortals. Navajo, 19th century (WFA/Schindler Collection, New York); **95br** Settet and Khnum, Ancient Egyptian gods depicted on the temple wall, Elephanta Island, Aswan (iS/Rafik El Raheb); **96l** *Venus*, by Lucas Cranach the Elder, early 16th century (BAL/Stadelsches Kunstinstitut, Frankfurt-am-Main); **96r** Buddhist stupa (detail) at Palgor Chorten monastery, Gyantse, Tibet (iS/Terraxplorer); **97tr** Iaia of Cyzicus (Marcia) with comb and mirror; illumination from a French translation of Boccaccio's *Opus de claris mulieribus* (*On Famous Women*), early 15th century (AKG/BL – Ms. Royal 16 G V, fol. 80); **97bl** Opening the Mouth ritual – wall relief of gods in a temple, Saqqara, Egypt (Sh/Quintanilla); **97bc** Punic mask of man grimacing, terracotta, 4th century BCE, from Carthage, Tunisia (AA/Bardo Museum, Tunis/GDO); **97br** Carved wooden decoration on a Maori meeting house, New Zealand (BSP/Chris Jewiss); **98tl** Planet Man, from a Book of Hours printed by Philippe Pigouchet for Simon Vostre, 1498 (BAL/Lambeth Palace Library, London); **98tr** Detail of the two breezes from *The Birth of Venus* by Botticelli, ca.1485 (AA/Galleria degli Uffizi, Florence/ADO); **98bc** The heart is removed from the sacrificial victim and offered to the sun, from a facsimile of the *Florentine Codex* by Friar Bernardino de Sahagún, mid-16th century, Mexico (AA/Templo Mayor Library, Mexico/GDO); **98br** Angel on stained glass holding heart (iS/Victoria Wren); **99tr** Statue of Augustus, Rome (Sh/Jonathan Larsen); **99bl** Bronze hand of Buddha from the temple of Nakhon Pathom, Thailand (iS/wrangle); **100tl**

Vishnu from French manuscript *Book of the Moghul*, 17th century (AA/Biblioteca Nazionale Marciana, Venice/GDO); **101c** Attitudes and postures practiced by Hindu devotees, 18th century (AA/BL); **102tl** *The Nightmare*, oil on canvas, Henry Fussli, 1781 (BAL/The Detroit Institute of Arts/Founders Society purchase with Mr and Mrs Bert L.Smokler and Mr and Mrs Lawrence A. Fleischman funds); **102bl** Venus of Willendorf (Corbis/Ali Meyer); **102br** *Yoni-lingam* (Alamy/Nikreates); **103tl** Tibetan *yantra* in monastery in Kathmandu, Nepal (BSP/Paul Prescott); **103tr** *Yab-yum* statuette (Sh/Jun Mu); **103bl** Gold cup in the shape of an acorn, with two rams holding up a coat of arms, surmounted by the Latin inscription "IHS", for *In Hoc Signo* (by this sign), British, ca.1610 (AKG/EL); **103br** Hillside carving of the Cerne Abbas Giant, an ancient fertility symbol, England (Corbis/Skyscan); **105b** Relief at Deir el Bahri, Egypt (iS/Achim Prill); **106tl** Marble statue of Artemis in Selchuk, Turkey (Sh/Valery Shanin); **106tc** Sky goddess Nut, studded with stars, is created by Geb, god of the Earth, papyrus after tomb painting in Valley of the Kings, Thebes, Egypt (AA/Ragab Papyrus Institute, Cairo/GDO); **106tr** Copy of a 9th-century statue of the Viking god Thor and his hammer Mjolnir, found in Iceland (Dr/Gaja); **106b** Amaterasu emerges from her cave, Ama-no-Iwato in southern Honshu, and restores sunshine to the world. Triptych, 19th century (DBP/Japanese Art Gallery); **107tr** Lord Vishnu and goddess Lakshmi (Dr/Sundeep Goel); **107b** Golden Brahma statue (iS/Hector Joseph Lumang); **108tl** Chinese antique lacquer statue of Avalokiteshvara, ca.1800s (iS/Yungshu Chao); **108tr** Wall painting in KV19 tomb of Mentuherkhepeshef, Thebes (Gabana Studios Germany/Carola Schneider Germany); **108b** Uluru (Ayers Rock) (Dr/728jet); **109tc** Pottery figure of Mictlantecuhtli, Lord of the Dead. On their way to his underworld the dead were reduced to skeletons by a wind of knives (WFA/Anthropology Museum, Veracruz University, Jalapa); **109tr** Wood carving of Rama and his wife Sita, Hindu (Sh/Dmitry Rukhlenko); **109bl** The planet Mars, from the *Manuscript of the Spheres* (AA/Biblioteca Estense, Modena/ADO); **110l** Stained glass St. Michael, detail from the East Window in St. Mary's, Buckland, Oxfordshire by Henry Holiday (1839–1927) (Br Lawrence Lew, OP); **110r** *Bodhisattvas* painted on a temple door, Thailand (iS/Itsara Indrakamhaeng); **111t** Angels and archangels turning around God, Provençal codex *Breviare d'Amour* (*Breviary of Love*), by Master Ermengol of Beziers, late 13th–early 14th century (AA/Real Biblioteca de lo Escorial/GDO); **111bl** Detail from the ascension of the Prophet Mohammed, Persian. Islamic School, 16th century (BAL/Giraudon/Seattle Art Museum, Seattle); **111bc** Abdiel and Satan, a scene from Milton's *Paradise Lost*, engraving by Gustave Dore, 1870 (iS/Duncan Walker); **112tl** Tibetan mandala painting on monastery ceiling, Upper Pisang, Nepal (Sh/Paul Prescott); **112bl** Decoration on the roof of the Jokhang temple in Lhasa, Tibet (iS/Grigory Kubatyan); **112–113c** Buddha statue, Dalada Maligava, Temple of the Tooth, Kandy, Sri Lanka, early 19th century (AKG/Ullstein Bild); **113br** Footprint of Buddha with various auspicious symbols, India (Sh/Paul

Prescott); **115b** Tibetan sand *mandala* (Sh/Bestweb); **116tl** *Sadhu* painted with ash, Nepal (Getty Images/Image Bank/Ian Winstanley); **116tlc** Detail of St. Francis preaching to the birds, by Giotto, one panel in a fresco that illustrates the life of St. Francis, in the upper basilica, Assisi, 1297–1299 (Corbis/Sygma/Fabian Cevallos); **116tcr** Hand of a Buddha statue draped in orange fabric, Thailand. (iS/wrangle); **116tr** Decorated Bodhi tree at Ayuthaya, Thailand (Sh/Valery Shanin); **116b** Red brocade with a Chinese design (iS/Yougen); **117tc** The Risen Lord appears to St. Mary Magdalene. Victorian stained glass window in the church of St. Nicholas, Islip, Oxfordshire (Br Lawrence Lew, OP); **117b** Icon representing the Virgin Mary praying, 19th century (Sh/Bogdan Vasilescu); **118tl** Clay tablet from Iraq, listing quantities of various commodities in archaic Sumerian (early cuneiform script) ca.3200–3000BCE (BAL/Ashmolean Museum, University of Oxford); **118bcl** Number one lane on a race track (iS/tillsonburg); **118bcr** Typewriter key 2 (iS/Maria Toutoudaki); **118br** Trie Cassyn, Isle of Man symbol (Sh/Fabrizio Zanier); **119tr** Three-leafed clover (iS/ooyoo); **119bcl** 5Kc coin of Czech Republic (Sh/Castka); **119bcr** White dice (iS/pixhook); **120t** Bronze mirror back with the Five Directions, decorated with floating mountains, China, Tang dynasty, 618–907CE (AKG/National Palace Museum, Taipei); **120bl** Buddhist wheel, stone relief in the Forbidden City, Beijing (Sh/Photobank); **120bc** Digital number nine (Sh/Aleksandr Kurganov); **121br** Roman X on a blackboard (Sh/Stephen Aaron Rees); **121tc** Silver coin with the head of Nero, 37–68CE, from the Caphernaum treasure. (AKG/EL); **121bl** Number 11 painted on a church pew (Sh/Katharina Wittfeld); **121bc** Close-up of an old clock face at one minute before twelve (Sh/Wellford Tiller); **121br** Fence with the number 13 (Sh/motorolka); **122bl** Nine of Cups, Ten of Coins, Ace of Staves, and Ace of Swords with Visconti motto "a bon droit", "common" cards – Italian tarot cards, made for the Visconti-Sforza family, 15th century (Sc/Art Resource/Pierpont Morgan Library – M.630); **122tr, br** and **123** Collection of Tarot cards, colored lithograph, French School, 19th century (BAL/Archives Charmet/PC); **124c** Aerial view of the maze at Longleat House, England (Dr/Martin Crowdy); **124t** Turf maze in the "Cretan" pattern (Sh/clearviewstock); **125t** Chartres labyrinth, 13th century (Photolibrary.com/J-C&D Pratt); **125cl** A celtic knot design from the church at Croick in the Highlands of Scotland (iS/Pawel Kowalczyk); **126t** Looking up from the center of an open air Grecian-style temple, built in the 1930s near San Francisco (iS/Eliza Snow); **126bl** Ammonite fossil (iS/Heiko Grossmann); **126bcl** Cross-section of a pine tree trunk (iS/Joze Pojbic); **126bcr** Painted egg sculpture, Lithuania (Dr/Gediminas Packevicius); **126br** Ceiling of the Hall of Prayers, Temple of Heaven, Beijing (Photolibrary.com/Luis Castaneda); **127t** A medicine wheel at Sedona, Arizona (Corbis/George HH Huey); **127b** The Kaaba Stone, Mecca, Saudi Arabia (Sh/Sufi); **128t** Giza pyramids, Egypt (iS/Volker Kreinacke); **128bl** Abstract triangular sky light of a hotel in Hawaii (Dr/Rboncato); **128br** Star of David on an old synagogue gate, Jerusalem (Dr/Aron

Brand); **129tl** Circular rooflight with a star design (Dr/Jordan Tan); **129cl** Tiles in Topkapi Palace, Istanbul (Sh/almond); **129bl** Pentagram on a manhole cover (Dr/Bjarne Henning Kvaale); **129br** The Dome of the Treasury (Qubbat al-Khazna), Omayyad Mosque, Damascus, Syria (Sh/WitR); **130tl** Lithograph of Mecca, 19th century (Corbis/Philip de Bay); **130bl** Saudi Arabian flag (Sh/JackF); **131c** Tiles decorating a mosque, Bukhara, Uzbekistan (Sh/Galyna Andrushko); **132l** *Icon of the Crucifixion*, in St Catherine's Monastery, Sinai, 12th century, within a frame depicting busts of eighteen saints (AA/Boistesselin/Kharbine-Tapabor); **132r** Reliquary cross, gold and gemstones, Limoges, late 13th century (AKG/Musée National de l'Hôtel de Cluny/François Guénet); **133tr** Mosaic in apse vault of the Basilica of San Apollinare in Classe, Ravenna, 6th century (AA/ADO); **135bc** Ploughing, October, folio of the Provençal *Breviary of Love*, 13th century (AA/Real Biblioteca de lo Escorial/GDO); **136tcr** United States airmail stamp with the Statue of Liberty, 1959–1961 (iS/Ray Roper); **136tr** Angels descending a ladder on the West façade of Bath Abbey (Sh/E Sweet); **136bl** Karo-Batak "Spirit Boat" banner from Sumatra, Indonesia (WFA/PC, New York); **137tl** St. Cuthbert digs a pit and obtains water by his prayers, manuscript illumination from Bede's *Vita Sancti Cuthberti* (*Life of St. Cuthbert*), English, Durham, late 12th century (AKG/BL – Ms. Additional 39943, fol.41 r); **137tc** Harvesting, Virgo, from Gothic manuscript *Beatae Elisabeth Psalter*, 13th century (AA/Archaeological Museum Cividale, Friuli/GDO); **137tr** Woodcut of an English blacksmith using an anvil in a forge, 1603 (iS/Hulton Archive); **137b** Fresco of libation jug bearers at Knossos Palace, Crete (Sh/scion); **138tr** Achaemenid "Eternal Soldiers" at Persepolis, Iran (Sh/John Said); **138cl** Sacrificial knife with mosaic handle, Aztec/Mixtec, Mexico, 15th–16th century (BM); **138bl** Ottoman engraved battle axe or halberd (iS/William Keith Wheatley); **139cl** Old English penny minted in 1900 (iS/Karen Mower); **139tr** Ottoman round shield (Sh/psamtik); **139b** Manuscript illumination of the Battle of Roncevaux Pass, from *Chroniques de France ou de Saint Denis*, French, 14th century (AA/BL); **140tl** Guardian statue at a temple, Thailand (iS/Adrian Hillman); **140tr** St. George killing the dragon, stained glass in the north chancel of St. Michael's, Hallaton, Leicestershire, by Richard Pook Collett, early 20th century (Sh/nachogalacho); **140bl** Rama (the hero of the epic *Ramayana*), on Hanuman, defeats the ten-headed demon Ravana, an album painting on paper, Tamil Nadu, India, ca.1820 (BM); **141tl** The Russian national emblem at the spire of the Resurrection Gate at Red Square in Moscow, Russia (iS/wrangle); **141cl** Francesco & Sperindio Cagnola, *Flagellation of Christ*, fresco, 15th century. "the poor man's Bible", Church of the Trinity, Piedmont (AA/GDO); **141r** Medieval armor (Sh/Michele Perbellini); **142tl** Hindu god statues on a temple, India (iS/Hung Meng Tan); **143l** Sandstone stele with a figure of Harihara, Indian, 10th century (AKG/EL); **143r** Wall painting showing the Hindu god Ganesh, Jaisalmer Fort, Rajasthan, India (Sh/ErickN); **144t** The coronation of Charles V of

France, miniature from the *Chronicles of Jean Froissart*, French, 14th century (iS/Hulton Archive); **144b** Native American man in traditional clothing (Sh/Caitlin Copeland); **145tr** *Mother of God of the Sign*, icon, Novgorod school (Sh/Vibrant Image Studio); **146tl** Ancient Egypt tomb painting depicting a banquet (Dr/Eishier/Metropolitan Museum, New York); **146cl** Illumination of Sacrificial bread being baked in an oven, Bible moralisé, France, early 13th century (AKG/Austrian National Library – *Codex Vindobonensis* 2554, fol.27v); **146c** Basket of bread and two fish, early Christian mosaic inside the Church of the Multiplication of the Loaves and the Fishes, Tabgha, Israel, 5th or 6th century (iS/Tomasz Parys); **146br** A tied bundle of grain, the attribute of Demeter, fragment of the architrave of the Sanctuary of Demeter, Eleusis, Greece, 50BCE (AKG/Hervé Champollion); **147t** Fertility offering of boiled rice made to Shinto gods, *Rice Cultivation Scroll* (*Tawarakasane kosaku emaki*), late 16th century (AA/Tokyo University/Granger Collection); **147b** Detail of a panel depicting the fortunes of the maize plant during the last two years of a four-year period. Tlaloc blesses the plant, which is shown as Chalchihuitlicue. From the *Codex Fejérváry-Mayer* (WFA/Liverpool Museum, Liverpool); **148t** Maestro Lienhart Scherhauff, *The Last Supper*, fresco, Italian, 1460 (AA/Museo Diocesano, Bressanone/GDO); **148br** Study of a Watermelon, gouache and gum arabic, late 18th century (BAL/PC/Bonhams, London); **149tc** Grape press, late Roman mosaic (Sh/Khirman Vladimir); **149tr** Indra being anointed with *soma*, gouache on paper, Indian School, 18th century (BAL/BN/Archives Charmet); **149bl** Amitayus (Tse-pameh), from Central Tibet, opaque watercolor on cotton, 15th century (BAL/Museum of Fine Arts, Boston, Massachusetts,/Gift of John Goelet); **150tl** The Gentleman Usher of the Black Rod at the entrance to the House of Lords ahead of the State Opening of Parliament in London (Getty Images/AFP/Leon Neal); **150bl** Mosiac of St. Edward king and confessor, by William Burges in the chapel of Worcester College, 19th century (Br Lawrence Lew, OP); **150bc** LadislasI (1040–1095) saint and king of Hungary, from *Chronicle of Hungary*, by Johan de Thwrocz, 1488 (AA/Biblioteca Nazionale Marciana, Venice/GDO); **150br** St. David, stained glass window in Great St Mary's, Cambridge (Br Lawrence Lew, OP); **151tr** Torah crown, silver with gem stones, Polish, 1729 (BAL / Israel Museum, Jerusalem/The Stieglitz Collection and donated with contribution from Erica & Ludwig Jesselson); **151cl** Fresco depicting St. Anastasia, healer of horses, with a bottle of oil in one hand and a cross in the other, from the Byzantine church of Our Lady of Asinou, Tradoos Mountains, Cyprus 12th century (AKG/De Agostini Picture Library); **151bc** King Solomon, Romanesque painted ceiling, church of St. Martin, Zillis, Switzerland, ca.1150 (AA/Church of Saint Martin, Zillis/GDO); **152tl** Army dress uniform of a decorated soldier at Arlington National Cemetery, USA (iS/Valerie Paganessi); **152bl** Seal of the President of the United States (Sh/Vladislav Gurfinkel); **152bcl** Coat of arms of Pope Benedict XVI (Sh/Clara); **152bcr** The symbol of the Most Noble Order of the Garter, a blue "garter" with the motto *Honi Soit Qui*

Mal Y Pense, the oldest British order of chivalry, founded in 1348 by King Edward III (Getty Images/Buyenlarge); **152br** The official badge (mandarin square) of a high-ranking civil servant in China, silk embroidery, late 17th century (WFA/PC); **153t** A detail of a wall painting in the tomb of Amen-her-khepeshef; the pharaoh wears an Amun crown, combining the red crown and a pair of tall feathers (WFA/E Strouhal); **153b** Fragment of wallpaper decorated with a French revolutionary rosette, cap and pick, 1793–1794 (AA/Musée de la Révolution Française, Vizille/GDO); **154tl** King David playing a psaltery accompanied by tuba, organ and cymbal players. From the *Psalterium Beatae Elisabeth*, illuminated manuscript, 13th century (AKG/EL); **154bl** Detail of an angel with tambourine from *Mary and Child and angels making music*, painting on wood panel by Sano di Pietro, ca.1448–1450. From the monastery S.Francesco in Colle Val d'Elsa (AKG/Pinacoteca Nazionale, Siena); **154bcl** Isis holding a sistrum, Abydos, Egypt (Corbis/Roger Wood); **154bcr** A court musician plays bagpipes, miniature painting from the *Cantigas of Alfonso X*, parchment codex with illuminated miniatures and musical scores, Spanish, 13th century (AA/Real Monasterio del Escorial Spain/Granger Collection); **154br** Krishna playing the flute to Radha beside a cow, tempera, Kangra, India, 1820–1825 (V&A); **155tr** Roman wall painting of Apollo Citharoedus (Apollo with lyre), Rome (BSP/LeonardoRC); **155c** Musician with pan pipes, Roman mosaic, Rome, 2nd century (AA/Museo della Civilta, Romana Rome/GDO); **155b** Detail of of an angel playing a trumpet, a window by Sir Edward Burne-Jones in Christ Church Cathedral, Oxford, ca.1877–1878 (Br Lawrence Lew, OP); **156tl** Chinese pagoda, Jurong Lake, Singapore (Sh/jasonleehl); **156bl** Chinese classical bridge, Beijing (Sh/sming); **156bc** Old temple door at Thikse monastery, Ladakh, India (Sh/Jeremy Richards); **156br** Rose window of the church of Sant'Agostino Rieti, Lazio, Italy (Sh/Claudio Giovanni Colombo); **157tl** US Capitol, Washington, DC (Sh/Condor 36); **157tc** Spiral staircase in the Bouzov castle, Czech Republic (Sh/nohanka); **157tr** Interior of Wells cathedral, Somerset (Sh/Matthew Collingwood); **157bl** Egyptian obelisk at the center of the Piazza del Popolo, Rome. A Catholic cross adorns the top (iS/Harry Thomas); **157bc** Qutb Minar ruins in Delhi, India (Sh/Sam D Cruz); **158tc** Freemason's medal (Dr/Rafael Laguillo); **158bl** Seal of the Grand Lodge, Rome, with pyramid and sphinx, from *The History of Freemasonry* by R.F. Gould, ca.1887 (PC); **158br** The pyramid and eye on the back of a US one dollar bill (Sh/James E Knopf); **159c** Apron of a master of the Saint-Julien Lodge in Brioude, painted leather, French, 19th century (BAL/Giraudon/Musée Crozatier, Le Puy-en-Velay); **161b** The churning of the sea of milk, Indian painting, 19th century (AA/Victoria and Albert Museum, London/Eileen Tweedy); **162tl** Krishna in cosmic form, Indian painting, Rajasthan, 1890 (BAL/Victoria & Albert Museum, London); **162tc** Woodcut of the Creation of Adam, from the *Nuremberg Chronicles*, ca.1493 (iS/nicoolay); **162tr** European print after a drawing of Pan Gu holding the *taiji* symbol. Engraved in color on paper, ca.1790 (BM); **162bc** Inherkha worshiping the sacred Benu bird of Heliopolis, Deir el-Medina, West Thebes, Egyptian, 20th Dynasty, 1186–1069BCE (AKG/James Morris); **162br** Mythical creature in a glazed brick relief, detail of the Ishtar Gate from Babylon, built under Nebuchadnezzar II, 604–561BCE (Dr/Lord.max/ Pergamon-Museum, Berlin); **163tr** Dreamtime Aboriginal painting of a serpent, Australian, 20th century (BAL/Horniman Museum, London/Heini Schneebeli); **163cl** Bronze head of a snake, from one of the gate-towers of the Oba's palace, Benin City, Nigeria (BAL/BM); **163bc** Viking picture stone with Odin (Wotan) on his horse Sleipnir welcomed by a Valkyrie with a drinking horn. Lillbjors, Gotland, Sweden, 8th century (AKG/EL/Historiska Museet, Stockholm); **164tr** *Noah's Ark*, Ottoman miniature of the Anatolian School, 16th century (AA/Topkapi Library, Istanbul/GDO); **164bl** First avatar of Vishnu as Matsya "The Fish", painted and gilded wood, Indian, 19th century (BAL/Musée Guimet, Paris/Bonora); **164br** Deucalion and Pyrrha repopulate the world after the Flood, illuminated by the Master of the Prayer Books, Bruges ca.1500 (BAL/BL – Harl 4425 f.153); **165tl** Engraved frontispiece of the fifth volume of Jansson's *Atlas Novus*, published in Amsterdam, 1650 (BAL/PC); **165bl** Ceramic vase, with a representation of the water goddess Chalchiuhtlicue, Aztec, Mexico (AA/Museo del Templo Mayor, Mexico/GDO); **165cr** Cylinder-seal impression of the water god Ea (right) with streams flowing from his body. It illustrates the myth in which the bird-man Zu is led before his judge Ea, because of his attempt to usurp the authority of the supreme Enlil by stealing the "tablet of destiny" upon which was insribed the fates of all gods and man. The god of agriculture, identified by the plough over his shoulder, represents the deities of vegetation injured by the theft. Akkadian, 2250BCE (WFA/BM); **166l** Painted limestone relief of a high priest dressed in a panther skin making a sacrifice in front of the funerary chamber in the tomb of Ramesses IX, Valley of the Kings, Thebes, 20th Dynasty, 1126–1108BCE (AA/GDO); **166r** Ancient sacrificial rite in honor of God, French manuscript illumination, 14th century (AA/Biblioteca Nazionale Marciana, Venice/ADO); **167tl** Abraham preparing to sacrifice his son Ishmael when he is pre-empted by an angel (below, King Nimrod persecutes Abraham by burning him at the stake), from *The Fine Flower of Histories*, or *Zubdat al-Tawarikh*, by Seyyid Loqman Ashuri, 1583. (AA/Turkish and Islamic Art Museum, Istanbul/ADO); **167tcl** Aztec human sacrifice (AA/Museo Ciudad, Mexico/ADO); **167tcr** *Sati*, illustration in *The Book of the Mogul*, 17th century (AA/Biblioteca Nazionale Marciana, Venice/ADO); **167tr** Orestes and sister Iphigenia in the temple of Artemis at Tauris, Attic red-figure *krater* by Iphigenia painter 4th century BCE (AA/Archaeological Museum Spina, Ferrara/ADO); **168tl** Lamb of God with gold cross, relief (Sh/Oculo); **168b** Detail of the reredos by Sir Ninian Comper, in the missionary chapel of St. George's Catholic Cathedral, Southwark ca.1928–1931 (Br Lawrence Lew, OP, by kind permission of the Dean of St George's Cathedral Southwark); **169c** East window, showing the splendor of the saints who gather around the Cross, St. George's Cathedral Southwark

(Br Lawrence Lew, OP, by kind permission of the Dean of St. George's Cathedral Southwark); **170tl** *The Golden Age* by Lucas Cranach the Elder, oil on panel, 1530 (Getty images/BAL/Alte Pinakothek, Munich); **170cl** Grim Reaper (Sh/Pres Panayotov); **170bl** Three-sided relief sculpture, Greek, early Classical (Corbis/Burstein Collection); **170br** Día de los Muertos (Day of the Dead) celebrations on Olevera Street, Los Angeles, California (Sh/Bobby Deal/RealDealPhoto); **171tl** Valhalla and the Midgard Serpent, Icelandic, 1680 (BAL/Arni Magnusson Institute, Reykjavik); **171tr** Nicolas Poussin, *Les bergers d'Arcadie* (*Shepherds of Arcadia*), also called *Et in Arcadia Ego*, oil on canvas, 1637–1638 (AA/ML/GDO); **171cl** Hades and Persephone, painting on a Greek vase, Apulian, found at Canosa di Puglia, Italy, 330BCE (AKG/Staatlische Antikensammlungen & Glyptothek, Munich/EL); **171bl** Reading out the rituals – a young woman carrying a plate with offerings, detail from a wall painting about the initiation of women into the cult of Dionysus, Villa of Mysteries, Pompeii, Roman, mid-1st century BCE (AKG); **171br** Scene with the god Mercury or Hermes holding a caduceus and carrying away a dead child in the Elysian Fields, wall painting from *hypocaust* of Octavius, 3rd century (AA/Museo Nazionale Romano, Rome/ADO); **172tl** The labour of Sisyphus in Tartaros, Greek vase painting, Apulian, found at Canosa di Puglia, Italy, 330BCE (AKG/Staatlische Antikensammlungen & Glyptothek, Munich/EL); **172tr** *Descent of the Buddha Amida with two attendant* bodhisattvas, a hanging scroll painting by Katô Nobukiyo, Japan, Edo period, 1796 (BM); **172b** Fowling in the marshes: fragment of wall painting from the tomb of Nebamun. Thebes, Egypt. 18th Dynasty, ca.1350BCE (BM); **173tl** Inanna-Ishtar (winged goddess of heaven, Earth and underworld), also associated with Lilith (wife of Adam), wearing a crown of lunar horns and a rainbow necklace with lions and owls, terracotta relief from Mesopotamia, ca.2000BCE (AA/PC/Eileen Tweedy); **173tc** Jolly Roger flag (iS/Kostas Koutsoukos); **173bl** The Fire Temple at Isfahan, Iran. These temples were the most important places of worship for Zoroastrians, the sacred fire burning inside them symbolizing the battle against evil (WFA/Euan Wingfield); **173br** Daoist mountain paradise on Penglai, polychrome and gilded stoneware made at the Shiwan kilns, Guangdong, China, late 19th century (BAL/National Museums of Scotland); **174tl** Egyptian relief of ibis-headed god Thoth (iS/Okrad); **175c** Pectoral with a bird-scarab, from the tomb of Tutankhamun, gold cloisonné decorated with semi-precious stones & glass paste, Egyptian, New Kingdom, ca.1370–1352BCE (Sc/EM); **176l** *Perseus with the head of Medusa*, by Benvenuto Cellini, in the Loggia de' Lanzi, Piazza della Signoria, Florence, 1545–1554 (Sh/Timur Kulgarin); **176r** Colossal statue of a heroic lion tamer – often thought to be Gilgamesh, stone relief from the entrance to the throne room of the palace of King Sargon II in Khorsabad (modern Iraq), Assyrian, 722–705BCE (AKG/ML/EL); **177tr** Round Table with the Holy Grail, from *L'Estoire de Saint Graal* by Robert de Boron, manuscript illumination, French, 15th century (AKG/BN – Ms. fr. 116, fol. 610 v); **177bl** Ulysses and the Sirens,

Roman mosaic from Dougga, Tunisia, 3rd century (Sh/Tomasz Szymanski/Bardo Museum, Tunis; **177bc** St. Brendan the Navigator, Irish monk (ca.486–575), manuscript illumination ca.1200 (AA/BL); **177br** *The Demons of Blackwater River Carry Away the Master* (an episode in *Journey to the West*), color lithograph from *Myths and Legends of China* by Edward T.C. Werner, 1922 (BAL/PC); **178tr** Herakles choking the Nemean lion, bronze medal, partially gilded, by Pier Jacopo Alari Bonacolsi Antico, ca.1460–1528 (AKG/Museo Nazionale del Bargello, Florence/Orsi Battaglini); **178bc** Herakles and Telephus, marble, from Tivoli 1st–2nd century (AA/ML/GDO); **178br** Eurysthenes, king of Trizina, guarding the kettle, detail of a hydra, Greek vase painting, ca.500BCE (AKG/ML/EL); **179tl** Herakles diverting the river to clean the Augean stables, mosaic from the Roman city of Volubilis, Mauretania Tingitania, Morocco ca.50BCE–24CE (AA/GDO); **179tr** Limestone relief of Herakles smiting Acheloos in the form of a bull, from Oxyrhynchus, Egypt, ca.300–500 (BAL/Brooklyn Museum of Art, New York/Charles Edwin Wilbour Fund); **179cl** Herakles and the Stymphalian birds, engraving from a Greek vase now in Boulogne museum (AA/Bibliothèque des Arts Décoratifs, Paris/GDO); **179cr** Herakles killing Diomedes on horseback, mosaic from the Roman city of Volubilis, Mauretania Tingitania, Morocco ca.50BCE–24CE (AA/GDO); **179b** Statue of Herakles killing the centaur, by Giambologna in the Loggia dei Lanzi on the Piazza della Signoria, Florence, 1599 (Sh/edobric); **180tl** *Anastasis*, or *Harrowing of Hell*, Christ's descent into Limbo, exterior fresco from the monastery of Moldovita, Moldavia, Romania, 1537 (AA/Moldovita Monastery, Romania/ADO); **180bl** *The Madonna of Mercy*, central panel from the Misericordia altarpiece, tempera on panel, by Piero della Francesca, 1445 (BAL/Pinacoteca, Sansepolcro); **180br** Stone figure of Brahma the Hindu creator god, Chola dynasty, from Tamil Nadu, southern India, ca. 1110–1150 (BM); **181tr** *Expulsion of Adam and Eve from the Garden of Eden*, left half of a panel painting depicting the confrontation between the old and the new Adam (Law and Grace) by Lucas Cranach the Elder, after 1529 (AKG/Germanisches Nationalmuseum, Nuremberg); **181cl** Illumination of the devil breathing poison from *Scivias* (*Know the ways of the Lord*), by Hildegard von Bingen, facsimile copy of the *Rupertsberg Codex*, 12th century. Original, formerly in Wiesbaden, disappeared during World War II (AKG/EL); **181c** The aged moon goddess, identified with the waning moon (the water issuing from her body and the serpent headdress are references to the rainy season), illustration from the *Codex Troana Cortesianus*, also know as the *Madrid Codex*. One of only four surviving Mayan codices it is composed entirely of almanacs organized in terms of the 260-day ritual calendar used throughout Mesoamerica for divination and prophecy. Mayan, ca.1230 (WFA/Museum of Americas, Madrid); **181br** Aztec sun stone, calendar with glyphs representing days, months and the sun, post-classical period Aztec (AA/NAM/GDO).